MUST-SEE MOVIES

AN ESSENTIAL GUIDE

66929

WARD CALHOUN

FALL
RIVER
PRESS

Art Directors: Gus Yoo, Brian MacMullen
Designers: Eunoh Lee, Eunho Lee
Editors: Amber Rose, Rachael Lanicci
Assistant Editors: Emma Frankel, Gabrielle Kappes
Photo Researcher: Benjamin DeWalt

Fall River Press
122 Fifth Avenue
New York, NY 10011

ISBN-13: 978-1-4351-0829-5
ISBN-10: 1-4351-0829-9

Printed and bound in China

1 3 5 7 9 10 8 6 4 2

Contents

Must-See Movies

1948
Abbott and Costello Meet Frankenstein

Overview

Genre: Comedy/ Horror
Duration: 83 min
Color: Black and White
Country: USA
MPAA Rating: Not Rated
Studio: Universal International Picture

Bud Abbott and Lou Costello are at it again, this time as two hapless deliverymen, Wilbur and Chick, who are charged with bringing two crates to a wax museum. Little do they know that one of those crates contains Count Dracula and the other, Frankenstein. Before you can say "boo!" Count Dracula escapes with Frankenstein back to his castle. What's worse, he plans to use Wilbur's brain to re-energize the monster. Coming to their aid is Lawrence Talbot, who is well aware of Dracula's evil plans. The only problem is, when the moon is full Talbot becomes the Wolf Man. Frightfully good fun, this film features horror legends Bela Lugosi as Dracula and Lon Chaney Jr. as the Wolf Man.

Cast

Bud Abbott: Chick Young
Lou Costello: Wilbur Grey
Lon Chaney Jr.: Larry Talbot / The Wolf Man
Bela Lugosi: Count Dracula
Glenn Strange: The Frankenstein Monster
Lénore Aubert: Dr. Sandra Mornay
Jane Randolph: Joan Raymond

Behind the Scenes

Director: Charles Barton
Writers: Robert Lees, Frederic I. Rinaldo, John Grant
Producers: Arlene Donovan, Scott Rudin
Executive Producer: Robert Arthur
Cinematographer: Charles Van Enger
Original Music: Frank Skinner

Awards

Added to National Film Registry in 2001

Trivia

• Walter Lantz (of Woody Woodpecker fame) drew the animation sequences of Dracula as a bat and his bat–vampire metamorphosis.

The African Queen

Overview

Genre: Drama/ Adventure
Duration: 105 min
Color: Color(Technicolor)
Country: USA and UK
MPAA Rating: Not Rated
Studio: United Artists

A chemistry experiment gone terribly right, *The African Queen* stars Katharine Hepburn as Rose Sayer, the headstrong sister of a British missionary who has been killed by German troops in World War I Africa. The minute Rose hooks up with her complete opposite, Humphrey Bogart's brusque steamboat captain Charlie Allnut, the sparks fly. After agreeing to transport Rose away from her destroyed village and back to safety, Charlie soon realizes he's taken on more than he's bargained for. The unlikely duo butt heads over all matter of things but slowly grow closer as together they battle the elements and the Germans. This top-notch adventure netted Bogart the Oscar.

Cast

Humphrey Bogart: Charlie Allnut
Katharine Hepburn: Rose Sayer
Robert Morley: Rev. Samuel Sayer
Peter Bull: Captain of the *Louisa*
Theodore Bikel: First Officer

Behind the Scenes

Director: John Huston
Writers: C.S. Forester (novel), James Agee, John Huston, Peter Viertel (uncredited), John Collier (uncredited)
Producers: Sam Spiegel and John Woolf
Executive Producer: Barbara McLean
Cinematographer: Jack Cardiff
Original Music: Allan Gray

Trivia

• Katharine Hepburn drank only water while filming to emphasize her disapproval of John Huston and Humphrey Bogart's heavy drinking. As an unfortunate result, she developed dysentery.
• The reed-filled riverbank scenes were not filmed in Africa but in Dalyan, Turkey.

Awards

Oscar Winner: Best Actor
Oscar Nominations: Best Actress, Best Director, Best Writing

1980
Airplane!

Overview

Genre: Comedy
Duration: 88 min
Color: Color
Country: USA
MPAA Rating: PG
Studio: Paramount
Pictures

This zany spoof of the *Airport* disaster stars Robert Hays as ex-pilot Ted Striker who finds himself the only man with flying experience aboard a doomed commercial airliner. After a bad in-flight meal (aren't they all?) disables most of the flight crew and many of the passengers, Striker is called to the cockpit. Still suffering from haunting war memories and a broken romance with Elaine—a stewardess on the plane—Striker shakily gets behind the controls. Along for the airborne antics are Peter Graves as an inappropriate captain, Lloyd Bridges as a substance-abusing air traffic controller, and Leslie Nielsen as a deadpan doctor. Fasten your seat belts for a laugh-filled takeoff.

Cast

Robert Hays: Ted Striker
Julie Hagerty: Elaine
Leslie Nielsen: Dr. Rumack
Robert Stack: Rex Kramer
Lloyd Bridges: McCroskey
Kareem Abdul-Jabbar: Roger Murdock (as Kareem Abdul-Jabaar)
Peter Graves: Captain Oveur
Lorna Patterson: Randy

Behind the Scenes

Director: Jim Abrahams, David Zucker, Jerry Zucker
Writers: Jim Abrahams and David Zucker, Jerry Zucker
Producer: Jon Davison, Howard W. Koch
Executive Producer: Jim Abrahams, David Zucker, Jerry Zucker
Cinematographer: Joseph F. Biroc

Trivia

• The airplane model used in the flying shots is on display at the museum in the Studios at Los Colinas (Texas).

Awards

Golden Globes Nominations: Best Motion Picture—Musical/Comedy

1979
Alien

Overview

Genre: Sci-Fi/Horror
Duration: 117 min
Color: Color
Country: USA
MPAA Rating: R
Studio: Twentieth Century Fox

When the commercial spaceship *Nostromo* receives a distress call from another craft, its crew members are sent to investigate. What they find is an empty ship housing thousands of strange-looking eggs. When crewmember Kane goes in for a closer look, one egg opens and something attaches itself to his head. Still alive, Kane is brought back onto *Nostromo* despite protests from acting commander Ripley, who wants him quarantined. Well, it turns out she was right. What they now have on their ship is a perfect organism capable of killing everyone onboard. They may not be able to hear you scream in space, as this movie's tagline suggested, but here on Earth they'll hear you loud and clear.

Cast

Tom Skerrit: Dallas
Sigourney Weaver: Ripley
Veronica Cartwright: Lambert
Harry Dean Stanton: Brett
John Hurt: Kane
Ian Holm: Ash
Yaphet Kotto: Parker

Behind the Scenes

Director: Ridley Scott
Writers: Dan O'Bannon and Ronald Shusett
Producers: Gordon Carroll, David Giler, Walter Hill
Cinematographer: Derek Vanlint
Original Music: Jerry Goldsmith

Awards

Oscar Winner: Best Effects—Visual
Oscar Nomination: Best Art Direction

Trivia

• The front of the alien's face was cast from a real human skull.

1951
All About Eve

Overview

Genre: Drama
Duration: 138 min
Color: Black and White
Country: USA
MPAA Rating: Not Rated
Studio: Twentieth Century Fox

Fasten your seat belts for this backstage drama starring Bette Davis as Broadway star Margo Channing and Anne Baxter as the conniving title character. After a seemingly innocent aspiring actress is taken under the wing of an established stage star, she soon reveals herself to be a wolf in sheep's clothing. Once introduced into the glamorous world of Ms. Channing, Eve Harrington will stop at nothing to make sure that she becomes a star herself. A cautionary tale of vanity, ambition, and betrayal, *All About Eve* features razor-sharp dialogue that suits its subject matter to a tee. The stellar cast also includes a brief appearance by Marilyn Monroe.

Cast

Bette Davis: Margo Channing
Anne Baxter: Eve Harrington
George Sanders: Addison DeWitt
Celeste Holm: Karen Richards
Gary Merrill: Bill Simpson
Hugh Marlowe: Lloyd Richards
Gregory Ratoff: Max Fabian

Behind the Scenes

Director: Joseph L. Mankiewicz
Writers: Mary Orr (story), Joseph L. Mankiewicz
Producer: Darryl F. Zanuck
Film Editor: Barbara McLean
Cinematographer: Milton R. Krasner
Original Music: Alfred Newman

Awards

Oscar Winners: Best Supporting Actor, Best Costume Design, Best Director, Best Picture, Best Sound, Best Writing

Trivia

• Bette Davis and co-star Gary Merrill fell in love during the film's production, and (after divorcing their respective spouses) the two married a few weeks after the film wrapped.

1930
All Quiet on the Western Front

Overview

Genre: Drama
Duration: 138 min
Color: Black and White
Country: USA
MPAA Rating: Not Rated
Studio: Universal Pictures

Adapted from a German novel, *All Quiet on the Western Front* is a searing World War I drama. After hearing an impassioned speech by their teacher on serving their country, a group of German students decide to join the cause. Their youthful exuberance is soon quelled as they witness, firsthand, the horrors of combat. One of the boys, Paul, is particularly affected as he experiences the loss of friend and enemy alike. He eventually returns home, only to find that little has changed and young men are still being encouraged to take up arms and join the good fight. *All Quiet on the Western Front* remains one of the most powerful indictments of war ever filmed.

Cast

Louis Wolheim: Kat Katczinsky
Lew Ayres: Paul Baümer
John Wray: Himmelstoss
Arnold Lucy: Professor Kantorek
Ben Alexander: Franz Kemmerich
Scott Kolk: Leer
Owen Davis Jr.: Peter

Behind the Scenes

Director: Lewis Milestone
Writers: George Abbott (screenplay), Maxwell Anderson and Del Andrews (adaptation)
Producer: Carl Laemmle Jr.
Film Editor: Edgar Adams
Cinematographer: Arthur Edeson

Awards

Oscar Winners: Best Director, Best Picture
Oscar Nominations: Best Cinematography, Best Writing—Achievement

Trivia

• Future director Fred Zinnemann was an extra on the film, but was soon fired for "impudence."

1976
All the President's Men

Overview

Genre: Drama
Duration: 138 min
Color: Color
(Technicolor)
Country: USA
MPAA Rating: PG
Studio: Warner Bros.
Pictures/Wildwood

Robert Redford and Dustin Hoffman star as Bob Woodward and Carl Bernstein, the two young *Washington Post* reporters who broke the story of the Watergate scandal. After a seemingly innocuous break-in at the Democratic Party headquarters in 1972, Woodward and Bernstein come across some information that may link the incident to a member of President Richard Nixon's staff and perhaps the president himself. As they continue to chase leads and gather information from sources such as the shadowy "Deep Throat," the reporters find that both the reputation of their paper and their very lives may be at stake. Based on true events, *All the President's Men* makes journalists into action heroes.

Cast

Dustin Hoffman: Carl Bernstein
Robert Redford: Bob Woodward
Jack Warden: Harry M. Rosenfeld
Jason Robards: Ben Bradlee
Martin Balsam: Howard Simons
Hal Holbrook: Deep Throat
Jane Alexander: Judy Hoback
Meredith Baxter: Debbie Sloane
Stephen Collins: Hugh W. Sloan Jr.

Behind the Scenes

Director: Alan J. Pakula
Writers: Carl Bernstein and Bob Woodward (book), William Goldman (screenplay)
Producer: Walter Coblenz
Film Editor: Robert L. Wolfe
Cinematographer: Gordon Willis
Original Music: David Shire

Trivia

• The real security guard who discovered the break-in at the Watergate complex, Frank Wills, plays himself in the film.
• This was the first film Jimmy Carter watched as president of the United States.

Awards

Oscar Winners: Best Supporting Actor, Best Art Direction, Best Sound, Best Writing—Adapted Screenplay
Oscar Nominations: Best Supporting Actress, Best Director, Best Film Editing, Best Picture

1984
Amadeus

Overview

Genre: Drama
Duration: 160 min
Color: Color
Country: USA
MPAA Rating: R
Studio: Orion
Pictures/The Saul
Zaentz Company

Originally a Broadway play, *Amadeus* follows the story of 18th-century Austrian composing prodigy Wolfgang Amadeus Mozart. Narrated by former court composer Antonio Salieri, Mozart's rise to prominence and eventual death is laid out by an old man in a mental asylum still consumed with jealousy over a person he considered his rival. So envious is Salieri of Mozart's gifts and accolades that he becomes obsessed with ridding the world of the man who has everything that he does not. Tom Hulce's wildly entertaining Mozart is the perfect complement to F. Murray Abraham's seething Salieri. And, of course, there's the music.

Cast

F. Murray Abraham: Antonio Salieri
Tom Hulce: Wolfgang Amadeus Mozart
Elizabeth Berridge: Constanze Mozart
Roy Dotrice: Leopold Mozart
Simon Callow: Emanuel Schikaneder/ Papageno in "Magic Flute"
Christine Ebersole: Katerina Cavalieri/ Constanza in "Abduction from the Seraglio"
Jeffrey Jones: Emperor Joseph II

Behind the Scenes

Director: Milos Forman
Writers: Peter Shaffer (play/screenplay)
Producer: Saul Zaentz
Executive Producers: Michael Hausman, Bertil Ohlsson
Cinematographer: Miroslav Ondricek

Trivia

• Though the music playing when Mozart is at the piano was prerecorded, Tom Hulce spent four hours a day rehearsing in order to appear convincing. Apparently, he was successful: several professors of music studied the film and noted that every key he struck was correct.

Awards

Oscar Winners: Best Picture, Best Actor, Best Art Direction, Best Costume Design, Best Director, Best Makeup, Best Sound, Best Writing—Adapted Screenplay
Oscar Nominations: Best Actor, Best Cinematography, Best Film Editing

1999
American Beauty

Overview

Genre: Drama
Duration: 122 min
Color: Color
Country: USA
MPAA Rating: R
Studio: DreamWorks

A lan Ball's complex and compelling screenplay explores the failures and successes of a single life and the hidden beauty found in all humanity. This film delves into the mind of Lester Burnham, played by Kevin Spacey, at a pivotal point in his existence. Deep in the throes of a midlife crisis, Lester seeks out the usual cosmetic solutions: new car, new job, and new body. But what he is really searching for is a deeper meaning to his life. Through a series of seemingly unconnected events, Lester slowly begins to understand inner peace and beauty. Exposing human failure, sadness, exhilaration, and redemption, *American Beauty* scratches beneath the surface and considers the awe-inspiring power of the individual.

Cast

Kevin Spacey: Lester Burnham
Annette Bening: Carolyn Burnham
Thora Birch: Jane Burnham
Wes Bentley: Ricky Fitts
Mena Suvari: Angela Hayes
Chris Cooper: Col. Frank Fitts
Peter Gallagher: Buddy Kane
Allison Janney: Barbara Fitts

Behind the Scenes

Director: Sam Mendes
Writer: Alan Ball
Producers: Bruce Cohen, Dan Jinks
Cinematographer: Conrad L. Hall
Original Music: Thomas Newman

Trivia

• Director Sam Mendes used three distinct visual styles—a very formal style for the bulk of the film, a more graceful style for the fantasy scenes, and a handheld look for the video footage.

Awards

Oscar Winners: Best Actor, Best Cinematography, Best Director, Best Picture, Best Writing
Oscar Nominations: Best Actress, Best Editing, Best Music

1973
American Graffiti

Overview

Genre: Comedy/Drama
Duration: 110 min
Color: Color
(Technicolor)
Country: USA
MPAA Rating: PG
Studio: Universal
Pictures

As the summer of '62 comes to a close in a small California town four young men enjoy one final night cruising the strip and chasing women while thinking about their futures. Steve Bolander and Curt Henderson are both leaving for college and each has his doubts. Steve frets over possibly breaking up with his girlfriend Laurie while Curt tries to hang on to the moment by chasing an elusive blonde in a white Thunderbird. Meanwhile, nerdy Terry has a hot date and drag racer John is looking for a showdown but instead finds himself saddled babysitting a 13-year-old girl. Drive-in signs flicker and radios blare classic rock 'n' roll hits in the gloaming of American innocence.

Cast

Richard Dreyfuss: Curt Henderson
Ron Howard: Steve Bolander
Paul Le Mat: John Milner
Charles Martin Smith: Terry "The Toad" Fields
Cindy Williams: Laurie Henderson
Candy Clark: Debbie Dunham

Behind the Scenes

Director: George Lucas
Writers: George Lucas, Gloria Katz, Willard Huyck
Producers: Francis Ford Coppola, Gary Kurtz
Film Editors: Verna Fields, Marcia Lucas, George Lucas (uncredited)

Awards

Oscar Nominations: Best Supporting Actress, Best Director, Best Film Editing, Best Picture, Best Writing\

Trivia

• Suzanne Somers played the role of the blonde in the T-Bird.

1951
An American in Paris

Overview

Genre: Musical/Romance
Duration: 113 min
Color: Color (Technicolor)
Country: USA
MPAA Rating: Not Rated
Studio: Metro-Goldwyn-Mayer (MGM)

Gene Kelly is Jerry Mulligan, an ex-U.S. soldier living the bohemian life of a painter in post–World War II Paris. He has no shortage of friends but struggles to make ends meet. One day he encounters a wealthy American patron of the arts who vows to help his career, though she clearly fancies Jerry more than his work. Around this same time he falls for a pretty young girl named Lise, played by Leslie Caron. What Jerry doesn't know is that his friend Henri also is quite taken with the girl. The story plays out to the marvelous music of George and Ira Gershwin and features incredible dancing including a hypnotic finale with Kelly and Caron.

Cast

Gene Kelly: Jerry Mulligan
Leslie Caron: Lise Bouvier
Oscar Levant: Adam Cook
Georges Guetary: Henri "Hank" Baurel
Nina Foch: Milo Roberts

Behind the Scenes

Director: Vincente Minnelli
Writer: Alan Jay Lerner (screenplay and story)
Producer: Arthur Freed
Film Editor: Adrienne Fazan
Cinematographers: John Alton, Alfred Gilks

Awards

Oscar Winners: Best Art Direction—Color, Best Cinematography—Color, Best Costume Design—Color, Best Music, Best Picture, Best Writing—Story and Screenplay

Trivia

• The final scene, a 17-minute dance sequence, took a month to film and cost the producers half a million dollars.

1978
Animal House

Overview

Genre: Comedy
Duration: 109 min
Color: Color
Country: USA
MPAA Rating: R
Studio: Universal
Pictures

Stocked with drunks and delinquents, Delta House is the worst fraternity at Faber College. It's also the only frat that's willing to accept nerdy freshmen like Larry Kroger and Kent Dorfman. While the Deltas party like there's no tomorrow, a fed-up Dean Wormer has them on something called double-secret probation. Just waiting for his chance to get the Deltas thrown off campus, Wormer recruits the insufferable WASPs of Omega House to do his dirty work. But once Boone, Bluto, Otter and the rest of the Deltas realize that their lackadaisical lifestyle is being threatened, they're not going to take this lying down. The movie that paved the way for countless campus comedies to follow, *Animal House* is more fun than a keg party.

Cast

John Belushi: John "Bluto" Blutarsky
Tim Matheson: Eric "Otter" Stratton
John Vernon: Dean Vernon Wormer
Verna Bloom: Marion Wormer
Tom Hulce: Larry "Pinto" Ktoger
Peter Riegert: Donald "Boon" Schoenstein
Karen Allen: Katy
Stephen Furst: Kent "Flounder" Dorfman
Donald Sutherland: Professor Dave Jennings

Behind the Scenes

Director: John Landis
Writers: Harold Ramis, Douglas Kennedy, Chris Miller
Producers: Ivan Reitman, Matty Simmons
Film Editor: George Folsey Jr.
Cinematographer: Charles Correll
Original Music: Elmer Bernstein

Trivia

• The only physical damage to the real frat house the cast and crew caused was the hole in the wall John Belushi makes with the guitar. Rather than repairing the hole, the fraternity placed a frame and an engraved brass tag around the hole to commemorate the film.

Awards

Added to National Film Registry in 2001

1977
Annie Hall

Overview

Genre: Comedy/ Romance
Duration: 93 min
Color: Color
Country: USA
MPAA Rating: PG
Studio: United Artists

W oody Allen's at the top of his game in this winning romantic comedy about the lives and loves of two neurotic New Yorkers. Woody stars as Alvy Singer, a nebbishy comedy writer who grew up under a rollercoaster in Coney Island. Diane Keaton is Annie, a flighty WASP with dreams of becoming a singer. The story of this unlikely couple is told in a series of hysterical vignettes employing such absurd techniques as subtitles, splitscreens, animation, and addressing the camera directly. It all works to perfection as we really get to see who these two people are, how they came to meet, and where this relationship is going. A cinematic gem, *Annie Hall* delivers laughs from beginning to end.

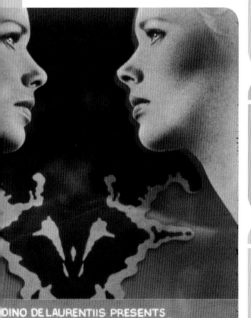

DINO DE LAURENTIIS PRESENTS
INGMAR BERGMAN'S
"FACE TO FACE"
Starring
LIV ULLMANN

Cast

Woody Allen: Alvy Singer
Diane Keaton: Annie Hall
Tony Roberts: Rob
Carol Kane: Allison
Paul Simon: Tony Lacey
Shelley Duvall: Pam
Christopher Walken: Duane Hall
Mordecai Lawner: Mr. Singer

Behind the Scenes

Director: Woody Allen
Writers: Woody Allen and Marshall Brickman
Producers: Charles H. Joffe, Jack Rollins
Executive Producer: Robert Greenhut
Cinematographer: Gordon Willis

Trivia

• The scene of Annie and Alvy visiting hell never made it into the final cut of the movie. The scene was rewritten and later used for Allen's *Deconstructing Harry*.
• The jokes Allen delivers to the University of Wisconsin audience and on *The Dick Cavett Show* are from his stand-up comic days.

Awards

Oscar Winners: Best Actress, Best Director, Best Picture, Best Writing
Oscar Nominations: Best Actor

1960
The Apartment

Overview

Genre: Comedy/ Romance
Duration: 125 min
Color: Black and White
Country: USA
MPAA Rating: Not Rated
Studio: Mirisch Company/United Artists

C.C. "Bud" Baxter is an anonymous drone at a large insurance company. Hoping to fast-track himself to a more high-profile position, Bud makes the big mistake of loaning out his Manhattan apartment to several executives for their extramarital affairs. So popular is his apartment that Bud can hardly find the time to sleep there himself, and he's still stuck in his same job. The lone bright spot in his day is office elevator girl Fran Kubelik. But when personnel manager Jeff Sheldrake offers Bud an honest-to-goodness promotion in exchange for the key to his apartment, it seems his ship has finally come in. The problem is, Fran may be setting sail with someone else.

Cast

Jack Lemmon: C. C. "Bud" Baxter
Shirley MacLaine: Fran Kubelik
Fred MacMurray: Jeff D. Sheldrake
Ray Walston: Joe Dobisch
Jack Kruschen: Dr. Dreyfuss
David Lewis: Al Kirkeby
Hope Holiday: Mrs. Margie MacDougall

Behind the Scenes

Director: Billy Wilder
Writers: Billy Wilder, I.A.L. Diamond
Producers: Billy Wilder, I.A.L. Diamond
Film Editor: Daniel Mandell
Cinematographer: Joseph LaShelle
Original Music: Adolph Deutsch

Trivia

• This was the last black and white film to win Best Picture at the Academy Awards for over 30 years, until *Schindler's List* in 1993.
• While filming the scene in which C.C. Baxter sleeps in Central Park in the rain, director Billy Wilder had to have Jack Lemmon sprayed with anti-freeze to prevent him from freezing.

Awards

Oscar Winners: Best Art Direction, Best Director, Best Picture, Best Writing
Oscar Nominations: Best Actor, Best Supporting Actor, Best Actress, Best Cinematography, Best Sound

1979
Apocalypse Now

Overview

Genre: Drama/Action
Duration: 153 min
Color: Color
Country: USA
MPAA Rating: R
Studio: United Artists

The madness of the Vietnam War as seen through the eyes of a special forces officer. Captain Benjamin Willard is sent on an insane mission into the jungles of Cambodia to find and terminate an army colonel who has deserted the war and reportedly positioned himself as some sort of almighty ruler among the local tribes. At the breaking point himself, Willard sets out to meet his objective and encounters all manner of disorder and destruction along the way. The closer he gets to his target, the more Willard seems to understand the man he's supposed to kill. Based on the novella *Heart of Darkness*, the actual filming of *Apocalypse Now* was every bit as chaotic as the movie itself.

Cast

Marlon Brando: Colonel Walter E. Kurtz
Martin Sheen: Captain Benjamin L. Willard
Robert Duvall: Lieutenant Colonel Bill Kilgore
Frederic Forrest: Jay "Chef" Hicks
Sam Bottoms: Lance B. Johnson
Laurence Fishburne: Tyrone "Clean" Miller
Harrison Ford: Colonel Lucas

Behind the Scenes

Director: Francis Ford Coppola
Writers: Joseph Conrad (novel), John Milius and Francis Ford Coppola (screenplay)
Producers: Kim Aubry, Francis Ford Coppola
Cinematographer: Vittorio Storaro

Awards

Oscar Winners: Best Cinematography, Best Sound

Trivia

• Martin Sheen had a heart attack while filming and had to spend months recuperating in a nearby hospital. A body double had to film his remaining scenes.

1995
Apollo 13

Overview

Genre: Drama/ Adventure
Duration: 140 min
Color: Color
Country: USA
MPAA Rating: PG
Studio: Universal Pictures/Imagine Entertainment

On April 11, 1970, NASA mission *Apollo 13* launches three men to the moon. Tom Hanks plays mission commander James Lovell, whose fateful report to ground control—"Houston, we have a problem"—indicates the first sign of trouble on a spacecraft already 200,000 miles away from Earth. As he speaks, Lovell watches the ship's oxygen supply leak into endless space. Nor is this the extent of the problems, for it soon becomes apparent that the same explosion that caused the gas tank to rupture has damaged the ship's propulsion engines to the point where, without a great deal of luck and ingenuity, the crew would indeed make it to the moon—but they would never be coming home.

Cast

Tom Hanks: Jim Lovell
Bill Paxton: Fred Haise
Kevin Bacon: Jack Swigert
Gary Sinise: Ken Mattingly
Ed Harris: Gene Kranz
Kathleen Quinlan: Marilyn Lovell
Tracy Reiner: Mary Haise

Behind the Scenes

Director: Ron Howard
Writers: Jim Lovell and Jeffrey Kluger (book), William Broyles Jr. and Al Reinert (screenplay)
Producers: Lorne Orleans, Brian Gazer
Executive Producer: Todd Hallowell

Awards

Oscar Winners: Best Film Editing, Best Sound

Trivia

• Many thought the scene in which Marilyn Lovell dropped her wedding ring down the drain seemed contrived, but this actually happened in real life.

1981
Arthur

Overview

Genre: Comedy/ Romance
Duration: 97 min
Color: Color (Technicolor)
Country: USA
MPAA Rating: PG
Studio: Orion Pictures

Millionaire playboy Arthur Bach has a pretty good life. While everyone else works for a living, Arthur boozes, plays with toys, and generally lives in a state of arrested adolescence. One day while shopping with his butler and best friend Hobson, Arthur meets Linda, a feisty waitress who has been caught shoplifting at a department store. Immediately smitten, Arthur plans to see a lot more of Linda. Those plans are quickly extinguished when Arthur's family announces that they will cut him off financially unless he marries his current wealthy, boring girlfriend. It's up to Arthur to decide between his lavish, carefree lifestyle and the one thing that money can't buy.

Cast

Dudley Moore: Arthur Bach
Liza Minelli: Linda Marolla
John Gielgud: Hobson
Geraldine Fitzgerald: Martha Bach
Jill Eikenberry: Susan Johnson
Stephen Elliott: Burt Johnson
Barney Martin: Ralph Marolla

Behind the Scenes

Director: Steve Gordon
Writer: Steve Gordon
Producer: Robert Greenhut
Executive Producer: Charles H. Joffe
Cinematographer: Fred Schuler
Original Music: Burt Bacharach, Christopher Cross, Carol Bayer Sager, Peter Allen

Awards

Oscar Winners: Best Supporting Actor, Best Music—Original Song
Oscar Nominations: Best Actor

Trivia

• John Gielgud refused the part of Hobson several times until the salary proved so substantial—and tempting—that he couldn't pass it up.

1997
As Good as It Gets

Overview

Genre: Comedy/Drama
Duration: 139 min
Color: Color
Country: USA
MPAA Rating: PG-13
Studio: TriStar
Pictures/Gracie Films

W here practical meets paranoid and sane meets schizophrenic you'll find the unlikely love story of Melvin Udall and Carol Connelly. A young waitress and single mother, Carol is fiery, honest, and determined to make it on her own. But, when she is forced to accept the help of a difficult and emotionally unbalanced customer she realizes she must reevaluate her standards and accept her limitations. Jack Nicholson and Helen Hunt shine in their Academy Award-winning roles in this heartwarming comedy that reminds us never to judge a book by its cover and to always take a chance on love.

Cast

Jack Nicholson: Melvin Udall
Helen Hunt: Carol Connelly
Greg Kinnear: Simon Bishop
Cuba Gooding Jr.: Frank Sachs
Skeet Ulrich: Vincent Lopiano
Shirley Knight: Beverly Connelly
Yeardley Smith: Jackie Simpson

Behind the Scenes

Director: James L. Brooks
Writers: Mark Andrus (story), Mark Andrus and James L. Brooks (screenplay)
Producers: James L. Brooks, Bridget Johnson, Kristi Zea
Executive Producers: Laura Ziskin, Richard Sakai, Laurence Mark
Cinematographer: John Bailey

Trivia

• Verdell the dog was played by six Brussels Griffons.
• The Monty Python song "Always Look on the Bright Side of Life" is performed for the soundtrack by Art Garfunkel.

Awards

Oscar Winners: Best Actor, Best Actress
Oscar Nominations: Best Supporting Actor, Best Film Editing, Best Music, Best Picture, Best Writing

1997
Austin Powers: International Man of Mystery

Overview

Genre: Comedy/ Adventure
Duration: 94 min
Color: Color
Country: USA
MPAA Rating: PG-13
Studio: New Line Cinema

Austin Powers, a British secret agent from the swinging '60s, has been cryogenically frozen. In the '90s he is thawed out to help bring down the notorious Dr. Evil, who is holding the world hostage with a nuclear threat to the tune of $100 billion. Powers, a walking anachronism, teams up with beautiful British agent Vanessa Kensington as they attempt to foil Dr. Evil's nefarious plans. Along the way they must contend with a veritable rogues' gallery of bumbling henchmen and kooky killers including Number Two, Alotta Fagina, Random Task, and the Fembots. Wild costumes and sight gags abound in this silly spy parody.

Cast

Mike Myers: Austin Powers / Dr. Evil
Elizabeth Hurley: Vanessa Kensington
Michael York: Basil Exposition
Mimi Rogers: Mrs. Kensington
Robert Wagner: Number Two
Seth Green: Scott Evil
Fabiana Udenio: Alotta Fagina

Behind the Scenes

Director: Jay Roach
Writer: Mike Myers
Producers: Demi Moore, Mike Myers, Jennifer Todd, Suzanne Todd
Executive Producers: Eric McLeod, Claire Rudnick Polstein
Original Music: George S. Clinton

Awards

MTV Movie Award: Best Dance Sequence, Best Villain

Trivia

• The shoe-throwing villain, Random Task, is based on the character Oddjob from the James Bond film *Goldfinger* (1964).

1955
Bad Day at Black Rock

Overview

Genre: Drama/Thriller
Duration: 81 min
Color: Color (Eastmancolor)
Country: USA
MPAA Rating: Not Rated
Studio: Metro-Goldwyn-Mayer (MGM)

When a one-armed man gets off a train in the tiny western town of Black Rock, he finds himself a most unwelcome guest. Apparently no one has visited this remote locale in quite some time, but that doesn't account for the overly unfriendly behavior of the locals toward John J. Macreedy. They offer no help as he attempts to visit an area known as Adobe Flat. But when he eventually states his purpose and makes it clear that he intends to see it though, things start getting tense. Not only may Macreedy not find what he's looking for in Black Rock, he may not make it out alive.

Cast

Spencer Tracy: John J. Macreedy
Robert Ryan: Reno Smith
Anne Francis: Liz Wirth
Dean Jagger: Sheriff Tim Horn
Walter Brennan: Doc T.R. Velie Jr.
John Ericson: Pete Wirth
Ernest Borgnine: Coley Trimble

Behind the Scenes

Director: John Sturges
Writers: Howard Breslin (story), Millard Kaufman and Don McGuire (screenplay)
Producer: Dore Schary
Film Editor: Newell P. Kimlin
Cinematographer: William C. Mellor

Awards

Oscar Nominations: Best Actor, Best Director, Best Writing

Trivia

• Spencer Tracy bought himself the suit that his character Macreedy wears throughout the film.

1976
The Bad News Bears

Overview

Genre: Comedy/ Sports
Duration: 102 min
Color: Color
Country: USA
MPAA Rating: PG
Studio: Paramount Pictures

What happens when a boozy pool cleaner agrees to coach of a bunch of little league misfits? When ex–minor leaguer Morris Buttermaker gets paid by a city councilman to take over the Chico's Bail Bonds Bears he finds his roster filled with nothing but awful ballplayers and bad attitudes. After the Bears get crushed in their first couple of games, both the kids and their parents are ready to call it a season. Instead, Buttermaker convinces his ex-girlfriend's hard-throwing daughter Amanda to be the team's new pitcher, and adds local punk Kelly Leak as an all-around ringer. But are two superstars enough to overcome the deficiencies of a talentless team and ne'er-do-well coach?

Cast

Walter Matthau: Coach Morris Buttermaker
Chris Barnes: Tanner Boyle
Tatum O'Neal: Amanda Whurlitzer
Erin Blunt: Ahmad Abdul Rahim
Jackie Earle Haley: Kelly Leak
Gary Lee Cavagnaro: Engelberg
Jaime Escobedo: Jose Agilar

Behind the Scenes

Director: Michael Ritchie
Writer: Bill Lancaster
Producer: Stanley R. Jaffe
Film Editor: Richard A. Harris
Cinematographer: John A. Alonzo
Original Music: Jerry Fielding

Awards

BAFTA Nomination: Best Actor

Trivia

• Writer Bill Lancaster supposedly based the character of Buttermaker on his famous father Burt Lancaster.

2003
Bad Santa

Overview

Genre: Comedy/
Crime
Duration: 91 min
Color: Color
Country: USA
MPAA Rating: R
Studio: Dimension
Films/Triptych Pictures

This film's title is quite possibly the understatement of all time. Billy Bob Thornton stars as Willie, the most debauched department store Santa Claus in the history of film or any other medium. A smalltime crook, Willie makes just enough money to keep him drunk, horny, and miserable. Each Christmas season he partners up with Marcus, a little person who plays elf to Willie's Santa as the two knock over the store where they work. Adding a touch of innocence to the felonious festivities is an awkward young boy who desperately wants to be Santa's friend. A deliciously dark comedy, *Bad Santa* is the antidote to too much Christmas cheer.

Cast

Billy Bob Thornton: Willie
Tony Cox: Marcus
Brett Kelly: The Kid
Lauren Graham: Sue
Lauren Tom: Lois
Bernie Mac: Gin
John Ritter: Bob Chipeska

Behind the Scenes

Director: Terry Zwigoff
Writers: Glenn Ficarra, John Requa
Producers: Sarah Aubrey, John Cameron,
Bob Weinstein
Executive Producers: Ethan Coen and Joel
Coen
Original Music: David Kitay

Awards

Golden Globe Nomination: Best
Actor—Musical or Comedy

Trivia

• This film marked John Ritter's final film
appearance and is dedicated to his memory.

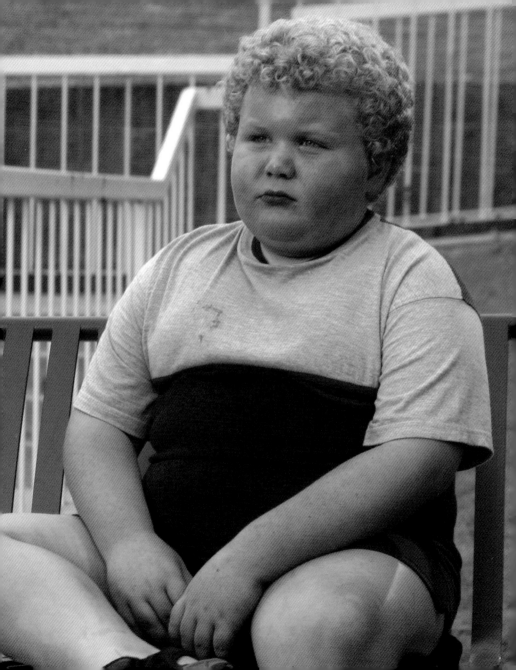

1942
Bambi

Overview

Genre: Family/Drama
Duration: 70 min
Color: Color
Country: USA
MPAA Rating: G
Studio: Walt Disney Productions

As the dawn breaks deep in the woods, the young rabbit Thumper and other forest creatures gather around to meet the new prince, a fawn named Bambi. This charming animated film follows Bambi as he grows up alongside Thumper and a new friend, Flower the skunk, and meets other deer like the bold Faline and the majestic Great Prince of the Forest. When tragedy strikes, Bambi must continue his ascent to the role of prince without his mother. As the cycles of seasons pass, Bambi will learn how to be brave, so he can lead his friends to safety and may even find love.

Cast

Hardie Albright: Adolescent Bambi (voice)
Stan Alexander: Young Flower (voice)
Peter Behn: Young Thumper (voice)
Thelma Boardman: Mrs. Quail (voice)
Donnie Dunagan: Young Bambi (voice)
Sam Edwards: Adult Thumper (voice)
Sterling Holloway: Adult Flower (voice)

Behind the Scenes

Director: David Hand
Writers: Felix Salten (novel), Larry Morey and Perce Pearce (story)
Producer: Walt Disney
Cinematography: Maxwell Morgan
Original Music: Edward H. Plump

Awards

Oscar Nominations: Best Music—Original Song, Best Music

Trivia

• The movie lost money during its first release in 1942, but was a box-office hit when re-released in 1947.

1940
The Bank Dick

Overview

Genre: Comedy
Duration: 73 min
Color: Color
Country: Black and White
MPAA Rating: Not Rated
Studio: Universal Pictures

The marvelous W.C. Fields stars as Egbert Sousé, a man whose life consists of smoking cigarettes in his room, drinking at an establishment called the Black Pussy Cat Café, and generally being a source of contempt among his family. Outside of his wretched home life, Sousé somehow manages to talk himself onto a movie set as the replacement for an inebriated director and also unwittingly foils a bank robbery. As a result of the latter, he is given a job as a bank guard. What follows is a series of gaffes, gags, and hilarious dialogue. In the end, what makes this movie so good is Fields himself. He's a comedic genius of the highest order.

Cast

W.C. Fields: Egbert Sousé
Cora Witherspoon: Agatha Sousé
Una Merkel: Myrtle Sousé
Evelyn Del Rio: Elsie Mae Adele Brunch Sousé
Jessie Ralph: Mrs. Hermisillo Brunch
Franklin Pangborn: J. Pinkerton Snoopington
Shemp Howard: Joe Guelpe, Bartender

Behind the Scenes

Director: Edward F. Cline
Writer: W.C. Fields
Executive Producer: Cliff Work (uncredited)
Cinematographer: Milton R. Krasner
Original Music: Frank Skinner (uncredited)

Awards

Added to National Film Registry in 1992

Trivia

- After Universal's censors turned down W.C. Fields's original script, director Edward Cline suggested that they film Fields's script anyway. Universal's front office never noticed.

1979
Being There

Overview

Genre: Comedy/Drama
Duration: 130 min
Color: Color
(Technicolor)
Country: USA
MPAA Rating: PG
Studio: Lorimar Pro-
ductions/United Artists

When a rich old man dies, a middle-aged, simple-minded gardener named Chance is forced to find somewhere else to work and live. Wandering the streets of Washington, D.C., Chance gets injured when he walks behind the limousine of powerful businessman Ben Rand. Taken to the Rand mansion, Chance's gentle demeanor and limited vocabulary soon endear him to both the terminally ill Ben and his wife Eve. The funny thing is, Ben and Eve and their well-connected friends all seem to mistake Chance's simplistic statements for quiet genius. The more he spouts odd gardening statements and repeats things he's seen on TV, the more popular he becomes. Peter Sellers delivers a terrific deadpan performance in this quirky comedy.

Cast

Peter Sellers: Chance
Shirley MacLaine: Eve Rand
Melvyn Douglas: Benjamin Rand
Jack Warden: President "Bobby"
Richard Dysart: Dr. Robert Allenby
Richard Basehart: Vladimir Skrapinov
David Clennon: Thomas Franklin

Behind the Scenes

Director: Hal Ashby
Writer: Jerzy Kosinski (novel and screenplay)
Producer: Andrew Braunsberg
Executive Producer: Jack Schwartzman
Cinematographer: Caleb Deschanel
Original Music: Johnny Mandel

Trivia

• Sellers repeatedly asked the producers to take the outtakes (shown during the end credits) out of the film when they submitted it to Cannes and released it to theaters, because he felt it "broke the spell" of the film.
• The inscription on Rand's tomb reads "Life is a state of mind," and these words also are the last line of the film. When Sellers died a year after the film's release, they were inscribed on Sellers's gravestone as well.

Awards

Oscar Winners: Best Supporting Actor
Oscar Nominations: Best Actor

1946
The Best Years of Our Lives

Overview

Genre: Drama/Romance
Duration: 172 min
Color: Black and White
Country: USA
MPAA Rating: Not Rated
Studio: Samuel Goldwyn Company

Three World War II vets from three different branches of the armed forces return to their Midwestern town and discover that their lives have changed dramatically. Al Stephenson, Fred Derry, and Homer Parrish meet on the transport plane home. Upon arriving in Boone City each man faces significant hurdles in his life. Al's banking position makes him sympathetic toward veterans that can't get loans. Fred returns to a damaged marriage and a dead-end job. And Homer, who lost both hands, worries about how his handicap is perceived. A stunning departure from other "returning hero" pictures, *The Best Years of Our Lives* is as relevant today as it was then.

Cast

Myrna Loy: Milly Stephenson
Fredric March: Al Stephenson
Dana Andrews: Fred Derry
Teresa Wright: Peggy Stephenson
Virginia Mayo: Marie Derry
Cathy O'Donnell: Wilma Cameron
Harold Russell: Homer Parrish

Behind the Scenes

Director: William Wyler
Writers: MacKinlay Kantor (novel) and Robert E. Sherwood (screenplay)
Producer: Samuel Goldwyn
Film Editor: Daniel Mandell
Cinematographer: Gregg Toland
Original Music: Hugo Friedhofer

Awards

Oscar Winners: Best Actor, Best Supporting Actor, Best Director, Best Film Editing, Best Music, Best Picture, Best Writing

Trivia

• In one of the bar scenes, Homer asks Butch to play a song, and Butch performs "Lazy River." Hoagy Carmichael, who plays Butch, composed that song.

1983
The Big Chill

Overview

Genre: Drama/Comedy
Duration: 105 min
Color: Color
(Metrocolor)
Country: USA
MPAA Rating: R
Studio: Columbia
Pictures

Upon receiving the news that their friend Alex has committed suicide, former college classmates Sam, Michael, Nick, Meg, Karen, Sarah, and Harold gather for a memorable weekend. As they recount memories of their friend, they also confront current issues relating to themselves and each other. Sarah and Harold have still-fresh marital wounds while Karen is mired in a loveless marriage. At the same time that Sam is realizing the pitfalls of fame, Michael is tiring of writing about the famous. Meanwhile, Meg's biological clock is ticking and time is running out on Nick to straighten out his life. Together they'll eat, drink, laugh, cry, and try to make sense of it all.

Cast

Tom Berenger: Sam Weber
Glenn Close: Sarah Cooper
Jeff Goldblum: Michael Gold
William Hurt: Nick Carlton
Kevin Kline: Harold Cooper
Mary Kay Place: Meg Jones
Meg Tilly: Chloe
JoBeth Williams: Karen Bowens
Don Galloway: Richard Bowens

Behind the Scenes

Director: Lawrence Kasdan
Writers: Lawrence Kasdan, Barbara Benedek
Producer: Michael Shamberg
Executive Producers: Lawrence Kasdan, Marcia Nasatir
Film Editor: Carol Littleton
Cinematographer: John Bailey

Trivia

• Kevin Costner was meant to play Alex in flashbacks, but his scenes were all cut. He can still be seen as the body being dressed at the beginning of the film.
• The house used in the film is the same one in which *The Great Santini* was shot.

Awards

Oscar Nominations: Best Supporting Actress, Best Picture, Best Writing

1998
The Big Lebowski

Overview

Genre: Comedy/
Duration: 117 min
Color: Color
(Technicolor)
Country: USA
MPAA Rating: R
Studio: Polygram
Filmed Entertainment/
Working Title Films

All The Dude ever wanted was to wear comfortable clothes, bowl a few games, and drink the occasional White Russian. But when two punks mistake him for a much richer man and ruin his favorite rug, he's looking for restitution. With the support of his bowling partners Walter and Donny, The Dude sets out to get reimbursed by the man with whom he shares a name—Jeffrey Lebowski. In the course of rectifying this little matter he's pulled into a bizarre world of kidnapping, pornography, and nihilists. Yet, faced with an assortment of oddball characters and ridiculous circumstances, The Dude abides.

Cast

Jeff Bridges: Jeffrey Lebowski—"The Dude"
John Goodman: Walter Sobchak
Julianne Moore: Maude Lebowski
Steve Buscemi: Theodore Donald "Donny" Kerabatsos
David Huddleston: Jeffrey Lebowski—"The Big Lebowski"
Philip Seymore Hoffman: Brandt
Tara Reid: Bunny Lebowski
John Turturro: Jesus Quintana
Sam Elliott: The Stranger

Behind the Scenes

Director: Joel Coen, Ethan Coen (uncredited)
Writers: Ethan Coen, Joel Coen
Producers: Ethan Coen, Joel Coen (uncredited)
Executive Producers: Tim Bevan, Eric Fellner
Cinematographer: Roger Deakins
Original Music: Carter Burwell

Trivia

• The Coen brothers wrote the screenplay with Jeff Bridges, John Goodman, Steve Buscemi, and Sam Elliot in mind for the parts they all play in the film.
• In keeping with traditional film-noir style, The Dude is in every scene of the film, except briefly when the Nihilists are ordering pancakes.
• Jeff Bridges raided his own personal wardrobe for most of The Dude's outfits.

1996
Big Night

Overview

Genre: Drama
Duration: 107 min
Color: Color
Country: USA
MPAA Rating: R
Studio: Rysher
Entertainment/Timpano
Productions

When two immigrant brothers, Primo and Secondo, open an authentic Italian restaurant in New Jersey, they find themselves struggling to compete with an already established red sauce joint. While Secondo handles the business side of things, Primo is a master chef who sweats every last detail of his remarkable cuisine. Struggling to find the recipe for success, Secondo turns to their main competitor for advice. When he promises to help the brothers out by bringing a famous name into their establishment, they throw everything they have into one special dinner that will make or break their restaurant. Filled with great performances and incredible-looking food, *Big Night* will leave you hungry for more.

Cast

Tony Shalhoub: Primo
Stanley Tucci: Secondo
Marc Anthony: Cristiano
Minnie Driver: Phyllis
Isabella Rossellini: Gabriella
Ian Holm: Pascal
Allison Janney: Ann
Campbell Scott: Bob

Behind the Scenes

Director: Campbell Scott and Stanley Tucci
Writers: Joseph Tropiano and Stanley Tucci
Producers: Jonathan Filley
Executive Producers: David Kirkpatrick, Keith Samples
Cinematographer: Ken Kelsch
Original Music: Gary DeMichele

Trivia

• The woman performing at the rival restaurant is played by Christine Tucci—Stanley Tucci's sister.

Awards

Independent Spirit Award: Best First Screenplay
Independent Spirit Award Nominations: Best First Feature, Best Male Lead

1974
Blazing Saddles

Overview

Genre: Comedy/
Western
Duration: 93 min
Color: Color
(Technicolor)
Country: USA
MPAA Rating: R
Studio: Warner Bros.
Pictures

In order to clear out the town of Rock Ridge for railroad construction a corrupt politician named Hedley Lamarr appoints a black man as their new sheriff. Upon his arrival, the sophisticated and street-smart Bart is treated to one of the rudest welcoming ceremonies ever. After making it back to the jailhouse in one piece, he befriends a prisoner named Jim who counsels him on the ways of simple folk. But when Lamarr sends a horse-punching behemoth named Mongo to smash up the town, it's anybody's guess how Bart will stop him. Packed with sight gags, songs, and a knee-slapping final showdown, Mel Brooks leaves no stone unturned in this zany send-up of Westerns.

Cast

Cleavon Little: Bart
Gene Wilder: Jim
Slim Pickens: Taggart
Harvey Korman: Hedley Lamarr
Madeline Kahn: Lili Von Shtupp
Mel Brooks: Governor William J. Lepetomane/ Indian Chief
Burton Gilliam: Lyle
Alex Karras: Mongo

Behind the Scenes

Director: Mel Brooks
Writers: Andrew Bergman (story and screenplay), Mel Brooks, Norman Steinberg, Richard Pryor, and Alan Uger (screenplay)
Producer: Michael Hertzberg
Film Editor: Danford B. Greene
Cinematographer: Joseph F. Biroc
Original Music: John Morris

Trivia

• According to the filmmakers, this is the first film in history to feature the sound of farting. Mel Brooks and his fellow writers came up with the idea after watching cowboys consume only coffee and beans in old westerns, and they concluded that this combination must lead to farting.
• Gene Wilder (Jim) joined the cast on the condition that Mel Brooks use his idea for his next film. Brooks agreed, and Wilder's idea was the basis for *Young Frankenstein*.

Awards

Oscar Nominations: Best Supporting Actress, Best Film Editing, Best Music—Original Song

1986
Blue Velvet

Overview

Genre: Drama/Thriller
Duration: 120 min
Color: Color
Country: USA
MPAA Rating: R
Studio: De Laurentiis Entertainment Group

Upon finding a severed ear in his suburban hometown, Jeffrey Beaumont decides to investigate. After alerting the police to his find, Jeffrey takes up with Sandy, a detective's daughter, and the pair does some sleuthing of their own. Soon Jeffrey finds himself wrapped up in a dark underworld where a mysterious and beautiful nightclub singer may hold the key to the missing appendage. But there are others involved as well, most prominently an ether-inhaling psychopath named Frank Booth who isn't exactly a model of stability. The more Jeffrey pokes his nose into the case, the closer he gets to having it end up like that ear.

Cast

Isabella Rossellini: Dorothy Vallens
Kyle MacLachlan: Jeffrey Beaumont
Dennis Hopper: Frank Booth
Laura Dern: Sandy Williams
Hope Lange: Mrs. Williams
Dean Stockwell: Ben
George Dickerson: Detective John Williams

Behind the Scenes

Director: David Lynch
Writer: David Lynch
Producer: Fred C. Caruso
Executive Producer: Richard A. Roth
Original Music: Angelo Badalamenti
Cinematographer: Frederick Elmes

Awards

Oscar Nomination: Best Director

Trivia

• The prosthetic ear found by Kyle McLachlin's character at the beginning of the film is on display at Movie Madness Video and More in Portland, Oregon.

1981
Body Heat

Overview

Genre: Drama/Crime
Duration: 113 min
Color: Color (Technicolor)
Country: USA
MPAA Rating: R
Studio: The Ladd Company/Warner Bros.

Matty Walker is the type of woman most men would kill for, and attorney Ned Racine just may be one of those guys. When Walker saunters past Racine in the sizzling Florida heat, he's immediately interested in whatever she's selling. It's not long before the two are tearing at each other's clothes. But the one thing standing in the way of complete carnal nirvana is Matty's wealthy older husband. What to do about him? Surely two intelligent, attractive adults can figure something out. A modern film noir in the tradition of *Double Indemnity*, *Body Heat* is the perfect combination of crime and passion.

Cast

William Hurt: Ned Racine
Kathleen Turner: Matty Walker
Richard Crenna: Edmund Walker
Ted Danson: Peter Lowenstein
J.A. Preston: Oscar Grace
Mickey Rourke: Teddy Lewis
Kim Zimmer: Mary Ann Simpson

Behind the Scenes

Director: Lawrence Kasdan
Writer: Lawrence Kasdan
Producer: Fred T. Gallo
Executive Producer: George Lucas (uncredited)
Cinematographer: Richard H. Kline
Original Music: John Barry

Awards

Golden Globe Nomination: New Star of the Year in a Motion Picture (Turner)
BAFTA Nomination: Most Outstanding Newcomer to Leading Film Roles (Turner)

Trivia

• Christopher Reeve turned down the part of Ned Racine because he thought he wouldn't be convincing as a seedy lawyer.

1967
Bonnie and Clyde

Overview

Genre: Drama/Action
Duration: 112 min
Color: Black and White
Country: USA
MPAA Rating: R
Studio: Warner Bros.-
Seven Arts

There's nothing like a couple of attractive, fun-loving, gun-toting, bank robbers to get your attention. Starring Faye Dunaway and Warren Beatty as the sexy stick-up artists, *Bonnie and Clyde* is a wild and wooly ride loosely based on the true adventures of the Depression era duo. Once small-time crook Clyde Barrow catches Bonnie Parker's eye, the attraction is immediate and the results combustible. Hooked on each other and the rush of robbing banks, Bonnie and Clyde soon grab headlines and develop a cult following as a pair of latter-day Robin Hoods. But the law doesn't see it that way, and things just may get messy.

Cast

Warren Beatty: Clyde Barrow
Faye Dunaway: Bonnie Parker
Michael J. Pollard: C.W. Moss
Gene Hackman: Buck Barrow
Estelle Parsons: Blanche
Denver Pyle: Frank Hamer
Dub Tayor: Ivan Moss
Gene Wilder: Eugene Grizzard

Behind the Scenes

Director: Arthur Penn
Writers: David Newman, Robert Benton, Robert Towne (uncredited)
Producer: Warren Beatty
Film Editing: Dede Allen
Cinematographer: Burnett Guffey
Original Music: Charles Strouse

Trivia

• François Truffaut and Jean-Luc Godard were each offered the chance to direct the film, but they both turned it down.
• This film marked the silver screen debut of actor Gene Wilder.

Awards

Oscar Winners: Best Supporting Actress, Best Cinematography
Oscar Nominations: Best Actor, Best Supporting Actor, Best Actress, Best Costume Design, Best Director, Best Picture, Best Writing

1985
The Breakfast Club

Overview

Genre: Drama
Duration: 97 min
Color: Color
Country: USA
MPAA Rating: R
Studio: Universal Pictures

Detained in the longest, more important Saturday of their young lives, five stereotypes define the American teenage experience. Forced into close quarters and united in a common purpose—getting through detention, and also making it through the gauntlet of high school—they slowly, painfully discover what a jock, a rebel, a princess, an outcast, and a nerd have in common. Writer/Director John Hughes hit a nerve by exposing teenage cliques as false denominations among a unique generation. *The Breakfast Club* earned that rare distinction of transcending its teen drama genre and becoming an enduring American classic.

Cast

Emilio Estevez: Andrew "Andy" Clark
Anthony Michael Hall: Brian Ralph Johnson
Judd Nelson: John Bender
Molly Ringwald: Claire Standish
Ally Sheedy: Allison Reynolds
Paul Gleason: Principal Richard Vernon
John Kapelos: Carl the Janitor

Behind the Scenes

Director: John Hughes
Writer: John Hughes
Producer: John Hughes and Ned Tanen
Cinematographer: Thomas Del Ruth
Original Music: Keith Forsey

Trivia

• Writer/Director John Hughes has a brief cameo as Brian's father.

Trivia

• Ranked as the best high school movie by *Entertainment Weekly* in 2006, this film was shot completely in sequence.

1979
Breaking Away

Overview

Genre: Comedy/Sports
Duration: 100 min
Color: Color
Country: USA
MPAA Rating: PG
Studio: Twentieth Century Fox

Dave Stoller wants to be an Italian bike racer; the problem is, he lives in Indiana with his parents. Having a dream is one thing, but when Dave starts shaving his legs, listening to opera records, and speaking Italian, his father has had just about all he can stand. Living in the shadow of Indiana University, Dave and his friends Mike, Cyril, and Moocher are known derisively as "Cutters" by the privileged frat boys that take over their town every year. When the animosity between the students and Cutters reaches a boiling point, Dave and his friends decide to compete against the fraternities the only way they know how—on a bike.

Cast

Dennis Christopher: Dave Stoller
Dennis Quaid: Mike
Daniel Stern: Cyril
Jackie Earle Haley: Moocher
Barbara Barrie: Mrs. Stoller
Paul Dooley: Mr. Stoller
Robyn Douglass: Katherine

Behind the Scenes

Director: Peter Yates
Writer: Steve Tesich
Producer: Peter Yates, Art Levinson
Film Editor: Cynthia Scheider
Cinematographer: Matthew F. Leonetti
Original Music: Patrick Williams

Awards

Oscar Winners: Best Writing
Oscar Nominations: Best Supporting Actress, Best Director, Best Music, Best Picture

Trivia

• The movie's success spawned a short-lived series about Dave and his friends' lives in Bloomington.

1960
Breathless

Overview

Genre: Drama/Thriller
Duration: 90 min
Color: Black and White
Country: France
MPAA Rating: Not Rated
Studio: Les Productions Georges de Beauregard/ Société Bouvelle de Cinématographie (SNC)

Iconic of French New Wave films, *À Bout de souffle—Breathless*—pays tribute to the history of cinema while illustrating a love story with tragic results. Jean-Paul Belmondo plays small-time crook Michel Poiccard who is the epitome of cool. After Poiccard offhandedly kills a police officer, he takes refuge with his New Yorker girlfriend Patricia—the stunning Jean Seberg—an aspiring journalist. The two lovers hide from the authorities and when the tension mounts, betrayal seems likely. The handheld camera work provides Godard's flowing narrative with a documentary-like frame. *Breathless* is a thrilling modern masterpiece that will remain a staple of pop culture.

Cast

Jean-Paul Belmondo: Michel Poiccard
Jean Seberg: Patricia Franchini
Daniel Boulanger: Police Inspector Vital
Jean-Pierre Melville: Parvulesco
Henri-Jacques Huet: Antonio Berrutti
Van Doude: Himself
Claude Mansard: Claudius Mansard

Behind the Scenes

Director: Jean-Luc Godard
Writers: François Truffaut (story), Jean-Luc Godard (screenplay)
Producer: Georges de Beauregard
Original Music: Martial Solal
Cinematography: Raoul Coutard

Awards

BAFTA Nominations: Best Foreign Actress

Trivia

• Director Jean-Luc Godard could not afford a dolly for the camera, so he pushed the cinematographer around in a wheelchair through many scenes of the film.

1957
The Bridge on the River Kwai

Overview

Genre: Drama/Adventure
Duration: 161 min
Color: Color
Country: UK/USA
MPAA Rating: PG
Studio: Columbia Pictures

British POWs held in a Burmese prison camp are forced to build a strategic rail bridge in this gripping World War II drama. After their capture, British soldiers are ordered by their ruthless Japanese camp commander Colonel Saito to construct a bridge that will greatly aid the enemy. Sir Alec Guinness turns in an Oscar-winning performance as Colonel Nicholson, the British commanding officer who first stands up to Saito but finally agrees to build the bridge as a monument to the fortitude of his men. As the company reluctantly resume construction under Nicholson's direction, the Allies hatch a plan to destroy it. *The Bridge on the River Kwai* is a brilliant microcosm of the pure insanity of war.

Cast

William Holden: Shears
Jack Hawkins: Major Warden
Alec Guinness: Colonel Nicholson
Sessue Hayakawa: Colonel Saito
James Donald: Major Clipton
Geoffrey Horne: Lieutenant Joyce
André Morell: Colonel Green
Peter Williams: Captain Reeves

Behind the Scenes

Director: David Lean
Writers: Pierre Boulle (novel), Michael Wilson and Carl Foreman (screenplay)
Producer: Sam Spiegel
Film Editor: Peter Taylor
Cinematographer: Jack Hildyard
Original Music: Malcolm Arnold

Trivia

• The blacklisted screenplay writers Michael Wilson and Carl Foreman didn't receive credits when the film was first released. This resulted in French novelist Pierre Boulle, who didn't speak English, winning the Oscar for Best Adapted Screenplay.

Awards

Oscar Winners: Best Actor, Best Cinematography, Best Director, Best Film Editing, Best Music, Best Picture, Best Writing—Adapted Screenplay
Oscar Nomination: Best Supporting Actor

1995
The Bridges of Madison County

Overview

Genre: Drama/ Romance
Duration: 135 min
Color: Color (Technicolor)
Country: USA
MPAA Rating: PG-13
Studio: Warner Bros. Pictures

Robert Kincaid, a traveling photographer and worldly loner enters Madison County in the hopes of photographing its many covered bridges. What he finds there will change his life forever. Francesca Johnson, a lonely and misplaced housewife offers him tea, directions, and a place to stay for four fateful days. This short time turns her world upside down and leaves her torn between the life of stability she has and the new love she feels. As Francesca's story is discovered and recounted by her children after her death, it uncovers those universal truths about the choices that we make in life and the struggle between what seems right in the world and what you know to be right in your heart.

Cast

Clint Eastwood: Robert Kincaid
Meryl Streep: Francesca Johnson
Annie Corley: Carolyn Johnson
Victor Slezak: Michael Johnson
Jim Haynie: Richard Johnson
Sarah Kathryn Schmitt: Young Carolyn
Christopher Kroon: Young Michael

Behind the Scenes

Director: Clint Eastwood
Writers: Robert James Waller (novel), Richard LaGravenese (screenplay)
Producers: Clint Eastwood, Kathleen Kennedy
Film Editor: Joel Cox
Cinematographer: Jack N. Green

Awards

Oscar Nominations: Best Actress

Trivia

• Both the Cedar Bridge where Francesca and Robert meet and the house that was used as the set for Francesca's home burned down in two separate fires a year apart.

1988
Bull Durham

Overview

Genre: Comedy/ Sports
Duration: 108 min
Color: Color
Country: USA
MPAA Rating: R
Studio: Orion Pictures

Ebby Calvin "Nuke" LaLoosh is a talented young minor league pitcher with a million dollar arm but a five-cent head. In order to get LaLoosh's mechanics and mind in shape, the organization demotes reluctant veteran catcher Crash Davis from his Triple A team to show the kid the ropes. Also on hand to help LaLoosh is Annie Savoy, a beautiful fan of the struggling Durham Bulls who bestows "life wisdom" upon one lucky player each season. Crash can't stand LaLoosh but likes Annie. Annie wants Crash but is committed to "Nuke." They're all about to find out that turning a triple play is a lot easier on the field than it is off.

Cast

Kevin Costner: Crash Davis
Susan Sarandon: Annie Savoy
Tim Robbins: Ebby Calvin "Nuke" LaLoosh
Trey Wilson: Joe Riggins
Robert Wuhl: Larry Hockett
William O'Leary: Jimmy

Behind the Scenes

Director: Ron Shelton
Writer: Ron Shelton
Producers: Mark Burg, Thom Mount
Executive Producer: David V. Lester
Film Editors: Robert Leighton, Adam Weiss
Cinematographer: Bobby Byrne
Original Music: Michael Convertino

Awards

Oscar Nominations: Best Writing

Trivia

• The bull sign at the old baseball field was built for the film, but the Durham Bulls liked it so much that they put it into their new ballpark, where it is used to this day.

1968
Bullitt

Overview

Genre: Drama/Action
Duration: 114 min
Color: Color (Technicolor)
Country: USA
MPAA Rating: PG
Studio: Warner Bros.-Seven Arts/Solar Productions

The King of Cool, Steve McQueen stars as Detective Lieutenant Frank Bullitt. Set in the late-60s San Francisco, we follow Bullitt as he attempts to protect a witness from thugs who don't want him to rat. Then the rat takes it to the face from a sawed-off shotgun. But the rat isn't who we thought he was. The plot is almost inconsequential here. What matters is McQueen picking the thread, angry and sporting a souped up 390 Mustang. McQueen was his own wheelman for the majority of this production, and that gives the chase scenes an air of gritty authenticity. His performance is the archetype for the blank, nihilistic action hero . . . and cool baby, real cool.

Cast

Steve McQueen: Bullitt
Robert Vaughn: Chalmers
Jacqueline Bisset: Cathy
Don Gordon: Delgetti
Robert Duvall: Weissberg
Simon Oakland: Captain Bennet
Norman Fell: Captain Baker

Behind the Scenes

Director: Peter Yates
Writers: Robert L. Fish (novel), Alan Trustman and Harry Kleiner (screenplay)
Producer: Philip D'Antoni
Executive Producer: Robert E. Relyea
Cinematographer: William A. Fraker
Original Music: Lalo Schifrin

Awards

Oscar Winner: Best Film Editing
Oscar Nomination: Best Sound

Trivia

• Steve McQueen purposely kept his head close to the open car window during the famous car chase so that audiences would be able to tell that he was actually driving.

1969
Butch Cassidy and the Sundance Kid

Overview

Genre: Drama/Adventure
Duration: 110 min
Color: Color
Country: USA
MPAA Rating: PG
Studio: Twentieth Century Fox

This lively retelling of the story of the legendary bank robbing team stars Paul Newman as Butch and Robert Redford as Sundance. After Butch and his Hole in the Wall Gang rob the Union Pacific railroad one too many times, the railroad hires an all-star posse to track them down. But rather than chasing the entire gang, the posse only goes after Butch and Sundance. Their relentless pursuit of these two anti-heroes has Butch repeatedly asking the question "who are those guys?" After a narrow escape, the likable duo decide to take their act to another country. But this new venue will take some getting used to.

Cast

Paul Newman: Butch Cassidy
Robert Redford: The Sundance Kid
Katharine Ross: Etta Place
Strother Martin: Percy Garris
Henry Jones: Bike salesman
Jeff Corey: Sheriff Bledsoe
George Furth: Woodcock

Behind the Scenes

Director: George Roy Hill
Writer: William Goldman
Producer: John Foreman
Executive Producer: Paul Monash
Cinematographer: Conrad L. Hall
Original Music: Burt Bacharach

Awards

Oscar Winners: Best Cinematography, Best Original Song, Best Original Score, Best Writing
Oscar Nominations: Best Director, Best Picture, Best Sound

Trivia

• The real name of Butch's gang was The Wild Bunch, but a change to the Hole in the Wall Gang avoided any confusion with Sam Peckinpah's *The Wild Bunch* (1969).

1972
Cabaret

Overview

Genre: Musical/Drama
Duration: 124 min
Color: Color (Technicolor)
Country: USA
MPAA Rating: PG
Studio: ABC Pictures

As the Nazis rise to power in Berlin, the dark, burlesque-style Kit Kat Klub parties on into the wee hours of night. One of its star entertainers, Sally Bowles, struggles with her personal demons and a precarious relationship while belting out show-stopping song and dance numbers. This musical also serves as a commentary on the social unrest of the Second World War and the desperation and need for escape felt by those living in a changing Germany. As one of the most exciting cities in Europe begins its dark descent into political dysfunction, the gritty Kit Kat Klub—led by Liza Minelli's Sally and Joel Grey as the all-seeing Master of Ceremonies—serves as a raging, yet impotent voice against the inevitable.

Cast

Liza Minnelli: Sally Bowles
Michael York: Brian Roberts
Helmut Griem: Maximilian von Heune
Joel Grey: Master of Ceremonies
Fritz Wepper: Fritz Wendel
Marisa Berenson: Natalia Landauer

Behind the Scenes

Director: Bob Fosse
Writers: Christopher Isherwood (story), John Van Druten (play), Joe Masteroff (book), Jay Presson Allen (screenplay)
Producer: Cy Feuer
Film Editor: David Bretherton
Cinematographer: Geoffrey Unsworth
Original Music: John Kander

Trivia

• The song "Tomorrow Belongs to Me," is now thought to be a real Nazi anthem, but it was created specifically for *Cabaret* by composer/lyricist team John Kander and Fred Ebb. It has led to accusations of anti-Semitism against the two of them, though both are Jewish.

Awards

Oscar Winners: Best Supporting Actor, Best Actress, Best Art Direction, Best Cinematography, Best Director, Best Film Editing, Best Music, Best Sound
Oscar Nominations: Best Picture, Best Writing—Adapted Screenplay

1980
Caddyshack

Overview

Genre: Comedy/Sports
Duration: 98 min
Color: Color
(Technicolor)
Country: USA
MPAA Rating: R
Studio: Orion Pictures

Bushwood Country Club may employ some weirdos, but they sure don't want any as members. Caddy Danny Noonan's one chance to go to college may rely on him sucking up to Judge Smails, a snooty club member who awards an annual scholarship. But Danny still has time to chase girls, caddy for eccentric rich guy Ty Webb, and even play a few rounds himself. When boisterous millionaire developer Al Czervik shows up at Bushwood, the insults and wisecracks fly. Before long, it's war between Smails and Czervik with a golf match that could complicate things for Danny. But none of this may happen if wacko groundskeeper Carl Spackler doesn't win his own war against a pesky gopher.

Cast

Chevy Chase: Ty Webb
Rodney Dangerfield: Al Czervik
Ted Knight: Judge Elihu Smails
Michael O'Keefe: Danny Noonan
Bill Murray: Carl Spackler
Sarah Holcomb: Maggie O'Hooligan
Scott Colomby: Tony D'Annunzio
Cindy Morgan: Lacey Underall
Henry Wilcoxon: The Bishop

Behind the Scenes

Director: Harold Ramis
Writers: Harold Ramis, Brian Doyle-Murray, Douglas Kenney
Producers: Douglas Kenney, Stan Jolly
Executive Producer: Jon Peters
Film Editors: David Bretherton, William Carruth
Cinematographer: Stevan Larner
Original Music: Johnny Mandel

Trivia

• Writer/Director Harold Ramis told Bill Murray he wanted him to emulate a kid announcing his own fantasy sports moment, and that was all the direction Murray needed to improvise the famous "Cinderella story" sequence in just one take.
• Only one character in the film ever says the word "caddyshack"—Lou, who is played by the film's co-writer (and Bill Murray's brother) Brian Doyle-Murray.
• The chirping sound that the gopher makes is really the vocal track from a dolphin.

1942
Casablanca

Overview

Genre: Drama/ Romance
Duration: 99 min
Color: Black and White
Country: United States
MPAA Rating: PG
Studio: Warner Bros. Pictures

As World War II rages, exiles from all over Europe gather in the Moraccan city of Casablanca waiting for a chance to go to America. When two letters of transit fall into the hands of gruff expatriate and nightclub owner Rick Blaine, he finds himself holding the most valuable commodities in town. In no hurry to do anything with the letters, things change when Czech resistance leader Victor Laszlo shows up with Blaine's former love Ilsa Lund on his arm. Rick can help the duo escape the Nazis or he can continue to look after his own best interests. Filled with intrigue, romance, and suspense, Casablanca only gets better as time goes by.

Cast

Humphrey Bogart: Rick Blaine
Ingrid Bergman: Ilsa Lund
Paul Henreid: Victor Lazlo
Claude Rains: Louis Renault
Conrad Veidt: Major Strasser
Sydney Greenstreet: Ferrari
Peter Lorre: Ugarte
S.Z. Sakall: Carl

Behind the Scenes

Director: Michael Curtiz
Writers: Murray Burnett and Joan Alison (play), Julius J. Epstein, Philip G. Epstein and Howard Koch (screenplay), Casey Robinson (uncredited)
Producer: Hal B. Wallis
Executive Producer: Jack L. Warner
Cinematographer: Arthur Edeson
Original Music: Max Steiner

Trivia

• Dooley Wilson (Sam) was a professional drummer who faked playing the piano. The recorded music was by a performance by Elliot Carpenter, whose hand movements Wilson copied.

Awards

Oscar Winners: Best Director, Best Picture, Best Writing
Oscar Nominations: Best Actor, Best Supporting Actor, Best Cinematography, Best Film Editing, Best Music Score

1974
Chinatown

Overview

Genre: Drama/Thriller
Duration: 131 min
Color: Color
Country: USA
MPAA Rating: R
Studio: Paramount Pictures

Set in 1930s Los Angeles, Roman Polanski's wicked take on film noir centers around Jake Gittes, a private detective who works mostly on divorce cases. When he's hired by a woman to follow yet another possible stray husband, Gittes dutifully shadows the man and gets the goods on him. Just another day at the office until the man turns up dead and Gittes finds out that he wasn't hired by who he thought he was. As he digs to discover the truth, Jake finds a world bureaucratic corruption involving the city's water supply as well as some influential and dangerous people who would prefer he keep his nose out of their affairs.

Cast

Jack Nicholson: J.J. "Jake" Gittes
Faye Dunaway: Evelyn Cross Mulwray
John Huston: Noah Cross
Perry Lopez: Lieutenant Lou Escobar
John Hillerman: Russ Yelburton
Darrell Zwerling: Hollis I. Mulwray
Diane Ladd: Ida Sessions
Bruce Glover: Duffy
James Hong: Kahn

Behind the Scenes

Director: Roman Polanski
Writers: Robert Towne, Roman Polanski
Producers: Robert Evans, C.O. Erickson
Film Editor: Sam O'Steen
Cinematographer: John A. Alonzo
Original Music: Jerry Goldsmith

Trivia

• Faye Dunaway and Roman Polanski reportedly did not get along during production. One alleged incident had Polanski pulling out some of her hair during an argument.

Awards

Oscar Winner: Best Writing
Oscar Nominations: Best Actor, Best Actress, Best Art Direction, Best Cinematography, Best Costume Design, Best Director, Best Film Editing, Best Music, Best Picture, Best Sound

1983
A Christmas Story

Overview

Genre: Comedy
Duration: 94 min
Color: Color (Metrocolor)
Country: USA
MPAA Rating: PG
Studio: Metro Goldwyn Mayer (MGM)

All Ralphie wants for Christmas is an official Red Ryder BB rifle—is that too much to ask? Apparently so, as Ralphie's mother fears that he'll shoot his eye out. Undeterred, he'll use every bit of his imagination to help figure a way out of this BB conundrum, even if it means going to Santa himself. With Christmas fast approaching, Ralphie is running out of time to plead his case for this Holy Grail of all holiday gifts. Among the many obstacles standing in his way are his teacher, a neighborhood bully, and his lamp-obsessed father. Jean Shepherd wrote and narrates this timeless family Christmas tale.

Cast

Peter Billingsley: Ralphie Parker
Melinda Dillon: Mrs. Parker
Darren McGavin: Mr. Parker
Ian Petrella: Randy Parker
Scott Schwartz: Flick
R.D. Robb: Schwartz
Tedde Moore: Miss Shields

Behind the Scenes

Director: Bob Clark
Writers: Jean Shepherd (novel and screenplay), Leigh Brown and Bob Clark (screenplay)
Producers: Bob Clark, René Dupont
Film Editor: Stan Cole
Cinematographer: Reginald H. Morris
Original Music: Paul Zaza, Carl Zittrer

Awards

Writer's Guild of America (WGA) Nomination: Best Comedy Adapted from Another Medium

Trivia

• What seemed like nonsensical mutterings that Ralphie shouts as he beats up Scut Farkas were actually scripted word for word.

1990
Cinema Paradiso

Overview

Genre: Drama/Romance
Duration: 155 min
Color: Color
Country: Italy/France
MPAA Rating: PG
Studio: Cristaldi Pictures/Films Ariane/Forum Pictures/RAI 3

Upon hearing news from home, an Italian film director flashes back to his childhood in post–World War II Sicily. Growing up in a small village without much money, the precocious Salvatore (Toto) is fascinated with the movies. Alfredo, the gruff projectionist at the local cinema, befriends the boy. Even as he grows older, the young man is still drawn to the screen and his best friend. As the older Salvatore remembers the past, his village theater always seems to play a prominent role. Based on the true experiences of director Giuseppe Tornatore, *Cinema Paradiso* is a heartfelt valentine to the movies and the people who love them.

Cast

Philippe Noiret: Alfredo
Salvatore Cascio: Salvatore (Child)
Marco Leonardi: Salvatore (Adolescent)
Jacques Perrin: Salvatore (Adult)
Antonella Attili: Maria (Young)
Pupella Maggio: Maria (Older)

Behind the Scenes

Director: Giuseppe Tornatore
Writers: Giuseppe Tornatore (story and screenplay), Vanna Paoli (screenplay)
Producers: Franco Cristaldi, Giovanna Romagnoli
Film Editor: Mario Morra
Cinematographer: Blasco Giurato

Awards

Oscar Winner: Best Foreign Language Film

Trivia

• Director Giuseppe Tornatore makes a brief cameo appearance. He can be seen working the projection machine toward the end of the movie.

1941
Citizen Kane

Overview

Genre: Drama
Duration: 119 min
Color: Black and White
Country: United States
MPAA Rating: PG
Studio: Mercury Productions/RKO Radio Pictures

Orson Welles' 1941 masterpiece revolves around the life and death of newspaper tycoon Charles Foster Kane. The film opens with Kane's last breath and mysterious final word and then retraces the life of this fascinating mogul through newsreels, interviews, and flashback sequences. Who was this larger-than-life figure and how did he get where he was? Discovery is a recurring theme throughout. A life of sensational accomplishments and well-publicized failures only tell half the story. Orson Welles directed, starred in, and co-wrote the screenplay for *Citizen Kane*. Widely considered one of the greatest movies ever made, it's an absolute must for any self-respecting film buff.

Cast

Orson Welles: Charles Foster Cane
Joseph Cotten: Jedediah Leland
Dorothy Comingore: Susan Alexander Kane
Agnes Moorehead: Mary Kane
Ruth Warrick: Emily Monroe Norton Kane
Ray Collins: James W. Gettys
Erskine Sanford: Herbert Carter
Everett Sloane: Mr. Bernstein
William Alland: Jerry Thompson

Behind the Scenes

Director: Orson Welles
Writers: Orson Welles, Herman J. Mankiewicz
Producer: Orson Welles
Executive Producer: George Schaefer (uncredited)
Film Editors: Mark Robson, Robert Wise
Cinematographer: Gregg Toland
Original Music: Bernard Herrmann

Trivia

• During production, Orson Wells broke his ankle and was forced to direct from a wheelchair for two weeks. He wore metal braces when performing his lines.
• Cane is purportedly modeled after the legendary newspaper tycoon, William Randolph Hearst (1863–1951).

Awards

Oscar Winners: Best Writing
Oscar Nominations: Best Actor in a Leading Role, Best Art Direction, Best Cinematography, Best Director, Best Film Editing, Best Music Score, Best Picture, Best Sound

1972
A Clockwork Orange

Overview

Genre: Drama/Thriller
Duration: 136 min
Color: Color
Country: UK
MPAA Rating: R
Studio: Warner Bros. PIctures

In a futuristic England, Alex DeLarge and his droogs are one of many violent teenage gangs roaming the streets. Alex and company commit robberies, rapes, and dish out "ultra violence" on their hapless victims all in the name of fun. But when Alex's cohorts tire of his brutal leadership, they arrange for him to be caught by the police after one of his more insidious assaults. Facing a lengthy prison term, Alex tries to figure out any way to get his sentence shortened. An experimental government program that can cure criminals in as little as two weeks might be just the thing. But what kind of therapy is used to cure evil?

Cast

Malcolm McDowell: Alex DeLarge
Patrick Magee: Mr. Alexander
Michael Bates: Chief Guard
Warren Clarke: Dim
John Clive: Stage Actor
Adrienne Corri: Mrs. Alexander
Carl Duering: Dr. Brodsky

Behind the Scenes

Director: Stanley Kubrick
Writers: Anthony Burgess (novel), Stanley Kubrick (screenplay)
Producer: Stanley Kubrick
Executive Producers: Si Litvinoff, Max L. Raab
Film Editor: Bill Butler
Cinematographer: John Alcott

Trivia

• The language of Alex and his droogs is author Anthony Burgess's "Nadsat"—a mix of English, Russian, and slang. Stanley Kubrick did not want to use too much of it, because he did not want the film to be inaccessible to a mainstream audience.

Awards

Oscar Nominations: Best Director, Best Film Editing, Best Picture, Best Writing

1977
Close Encounters of the Third Kind

Overview

Genre: Sci-Fi/Drama
Duration: 137 min
Color: Color
(Metrocolor)
Country: USA
MPAA Rating: PG
Studio: Columbia
Pictures

When a power company employee is sent to check on a possible outage on a remote road, he has an up-close experience with a UFO. The half-sunburned face Roy Neary receives as a result of his encounter isn't the only impression left on him. He becomes consumed with these flying objects and his search to find out the truth about them may jeopardize his job, his family, and his very sanity. During his journey of discovery he crosses paths with other "believers" including a single mother whose son vanished during a separate encounter. Whether Roy and the others ever find what they are looking for may just hinge on how far they are willing to go.

Cast

Richard Dreyfuss: Roy Neary
François Truffaut: Claude Lacombe
Teri Garr: Ronnie Neary
Melinda Dillon: Gillian Guiler
Bob Balaban: David Laughlin
J. Patrick McNamara: Project Leader
Cary Guffey: Barry Guiler
Shawn Bishop: Brad Neary

Behind the Scenes

Director: Steven Spielberg
Writer: Steven Spielberg
Producers: Julia Phillips, Michael Phillips
Film Editor: Michael Kahn
Cinematographer: Vilmos Zsigmond
Original Music: John Williams

Trivia

• This film holds the record for the most cinematographers on a production (11).
• Flight 19, one of four planes that appear intact in the Mexican desert after being lost off Fort Lauderdale, is based in fact. The real "Lost Flight 19" left the naval base in December of 1945 and was never seen again.

Awards

Oscar Winners: Best Cinematography, Special Achievement Award—Sound Effects Editing
Oscar Nominations: Best Supporting Actress, Best Art Direction, Best Director, Best Effects—Visual, Best Film Editing, Best Music, Best Sound

1985
The Color Purple

Overview

Genre: Drama
Duration: 154 min
Color: Color
Country: USA
MPAA Rating: PG-13
Studio: Warner Bros.
Pictures

B ased on Alice Walker's Pulitzer Prize–winning book, *The Color Purple* follows the life of a young black girl growing up in the south during the turn of the 20th century. Celie Johnson is poor and uneducated, but she has great love in her life. When this love, her sister, is taken away, Celie must contend with a hateful father and abusive husband on her own. She learns early what she is made of and creates many enduring friendships due to her strength, kindness, and determination in the face of adversity. *The Color Purple* is a story about the African American woman and the spirit that leads one such woman—though broken and abused many times—toward love and salvation.

Cast

Danny Glover: Albert
Whoopi Goldberg: Celie Johnson
Margaret Avery: Shug Avery
Oprah Winfrey: Sofia
Willard E. Pugh: Harpo Johnson
Akosua Busia: Nettie Harris
Adolph Caesar: Old Mister Johnson
Rae Dawn Chong: Squeak
Laurence Fishburne: Swain

Behind the Scenes

Director: Steven Spielberg
Writers: Alice Walker (novel), Menno Meyjes
Producers: Steven Spielberg, Frank Marshall, Kathleen Kennedy, Quincy Jones
Executive Producers: Jon Peters, Peter Guber
Cinematographer: Allen Daviau
Original Music: Quincy Jones

Trivia

• Both Whoopi Goldberg and Oprah Winfrey made their on-screen debuts in this film, and both received Oscar nominations for their acting.
• Steven Spielberg banned producers Peter Gruber and Jon Peters from setting foot on the set because of their notoriety for offering "suggestions" of changes to make during production.

Awards

Oscar Nominations: Best Actress, Best Supporting Actress, Best Art Direction, Best Cinematography, Best Costume Design, Best Makeup, Best Music, Best Music—Original Song, Best Picture, Best Writing—Adapted Screenplay

1967
Cool Hand Luke

Overview

Genre: Drama
Duration: 126 min
Color: Color
(Technicolor)
Country: USA
MPAA Rating: Not
Rated
Studio: Warner Bros.
Pictures

Luke Jackson is a natural born world-shaker. After getting drunk one night and then cutting the heads off parking meters, he's sentenced to work on a chain gang. Laboring under the blistering sun doesn't bother Luke as much as the camp captain's proclamations that he needs to get his mind right. Not one to back down to anyone or anything, Luke would rather suffer a beating at the hands of a much stronger prisoner than give up. It's this never-say-die attitude and his cool demeanor that win him the unwanted idolization of his fellow inmates. But once Luke sets his mind on escaping, there will be no turning back—even if he's caught.

Cast

Paul Newman: Luke
George Kennedy: Dragline
J.D. Cannon: Society Red
Lou Antonio: Koko
Strother Martin: Captain
Dennis Hopper: Babalugats
Harry Dean Stanton: Tramp

Behind the Scenes

Director: Stuart Rosenberg
Writers: Donn Pearce (novel and screen-play), Frank Pierson (screenplay)
Producer: Gordon Carroll
Film Editor: Sam O'Steen
Cinematographer: Conrad L. Hall

Awards

Oscar Winners: Best Supporting Actor
Oscar Nominations: Best Actor, Best Music, Best Writing—Adapted Screenplay

Trivia

• Over the course of filming the road-tarring sequence, the actors actually blacktopped an entire mile-long stretch of highway for the county where they were filming.

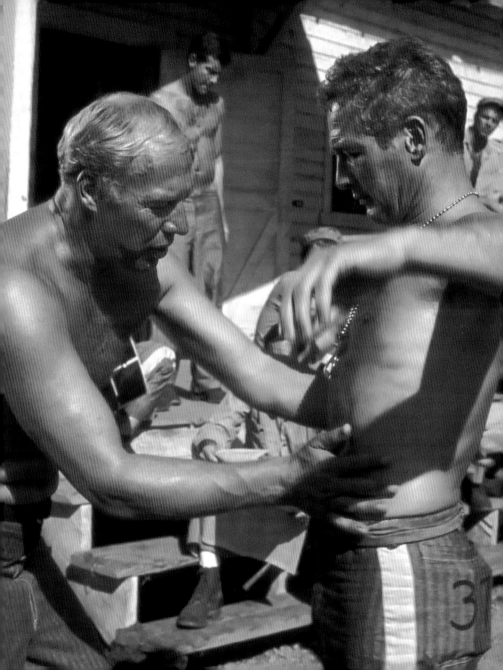

1990
Dances with Wolves

Overview

Genre: Drama/
Adventure
Duration: 180 min
Color: Color
Country: USA
MPAA Rating: PG-13
Studio: Orion Pic-
tures/Tig Productions

After he unintentionally helps rally Union troops to victory in a Civil War battle, Lt. John Dunbar is rewarded with his choice of next assignment. He chooses a remote post in South Dakota, far away from the war and all other civilization for that matter. At first his only companion is a curious wolf, but soon Dunbar finds that he is in the company of an even more curious tribe of Sioux Indians. Dunbar and his native hosts begin a period of mutual discovery that blossoms into a friendship. He feels a distinct kinship with the thoughtful Sioux, but other tribes and his own approaching army may jeopardize the life he's discovered on these plains.

Cast

Kevin Costner: Lieutenant John J. Dunbar
Mary McDonnell: Stands With a Fist
Graham Greene: Kicking Bird
Rodney A. Grant: Wind in His Hair
Floyd "Red Crow" Westerman: Ted Bears
Tantoo Cardinal: Black Shawl
Robert Pastorelli: Timmons
Charles Rocket: Lieutenant Elgin

Behind the Scenes

Director: Kevin Costner
Writer: Michael Blake (novel and screenplay)
Producers: Kevin Costner, Jim Wilson
Executive Producer: Jake Eberts
Cinematographer: Dean Semler
Original Music: John Barry

Trivia

• Takes of the climactic buffalo stampede could be filmed only once a day because the herd would usually run 10 miles, and wranglers would spend the remaining time rounding up the buffalo for the following day.
• This is the highest grossing Western of all time, with a domestic take of $184 million.

Awards

Oscar Winners: Best Cinematography, Best Director, Best Film Editing, Best Music, Best Picture, Best Sound, Best Writing—Adapted Screenplay
Oscar Nominations: Best Actor, Best Supporting Actor, Best Supporting Actress, Best Art Direction, Best Costume Design

1981
Das Boot

Overview

Genre: Drama/War
Duration: 149 min
Color: Color
Country: West Germany
MPAA Rating: R
Studio: Bavaria Film

Wolfgang Petersen's claustrophobic classic shows the other side of World War II as it follows a German U-boat during its dangerous missions in the Atlantic. Commanding the sub is a battle-tested captain played by Jürgen Prochnow. Under the captain's steady hand the young crew are faced with an underwater rollercoaster ride where hours of complete monotony are followed by moments where they face almost certain death. Giving perhaps one of the most complete views of what combat is like for soldiers of any army, *Das Boot* contrasts the horrors of battle with human elements, as these men grapple with their own mortalities—as well as those of the enemy—and the war itself.

Cast

Jürgen Prochnow: Captain Lieutenant Henrich Lehmann-Willenbrock/Der Alte
Herbert Grönemeyer: Lieutenant Werner/Correspondent
Klaus Wennemann: Chief Engineer Fritz Grade/Der Leitende
Hubertus Bengsch: First Lieutenant

Behind the Scenes

Director: Wolfgang Petersen
Writers: Lothar G. Buchheim (novel), Wolfgang Petersen (screenplay)
Producer: Günter Rohrbach, Michael Bittins
Film Editor: Hannes Nikel
Cinematographer: Jost Vacano
Original Music: Klaus Doldinger

Awards

Oscar Nominations: Best Cinematography, Best Director, Best Effects—Sound, Best Film Editing, Best Sound, Best Writing—Adapted Screenplay

Trivia

• *Das Boot* was filmed entirely in sequence, rare for a major motion picture.

1951
The Day the Earth Stood Still

Overview

Genre: Sci-Fi/Drama
Duration: 92 min
Color: Black and White
Country: USA
MPAA Rating: G
Studio: Twentieth Century Fox

During the height of the cold war, a space alien named Klaatu arrives in Washington, D.C., with a most important message for the people of Earth. He is promptly shot by a jittery soldier but is able to recover from his wounds. Upon telling government officials that he needs to address the leaders of the entire world, his request is met with political red tape. Hiding among the general population, Klaatu meets with a scientist and explains his mission: if Earth cannot learn to live in peace they will be deemed a threat to other planets and dealt with accordingly. Many sci-fi movies become hilariously dated as the years pass, but this one has aged like a fine wine.

Cast

Michael Rennie: Klaatu
Patricia Neal: Helen Benson
Hugh Marlowe: Tom Stevens
Sam Jaffe: Professor Jacob Barnhardt
Billy Gray: Bobby Benson
Frances Bavier: Mrs. Barley
Lock Martin: Gort

Behind the Scenes

Director: Robert Wise
Writers: Harry Bates (story), Edmund H. North
Producer: Julian Blaustein
Film Editor: William Reynolds
Cinematographer: Leo Tover
Original Music: Bernard Herrmann

Awards

Golden Globe Winners: Best Film Promoting International Understanding
Golden Globe Nominations: Best Motion Picture Score

Trivia

• Lock Martin was chosen to play Gort because he was so tall. However, he wasn't very strong and needed assistance to carry Patricia Neal and Michael Rennie.

1978
Days of Heaven

Overview

Genre: Drama/ Romance
Duration: 94 min
Color: Color
Country: USA
MPAA Rating: PG
Studio: Paramount Pictures

When a Chicago steelworker named Bill has a fatal confrontation with his boss, he takes off for Texas with his girlfriend Abby and his little sister Linda. With Bill and Abby pretending to be brother and sister, they eventually find work harvesting wheat for a sickly farmer. Over time, the farmer begins to fall for Abby, and Bill encourages the romance feeling that their ailing boss could be the answer to all of their problems. Young Linda sees all and tells the story of this awkward love triangle. Playing out against the amber fields of wheat, the beauty of their surroundings offers no protection against the forces of nature and those of man.

Cast

Richard Gere: Bill
Brooke Adams: Abby
Sam Shepard: The Farmer
Linda Manz: Linda
Robert J. Wilke: The farm foreman
Jackie Shultis: Linda's friend
Stuart Margolin: Mill foreman
Timothy Scott: Harvest hand

Behind the Scenes

Director: Terrence Malick
Writer: Terrence Malick
Producer: Bert Schneider and Harold Schneider
Executive Producer: Jacob Brackman
Film Editor: Billy Weber
Cinematographer: Néstor Almendros
Original Music: Ennio Morricone

Trivia

- The scene of locusts flying up to the sky was shot in reverse—the helicopter crew threw peanut shells down and the actors walked backwards.
- Much of the film was shot at "magic hour," dusk and dawn. Terrence Malick wanted to have a white sky without any sun.

Awards

Oscar Winner: Best Cinematography
Oscar Nominations: Best Costume Design, Best Music, Best Sound

1989
Dead Poets Society

Overview

Genre: Drama
Duration: 128 min
Color: Color
Country: USA
MPAA Rating: PG
Studio: Touchstone
Pictures

Professor John Keating has an unorthodox method of teaching, especially for the prim and proper ways of the Welton Academy for Boys. Once a student at the academy himself, Keating challenges the boys in his English class to seize the day and to try things they never imagined. His unconventional approach immediately captures their attention. He finds an individual's weakness and pushes until it's a strength. When roommates Neil Perry and Todd Anderson and their friends discover that Keating was a member of the Dead Poets Society, they inquire about its origins and rekindle the organization. Through the society, the boys become men and learn to question their place in life, not just accept it.

Cast

Robin Williams: John Keating
Robert Sean Leonard: Neil Perry
Ethan Hawke: Todd Anderson
Josh Charles: Knox Overstreet
Gale Hansen: Charlie Dalton
Dylan Kussman: Richard Cameron
Allelon Ruggiero: Steven Meeks
James Waterston: Gerard Pitts

Behind the Scenes

Director: Peter Weir
Writer: Tom Schulman
Producers: Steven Haft, Paul Junger Witt, Tony Thomas
Film Editors: William M. Anderson, Priscilla Nedd, Lee Smith
Cinematographer: John Seale
Original Music: Maurice Jarre

Trivia

• This film is loosely based on the experiences of private school students with Samuel Pickering, who is currently a professor of English at the University of Connecticut.

Awards

Oscar Winners: Best Writing
Oscar Nominations: Best Actor, Best Director, Best Picture

1979
The Deer Hunter

Overview

Genre: Drama/War
Duration: 182 min
Color: Color (Technicolor)
Country: USA
MPAA Rating: R
Studio: Universal Pictures

Michael Cimino's unforgettable war drama focuses on the lives of three Russian-American men from Western Pennsylvania who are leaving for Vietnam. Steve, Mike, and Nick are part of a group of friends who live in a blue-collar town and hunt together. Prior to joining the war they celebrate Steve's wedding and enjoy their last moments of bonding and innocence—their strengths and weaknesses as civilians soon to be tested in combat as soldiers. The horrors of what they experience in a POW camp will forever alter them individually and as friends. An absolutely haunting movie, *The Deer Hunter* won multiple Oscars including Best Picture.

Cast

Robert De Niro: Michael
John Cazale: Stan
John Savage: Steven
Christopher Walken: Nick
Meryl Streep: Linda
George Dzundza: John
Chuck Aspegren: Axel

Behind the Scenes

Director: Michael Cimino
Writers: Quinn K. Redeker (story), Michael Cimino and Louis Garfinkle (story and screenplay), Deric Washburn (screenplay)
Producers: Michael Cimino, Michael Deeley, John Peverall, Barry Spikings
Film Editor: Peter Zinner
Cinematographer: Vilmos Zsigmond

Trivia

• In the scene when Steven (played by John Savage) yells, "Michael, there's rats in here, Michael!" as he is stuck in the river, Savage was actually yelling to director Michael Cimino because he was afraid of rats and wanted to be pulled out. The scene felt so real that it was left in the film.

Awards

Oscar Winners: Best Supporting Actor, Best Director, Best Film Editing, Best Picture, Best Sound
Oscar Nominations: Best Actor, Best Supporting Actress, Best Cinematography, Best Writing

1991
Defending Your Life

Overview

Genre: Comedy/
Fantasy
Duration: 112 min
Color: Color
Country: English
MPAA Rating: PG
Studio: Warner Bros.
Pictures

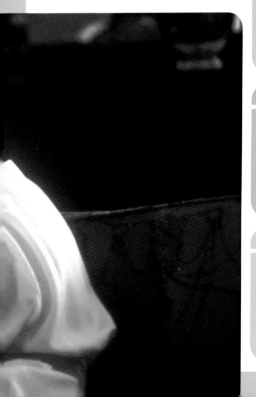

After dying in a car accident, Daniel Miller wakes up in a strange locale that somewhat resembles Los Angeles. He soon learns that he is in a place called Judgment City where he has to defend his life. In a nutshell, Daniel must prove that he has overcome his fears in order to "move on." If he doesn't he will be sent back to Earth to try again. All of this makes the neurotic Daniel feel like he's on trial, though he's assured that he is not. Complicating matters, he has fallen for a pretty defendant named Julia. As he's forced to view embarrassing moments from his life, Daniel starts to worry that Julia may be moving on without him.

Cast

Albert Brooks: Daniel Miller
Meryl Streep: Julia
Rip Torn: Bob Diamond
Lee Grant: Lena Foster
Buck Henry: Dick Stanley
Michael Durrell: Agency head
James Eckhouse: Jeep owner
Gary Beach: Car salesman

Behind the Scenes

Director: Albert Brooks
Writers: Albert Brooks, Monica Johnson
Producer: Michael Grillo
Executive Producer: Herb Nanas
Cinematographer: Allen Daviau
Original Music: Michael Gore

Trivia

• The Hall of Past Lives is the old Fluor Daniel building in Irvine, California.
• The trams used throughout the film are from Universal Studios Hollywood.

Awards

Saturn Award Nominations: Best Actress, Best Fantasy Film, Best Writing

2006
The Departed

Overview

Genre: Drama/Crime
Duration: 150 min
Color: Color
Country: USA
MPAA Rating: R
Studio: Warner Bros. Pictures

The Massachusetts State Police and an Irish-American gang fight a continuous battle for control of a crime-riddled Boston. The police select recent academy graduate Billy Costigan to infiltrate the gang, while the brutal mob boss Costello sends his young protégé Colin into the police academy under the guise of a straight-laced cop. As each group searches for the rat within its midst, both men face the blurred lines of crime and justice while their decisions are further complicated by their relationships with the same woman. Meanwhile, only two members of the police department know Costigan's identity, and they too are swept into the intrigue when there is a shake-up in the ranks of the department.

Cast

Leonardo DiCaprio: Billy Costigan
Matt Damon: Colin Sullivan
Jack Nicholson: Frank Costello
Mark Wahlberg: Sergeant Dignam
Martin Sheen: Captain Queenan
Ray Winstone: Mr. French
Vera Farmiga: Madolyn
Anthony Anderson: Brown
Alec Baldwin: Captain Ellerby

Behind the Scenes

Director: Martin Scorsese
Writers: William Monahan, Siu Fai Mak, Felix Chong
Producers: Brad Grey, Graham King, Gianni Nunnari, Brad Pitt
Executive Producers: G. Mac Brown, Doug Davidson, Kristin Hahn, Roy Lee
Cinematographer: Michael Ballhaus

Trivia

• Mark Wahlberg based his performance on the police officers who had arrested him in his youth and the reactions of his parents who had to come bail him out with their grocery money.
• Some Boston scenes were shot in New York City to take advantage of a tax credit.

Awards

Oscar Winners: Best Director, Best Editing, Best Picture, Best Writing—Adapted Screenplay
Oscar Nominations: Best Supporting Actor

1988
Die Hard

Overview

Genre: Action/ Adventure
Duration: 131 min
Color: Color
Country: USA
MPAA Rating: R
Studio: Twentieth Century Fox

It's Christmas Eve and New York City cop John McClane has just arrived in Los Angeles to spend the holidays with his estranged wife Holly and their kids. When he gets to Holly's office Christmas party in the Nakatomi Plaza high-rise, their reunion is put on hold when a gang of terrorists takes over the building. Led by Hans Gruber, the terrorists pose as a politically motivated group, but what they are really after is money. One thing is for sure, they mean business and won't hesitate to kill anyone who gets in their way. Having eluded the roundup of office hostages, McClane is faced with the impossible task of taking on Gruber's crew and getting everyone out alive.

Cast

Bruce Willis: Officer John McClane
Alan Rickman: Hans Gruber
Bonnie Bedelia: Holly Gennaro McClane
Alexander Godunov: Karl
Reginald VelJohnson: Sergeant Al Powell
Paul Gleason: Deputy Police Chief Dwayne T. Robinson
De'voreaux White: Argyle
William Atherton: Richard Thornburg

Behind the Scenes

Director: John McTiernan
Writers: Roderick Thorp (novel), Jeb Stuart and Steven De Souza (screenplay)
Producers: Lawrence Gordon, Joel Silver
Executive Producer: Charles Gordon
Film Editors: Frank Urioste, John F. Link II
Cinematographer: Jan de Bont
Original Music: Michael Kamen

Trivia

• This was Alan Rickman's feature film debut.
• In the scenes where John McClane must run through shards of glass in his bare feet (after Hans and his men shoot out the glass partitions), Bruce Willis actually wore fake rubber feet molded to look like his bare feet. As a result, his feet look unnaturally large in some of the shots.

Awards

Oscar Nominations: Best Effects—Sound, Best Effects—Visual, Best Film Editing, Best Sound

1982
Diner

Overview

Genre: Comedy/
Drama
Duration: 110 min
Color: Color
(Metrocolor)
Country: USA
MPAA Rating: R
Studio: MGM/United
Artists

Barry Levinson's nostalgic coming-of-age story centers around six friends in 1950s' Baltimore who are getting ready to see one of their crew married. Just days before Eddie's wedding, his best friend Billy returns from college to be best man. Meanwhile everyone in the group seems to be experiencing growing pains. Ladies' man Boogie has a gambling problem that could land him in hot water. Shrevie is going through a rough patch in his marriage. Fenwick has drinking and maturity issues. Billy is in a rocky relationship, and Eddie may just call off the wedding if his fiancée can't pass a football quiz. They all gather at the diner to eat some food and hash it out.

Cast

Steve Guttenberg: Edward "Eddie" Simmons
Daniel Stern: Laurence "Shrevie" Schreiber
Mickey Rourke: Robert "Boogie" Sheftell
Kevin Bacon: Timothy Fenwick Jr.
Tim Daly: William "Billy" Howard
Ellen Barkin: Beth Schreiber
Paul Reiser: Modell

Behind the Scenes

Director: Barry Levinson
Writer: Barry Levinson
Producer: Jerry Weintraub
Executive Producer: Mark Johnson
Film Editor: Stu Linder
Cinematographer: Peter Sova
Original Music: Bruce Brody, Ivan Kral

Trivia

• Contrary to speculation, no one character represents writer/director Barry Levinson. However, he has said that each of the main characters represents a small part of his youth.

Awards

Oscar Nominations: Best Writing

1987
Dirty Dancing

Overview

Genre: Drama/Romance
Duration: 100 min
Color: Color
Country: USA
MPAA Rating: PG-13
Studio: Vestron Pictures

Plucky Frances "Baby" Houseman arrives with her family for a summer vacation at a Catskills resort in 1963—but the summer proves more revolutionary than relaxing. As the moral virtues of the 1950s unwillingly retreat in the headwinds of 1960s' cultural change, Baby finds herself trapped between worlds, of upper and lower classes, of traditional roles and new opportunities, and between her father's desires and her own. When the resort's female dance lead, Penny, is forced to miss the rest of the season, Baby finds herself taking her place, opposite dance instructor Johnny Castle. Love, spoken in the universal language of dance, proves as incendiary as it is reactionary in this classic period-piece romance.

Cast

Jennifer Grey: Frances "Baby" Houseman
Patrick Swayze: Johnny Castle
Jerry Orbach: Dr. Jake Houseman
Cynthia Rhodes: Penny Johnson
Jack Weston: Max Kellerman
Jane Brucker: Lisa Houseman
Kelly Bishop: Marjorie Houseman
Lonny Price: Neil Kellerman

Behind the Scenes

Director: Emile Ardolino
Writers: Eleanor Bergstein
Producer: Linda Gottlieb
Executive Producers: Mitchell Cannold, Steven Reuther
Film Editors: Peter C. Frank, Farrel Jane Levy
Cinematographer: Jeff Jur
Original Music: John Morris

Trivia

• The scene where Johnny and Baby practice dancing and crawl toward each other on the floor was not intended to be part of the film— they were warming up before the shoot but the director liked it so much he kept it in the film.

Awards

Oscar Winner: Best Music—Original Song

1971
Dirty Harry

Overview

Genre: Crime/Action
Duration: 102 min
Color: Color (Technicolor)
Country: USA
MPAA Rating: R
Studio: Warner Bros. Pictures

San Francisco police inspector Harry Callahan hates criminals and likes doing things his own way. When a possible serial killer named Scorpio starts holding the city hostage and demanding a ransom, it's up to Harry to stop him. Armed with his trusty .44 Magnum and a sensible new partner named Chico, Callahan hits the streets looking for the madman. Between the elusive Scorpio and the heat he's getting from the department and mayor's office, Harry's had just about all he can take. Clint Eastwood's portrayal of rogue cop Dirty Harry created an instant archetype, contributed numerous catch phrases to popular culture, and spawned several sequels.

Cast

Clint Eastwood: Inspector Harry Callahan
John Vernon: The mayor
Andrew Robinson: Scorpio Killer
John Larch: The chief
John Mitchum: Inspector Frank DiGiorgio
Woodrow Parfrey: Mr. Jaffe
Josef Sommer: William T. Rothko

Behind the Scenes

Director: Don Siegel
Writers: Harry Julian Fink and Rita M. Fink (story and screenplay), Dean Riesner (screenplay)
Producer: Don Siegel
Executive Producer: Robert Daley
Cinematographer: Bruce Surtees

Trivia

• In one early scene, a theater marquee displays the 1971 movie *Play Misty For Me*, which starred and was directed by Eastwood.

Trivia

• This film was loosely based on the events surrounding the Zodiac Killer murders, which were still occurring during this time in San Francisco.

1989
Do the Right Thing

Overview

Genre: Drama
Duration: 120 min
Color: Color
Country: USA
MPAA Rating: R
Studio: Universal
Pictures

On one of the hottest days of the year in New York, one Brooklyn neighborhood is pushed to the brink. Mookie is the fast-talking delivery guy for Sal's Famous Pizzeria, a white-owned operation in black Bedford-Stuyvesant. As he makes his rounds we're introduced to other people from the block including volatile loud-mouth Buggin Out, boom box–toting Radio Raheem, and an old-timer known as Da Mayor. An uneasy alliance exists here, with longtime residents decrying the lack of black-owned businesses and local storeowners, especially Sal's son Pino, none too fond of the locals. The music of Public Enemy provides the soundtrack, as the entire neighborhood becomes a powder keg surrounded by flaring tempers.

Cast

Danny Aiello: Sal
Ossie Davis: Da Mayor
Ruby Dee: Mother Sister
Giancarlo Esposito: Buggin Out
Spike Lee: Mookie
John Turturro: Pino
Samuel L. Jackson: Mister Senor Love Daddy
Rosie Perez: Tina
Bill Nunn: Radio Raheem

Behind the Scenes

Director: Spike Lee
Writer: Spike Lee
Producer: Spike Lee
Film Editor: Barry Alexander Brown
Cinematographer: Ernest R. Dickerson
Original Music: Bill Lee

Trivia

• This was Martin Lawrence's feature film debut.
• The first line of the film, "Wake up," is also the last line of Spike Lee's previous movie, *School Daze*.

Awards

Oscar Nominations: Best Supporting Actor, Best Writing

1965
Doctor Zhivago

Overview

Genre: Drama/Romance
Duration: 197 min
Color: Color
Country: USA
MPAA Rating: PG-13
Studio: Metro-Goldwyn-Mayer (MGM)

Master of the epic David Lean strikes again, this time focusing his attention on the Russian Revolution. Omar Sharif stars as Yuri Zhivago, a doctor and poet who marries into an aristocratic family. Julie Christie is Lara, the beautiful daughter of a dressmaker. These two first meet under grave circumstances after a distraught Lara attempts suicide and Zhivago saves her. Though war, marriage, and a host of impossible circumstances conspire to keep them apart, the pair seems destined to be together. *Dr. Zhivago* contrasts the aching personal wants and emotions of its protagonists against a political movement that stresses the needs of the many over those of the individual.

Cast

Omar Sharif: Dr. Yuri Zhivago
Julie Christie: Lara
Geraldine Chaplin: Tonya
Rod Steiger: Komarovsky
Alec Guinness: Gen. Yevgraf Zhivago
Tom Courtenay: Pasha
Klaus Kinski: Kostoyed

Behind the Scenes

Director: David Lean
Writers: Boris Pasternak (novel) and Robert Bolt (screenplay)
Producer: Carlo Ponti
Executive Producer: Arvid Griffen
Cinematographers: Freddie Young and Nicolas Roeg (uncredited)

Awards

Oscar Winners: Best Art Direction, Best Cinematography, Best Costume Design, Best Music, Best Writing—Adapted Screenplay

Trivia

• Most of the film was shot in Spain. During the filming of the scene where the crowd chants the Marxist theme, police arrived on the set, thinking that there was a revolution.

1975
Dog Day Afternoon

Overview

Genre: Drama
Duration: 124 min
Color: Color (Technicolor)
Country: USA
MPAA Rating: R
Studio: Artists Entertainment Complex/ Warner Bros.

When two novices try to rob a Brooklyn bank, they unwittingly attract the attention of the entire city. Soon after Sonny Wortzik and his partner Sal enter the bank, everything starts going wrong. For starters, one of their accomplices loses his nerve and leaves. Next, they find that most of the bank's cash has already been picked up. Finally, there's a phone call; it's the police, and they want to know exactly what Sonny thinks he's doing. In the tense standoff that follows, crowds of people and the media gather outside as Sonny tries to negotiate a hostage situation. Based on a true story, *Dog Day Afternoon* is a first-rate crime drama with excellent performances by John Cazale as Sal and Al Pacino as Sonny.

Cast

Al Pacino: Sonny Wortzik
John Cazale: Sal
Charles Durning: Detective Sergeant Eugene Moretti
Chris Sarandon: Leon Shermer
Sully Boyar: Mulvaney
Penelope Allen: Sylvia
James Broderick: Sheldon
Carol Kane: Jenny

Behind the Scenes

Director: Sidney Lumet
Writers: P.F. Kluge and Thomas Moore (article), Frank Pierson (screenplay)
Producers: Martin Bregman, Martin Elfand
Film Editor: Dede Allen
Cinematographer: Victor J. Kemper

Trivia

• As in the movie, the real bank robber (John Wojtowicz) committed the robbery to pay for a sex-change operation for his lover. He did finally manage to finance the operation with part of his movie rights advance.

Awards

Oscar Winners: Best Writing
Oscar Nominations: Best Actor, Best Director, Best Film Editing, Best Picture, Best Supporting Actor

1944
Double Indemnity

Overview

Genre: Drama/Thriller
Duration: 107 min
Color: Black and White
Country: USA
MPAA Rating: Not Rated
Studio: Paramount Pictures

Walter Neff is a no-nonsense insurance salesman who knows all the angles. Phyllis Dietrichson is the type of woman a man would do anything for. When Walter calls on the Dietrichson house to renew Mr. Dietrichson's auto insurance the visitor's a dead duck the minute he lays eyes on Phyllis. It's not long before the two give into their desires, and that's when things get really interesting. It seems that Phyllis is in an abusive marriage and wants to take out an accident policy on her husband without his knowledge. Against his better judgement, Walter agrees to help her. It's too bad there's no insurance against women like Phyllis.

Cast

Fred MacMurray: Walter Neff
Barbara Stanwyck: Phyllis Dietrichson
Edward G. Robinson: Barton Keyes
Porter Hall: Mr. Jackson
Jean Heather: Lola Dietrichson
Tom Powers: Mr. Dietrichson
Byron Barr: Nino Zachetti

Behind the Scenes

Director: Billy Wilder
Writers: James M. Cain (novel), Billy Wilder, and Raymond Chandler (screenplay)
Producer: Joseph Sistrom (uncredited)
Executive Producer: Buddy G. DeSylva (uncredited)
Cinematographer: John F. Seitz

Awards

Oscar Nominations: Best Actress, Best Cinematography, Best Director, Best Music, Best Picture, Best Sound, Best Writing

Trivia

• It was Billy Wilder's idea for Barbara Stanwyck to wear a blonde wig. A month into production Wilder realized how bad it looked, but by then it was too late to re-shoot the earlier scenes.

1986
Down by Law

Overview

Genre: Comedy/Drama
Duration: 107 min
Color: Black and White
Country: USA
MPAA Rating: R
Studio: Island Pictures

Jim Jarmusch's moribund style burns brightly across every black and white frame of this under-appreciated gem. It's a classic take on the prison break picture that takes place in an abstracted New Orleans—a bayou of the mind. Sure you have your hapless jailbirds splashing through the swamp with baying hounds in hot pursuit, but this is Jarmusch's sad and beautiful world, so things take on an otherworldly air. The film charts the escape route and parallel descent of Jack, a third-rate pimp, Zack, an unemployed disc jockey, and Roberto, an Italian tourist. Imagine if the Marx Brothers were to bust out of the big house and you pretty much have *Down By Law*.

Cast

Tom Waits: Zack
John Lurie: Jack
Roberto Benigni: Roberto
Nicoletta Braschi: Nicoletta
Ellen Barkin: Laurette
Billie Neal: Bobbie
Rockets Redglare: Gig

Behind the Scenes

Director: Jim Jarmusch
Writer: Jim Jarmusch
Producer: Alan Kleinberg
Executive Producers: Carry Brokaw, Otto Grokenberger, Russell Schwartz
Cinematographer: Robby Muller
Original Music: John Lurie

Awards

Cannes Film Festival: Nominated for Golden Palm

Trivia

• Jim Jarmusch selected the shack in which the fugitives find refuge for its bunk beds, because he wanted their new quarters to look just like the prison cells they had escaped.

1964
Dr. Strangelove or: How I Learned to Stop Worrying and Love the Bomb

Overview
Genre: Comedy
Duration: 93 min
Color: Black and White
Country: UK
MPAA Rating: PG
Studio: Columbia Pictures

In the escalating military madness of the cold war, U.S. Air Force General Jack D. Ripper decides to take matters into his own hands and issues a command for one of his squadrons to launch a nuclear attack on the Soviet Union. As various military personnel scramble to call back the jets, a nervous U.S. president calls the Soviet Premier to inform him of the situation. Peter Sellers plays three roles in this hilarious black comedy, including the president, an anxious air force captain, and the bizarre title character, Dr. Strangelove. Who knew that the end of the world would come so soon and be so funny?

Cast

Peter Sellers: Group Captain Lionel Mandrake/ President Merkin Muffley/Dr. Strangelove
George C. Scott: General "Buck" Turgidson
Sterling Hayden: General Jack D. Ripper
Keenan Wynn: Colonel "Bat" Guano
Slim Pickens: Major T.J. "King" Kong
Peter Bull: Russian Ambassador Alexi de Sadesky
James Earl Jones: Lieutenant Lothar Zogg

Behind the Scenes

Director: Stanley Kubrick
Writers: Peter George (novel and screenplay), Stanley Kubrick and Terry Southern (screenplay)
Producer: Stanley Kubrick
Executive Producer: Leon Minoff (uncredited)
Film Editor: Anthony Harvey
Cinematographer: Gilbert Taylor
Original Music: Laurie Johnson

Trivia

• Stanley Kurbrick cast Slim Pickens as Kong, the gung-ho hick pilot. Pickens was never shown the script or told that the film was a dark comedy. As a result, he played the part straight as though it were a drama.

Awards

Oscar Nominations: Best Actor, Best Director, Best Picture, Best Writing—Adapted Screenplay

1931
Dracula

Overview

Genre: Horror
Duration: 75 min
Color: Black and White (tinted)
Country: USA
MPAA Rating: Not Rated
Studio: Universal Pictures

When an Englishman named Renfield travels to Transylvania to sell Carfax Abbey, the mysterious Count Dracula—unforgettably portrayed by Bela Lugosi—takes both the house and a bite out of Renfield. Upon arriving in England, Renfield is committed to an asylum while the Count moves into his new residence and starts feeding. Dracula's next-door neighbor, Dr. Seward, becomes alarmed when his daughter Mina's friend Lucy turns up dead. His concerns are confirmed by his colleague Van Helsing who suspects a vampire is in their midst. Together they must find a way to stop Count Dracula before he makes Mina his next victim.

Cast

Bela Lugosi: Count Dracula
Helen Chandler: Mina Harker
David Manners: John Harker
Dwight Frye: Renfield
Edward Van Sloan: Professor Abraham Van Helsing
Herbert Bunston: Dr. Jack Seward

Behind the Scenes

Director: Tod Browning
Writers: Bram Stoker (novel), John L. Balderston and Hamilton Dean (play), Garrett Fort (screenplay)
Producers: Tod Browning, Carl Laemmle Jr.
Film Editors: Milton Carruth, Maurice Pivar
Cinematographer: Karl Freund

Awards

Added to National Film Registry in 2000

Trivia

• When Bela Lugosi died in 1956, he was buried wearing the silk cape he wore in this film.

1933
Duck Soup

Overview

Genre: Comedy
Duration: 68 min
Color: Black and White
Country: USA
MPAA Rating: Not Rated
Studio: Paramount Pictures

When the tiny country of Freedonia falls on hard financial times, wealthy dowager Gloria Teasdale comes to its rescue but insists on naming wisecracking con man Rufus T. Firefly as the new leader. Firefly's freewheeling dictatorial approach quickly makes an enemy of Ambassador Trentino of bordering Sylvania. Trentino has designs on both Freedonia and Mrs. Teasdale and uses his two top spies Chicolini and Pinky to get the goods on Firefly. Soon Freedonia and Sylvania are on the brink of war, but Firefly, Chicolini, and Pinky seem more interested in hijinx than actual combat. *Duck Soup* is a madcap Marx Brothers comedy classic for kids of all ages.

Cast

Groucho Marx: Rufus T. Firefly
Harpo Marx: Pinky
Chico Marx: Chicolini
Zeppo Marx: Lieutenant Bob Roland
Margaret Dumont: Mrs. Gloria Teasdale
Raquel Torres: Vera Marcal
Louis Calhern: Ambassador Trentino of Sylvania

Behind the Scenes

Director: Leo McCarey
Writers: Bert Kalmar, Harry Ruby
Producer: Herman J. Mankiewicz (uncredited)
Film Editor: LeRoy Stone (uncredited)
Cinematographer: Henry Sharp
Original Music: Bert Kalmar, Harry Ruby

Trivia

• This film is Zeppo Marx's final appearance in a Marx Brothers film.
• During the battle, Groucho makes numerous costume changes, including both a Union soldier and Confederate general, a Boy Scout leader, and a Davy Crockett–like frontiersman.

Awards

Added to National Film Registry in 1990

1969
Easy Rider

Overview

Genre: Drama/ Adventure
Duration: 95 min
Color: Color (Technicolor)
Country: USA
MPAA Rating: R
Studio: Columbia Pictures

A landmark road movie, *Easy Rider* captures the freewheeling spirit of 1969 while documenting the clash of the counterculture and conservative class. Peter Fonda as Wyatt and Dennis Hopper as Billy together gun their cycles eastward, stop at a free-loving hippie commune, and get arrested in a Louisiana small town. In jail they befriend lawyer George Hanson, who gets caught between the two worlds of the liberals and the establishment with grave results. Wyatt and Billy end up in New Orleans where they revel in acid, women, and Mardi Gras, only to be faced with the harsh prejudice of what "dropping out" can really lead to. Featuring a stellar soundtrack, *Easy Rider* stands as an anthem for freedom in tumultuous times.

Cast

Peter Fonda: Wyatt
Dennis Hopper: Billy
Jack Nicholson: George Hanson
Antonio Mendoza: Jesus
Phil Spector: Connection
Luana Anders: Lisa
Sabrina Scharf: Sarah
Robert Walker Jr.: Jack

Behind the Scenes

Director: Dennis Hopper
Writers: Peter Fonda, Dennis Hopper, Terry Southern
Producer: Peter Fonda
Executive Producer: Bert Schneider
Film Editor: Donn Cambern
Cinematographer: Laszlo Kovacs

Trivia

• Hopper and Fonda modeled their movie after the Italian roadtrip film *Sorpasso, Il*, which made extensive use of pop music rather than a score written specifically for the film. Though this is common practice now, such a technique was very rare at the time.

Awards

Oscar Nominations: Best Supporting Actor, Best Writing

1963
8½

Overview

Genre: Comedy/Drama
Duration: 138 min
Color: Black and White
Country: Italy
MPAA Rating: Not Rated
Studio: Cineriz

When famed Italian movie director Guido Anselmi can't focus on his latest project he retreats to a spa and his imagination. Even there he is unable to escape the crushing pressures that surround him as he is bombarded by actors, a producer, and a difficult writer. On top of this, both his wife and his mistress are on the scene as well. As he floats in and out of the conscious world, his real-life problems manifest themselves in his dreams and his fantasies invade his real life. His personal and professional stalemate keeps the merry-go-round of so-called "Felliniesque" imagery whirling. In the end, what we have is a fascinating look inside the mind of the director himself.

Cast

Marcello Mastroianni: Guido Anselmi
Claudia Cardinale: Claudia
Anouk Aimée: Luisa Anselmi
Sandra Milo: Carla
Rossella Falk: Rossella
Barbara Steele: Gloria Morin
Caterina Boratto: La signora misteriosa

Behind the Scenes

Director: Federico Fellini
Writers: Federico Fellini and Ennio Flaiano (story and screenplay), Tullio Pinelli and Brunello Rondi (screenplay)
Producer: Angelo Rizzoli
Film Editor: Leo Cattozzo
Cinematographer: Gianni Di Venanzo

Awards

Oscar Winners: Best Costume Design, Best Foreign Language Film
Oscar Nominations: Best Art Direction, Best Director, Best Writing

Trivia

• To remind himself how he wanted the film to turn out, writer/director Federico Fellini attached a note under the camera's eyepiece that read "Remember, this is a comedy."

1966
The Endless Summer

Overview

Genre: Documentary/Sports
Duration: 95 min
Color: Color
Country: USA
MPAA Rating: PG
Studio: Bruce Brown Films

Universally recognized as the first motion picture to bring the sport and culture of surfing to the masses, Bruce Brown's documentary follows his journey with pals Mike Hynson and Robert August as they go looking for the perfect wave. As Brown narrates, Hynson and August skip across the globe following the summer season—surfboards in hand—landing in places like Africa, Tahiti, and Australia, among others. Sure, surfing is the main subject here but so too are the guys themselves and the interesting folks they meet along the way. Featuring fascinating footage from the world's most perfect beaches, *The Endless Summer* will have you wanting to "hang ten" yourself.

Cast

Michael Hynson: Principal surfer
Robert August: Principal surfer
Lord "Tally Ho" Blears: Himself
Bruce Brown: Narrator
Terence Bullen: South African guide
Wayne Miyata: Himself

Behind the Scenes

Director: Bruce Brown
Writer: Bruce Brown
Producer: Bruce Brown
Cinematographer: Bruce Brown
Original Music: The Sandals: John Blakeley, Gaston Georis, Walter Georis

Awards

Added to National Film Registry in 2002

Trivia

• This was one of the first "surfer movies" made, and it spawned several decades of similar documentaries since its release.

1973
Enter the Dragon

Overview

Genre: Action/Adventure
Duration: 98 min
Color: Color
Country: Hong Kong and USA
MPAA Rating: R
Studio: Concord Productions/Warner Bros. Pictures

When a reputed crime boss named Han hosts a martial arts tournament, intelligence officials hire a martial arts master named Lee to enter the contest and investigate Han's operation. A reluctant participant in both the contest and the covert mission, Lee has a change of heart when he finds out that Han may have been responsible for his sister's death. Newly energized, Lee will fight his way through the tournament and Han's entire army in order to bring the mastermind down. Featuring some of the most incredible martial arts fight scenes ever filmed, *Enter the Dragon* is a veritable highlight reel of the legendary Bruce Lee's considerable talents.

Cast

Bruce Lee: Lee
John Saxon: Roper
Kien Shih: Han
Ahna Capri: Tania
Angela Mao: Su Lin
Jim Kelly: Williams
Robert Wall: Oharra

Behind the Scenes

Director: Robert Clouse
Writer: Michael Allin
Producers: Paul M. Heller, Bruce Lee, Fred Weintraub, Leonard Ho
Film Editors: Kurt Hirshler, George Watters
Cinematographer: Gil Hubbs
Original Music: Lalo Schifrin

Awards

Added to National Film Registry in 2004

Trivia

• Kien Shih, who plays Han, didn't speak any English. Rather than speaking the lines phonetically, he simply mouthed them as best he could and another actor dubbed his dialogue for him.

1973
The Exorcist

Overview

Genre: Horror/Thriller
Duration: 122 min
Color: Color (Metrocolor)
Country: USA
MPAA Rating: R
Studio: Warner Bros. Pictures

The eternal battle between good and evil plays out in this chilling drama, made terrifying by its mundane setting in a small urban family. Troubled by a recent divorce, actress Chris MacNeil initially attributes the odd behavior of her 12-year-old daughter Regan to distress. But when doctors fail to find a cure for the girl, Chris turns to the Catholic Church. The priests' attempts to rid the girl of her demonic possessor are by turns terrifying and tragic. Legend would have it that the film itself also attracted its own unpleasant supernatural attention, with stories of fires, injuries, and odd occurrences coloring even the behind-the-scenes action with terror.

Cast

Ellen Burstyn: Chris MacNeil
Max von Sydow: Father Merrin
Lee J. Cobb: Lieutenant Kinderman
Jack MacGowran: Burke Dennings
Linda Blair: Regan MacNeil
Jason Miller: Father Karras
Kitty Winn: Sharon

Behind the Scenes

Director: William Friedkin
Writer: William Peter Blatty (novel and screenplay)
Producer: William Peter Blatty
Executive Producer: Noel Marshall
Cinematographers: Gerry Fisher, Owen Roizman, Billy Williams

Awards

Oscar Winners: Best Sound, Best Writing—Adapted Screenplay

Trivia

• When first released, the film terrified many moviegoers into bouts of hysteria in theaters, making it one of the most controversial films ever made. One man, fainting, broke his jaw.

1982
E.T.: The Extra-Terrestrial

Overview

Genre: Family/ Adventure
Duration: 115 min
Color: Color
Country: USA
MPAA Rating: PG
Studio: Universal Pictures

Elliot is a young boy who feels somewhat isolated until he meets an odd-looking space alien who's been left behind on Earth. The unlikely duo soon forges a special friendship as Elliot attempts to conceal the extra-terrestrial's existence while the cuddly E.T. tries his best to adapt to his new surroundings. A wonderful sci-fi adventure, *E.T.: The Extra-Terrestrial* turns the outer space visitor genre on its ear. Rather than earthlings on the run from alien invaders, it's E.T. and Elliot against a world populated by menacing adults. What this film captures better than almost any other, making it an instant classic, is the innocence and wonder of childhood.

Cast

Henry Thomas: Elliott
Dee Wallace: Mary
Robert MacNaughton: Michael
Drew Barrymore: Gertie
Peter Coyote: Keys
K.C. Martel: Greg
Sean Frye: Steve
C. Thomas Howell: Tyler

Behind the Scenes

Director: Steven Spielberg
Writers: Melissa Mathison and Satyajit Ray (uncredited)
Producer: Kathleen Kennedy, Steven Spielberg
Film Editor: Carol Littleton
Cinematographer: Allen Daviau
Original Music: John Williams

Trivia

• E.T.'s facial features were modeled after the poet Carl Sandburg, Albert Einstein, and a pug dog.
• The original dark concept for this film was soon after used to create the horror/thriller *Poltergeist*.

Awards

Oscar Winners: Best Effects—Sound, Best Effects—Visual, Best Music, Best Sound
Oscar Nominations: Best Cinematography, Best Director, Best Film Editing, Best Picture, Best Writing

1996
Fargo

Overview

Genre: Drama/Thriller
Duration: 98 min
Color: Color
Country: USA
MPAA Rating: R
Studio: Gramercy Pictures/PolyGram Filmed Entertainment

Minnesota auto dealer Jerry Lundegaard is a man at the end of his rope. Under the complete financial control of his wealthy father-in-law Wade, Jerry wants to carve out some sort of sweet deal for himself. Out of desperation, he hires two goons to kidnap his wife in hopes that Wade will pay a hefty ransom. Little does he know that these two thugs are already responsible for three murders being investigated by very pregnant police chief Marge Gunderson. As Margie doggedly pursues leads, Jerry's harebrained plans are unraveling. Is a pregnant cop any match for a couple of murderous kidnappers and a nervous car salesman? You betcha!

Cast

Frances McDormand: Police Chief Marge Gunderson
William H. Macy: Jerome "Jerry" Lundegaard
Steve Buscemi: Carl Showalter
Peter Stormare: Gaear Grimsrud
Kristin Rudrüd: Jean Lundegaard
Harvey Presnell: Wade Gustafson
Tony Denman: Scotty Lundegaard
Steve Reevis: Shep Proudfoot

Behind the Scenes

Directors: Joel Coen, Ethan Coen (uncredited)
Writers: Joel Coen, Ethan Coen
Producers: John Cameron, Ethan Coen, Joel Coen (uncredited)
Executive Producers: Tim Bevan, Eric Fellner
Film Editor: Roderick Jaynes
Cinematographer: Roger Deakins
Original Music: Carter Burwell

Trivia

• Contrary to popular belief, William H. Macy barely ad-libbed any of his lines. His character's stuttering mannerisms were almost entirely written in the script as they were performed.
• Film locations had to move around Minnesota, North Dakota, and Canada, because snow was melting due to a winter heatwave.

Awards

Oscar Winners: Best Actress, Best Writing
Oscar Nominations: Best Supporting Actor, Best Cinematography, Best Director, Best Film Editing, Best Picture

1982
Fast Times at Ridgemont High

Overview

Genre: Comedy/ Drama
Duration: 90 min
Color: Color (Technicolor)
Country: USA
MPAA Rating: R
Studio: Universal Pictures

A dapted from a book by Cameron Crowe, *Fast Times at Ridgemont High* follows the lives, loves, and all-around growing pains of several California teenagers. Stacy Hamilton is nice girl who can't seem to find a nice guy. Mark Ratner might be that guy, but he's getting lousy romantic advice from his sleazy ticket-scalping pal Mike Damone. Stacy's sexually experienced friend Linda is the object of everyone's desire, including Stacy's brother Brad. And all surfer Jeff Spicoli wants to do is catch some tasty waves and get stoned. It's all sex, drugs, and rock and roll . . . and no one has any money. If any of this sounds familiar, that's because it is—it's called high school.

Cast

Sean Penn: Jeff Spicoli
Jennifer Jason Leigh: Stacy Hamilton
Judge Reinhold: Brad Hamilton
Robert Romanus: Mike Damone
Brian Backer: Mark "Rat" Ratener
Phoebe Caes: Linda Barrett
Ray Walston: Mr. Hand
Vincent Schiavelli: Mr. Vargas
Forest Whitaker: Charles Jefferson

Behind the Scenes

Director: Amy Heckerling
Writers: Cameron Crowe (book and screenplay), Jonathan Roberts (screennplay)
Producers: Art Linson, Irving Azoff
Executive Producer: C.O. Erickson
Film Editor: Eric Jenkins
Cinematographer: Matthew F. Leonetti
Original Music: Joe Walsh

Trivia

• Sean Penn got so into character while shooting the film that he would only answer to the name Spicoli, and he had his name on the door of his dressing room changed to read "Spicoli."

Awards

WGA Nomination: Best Comedy Adapted from Another Medium
Added to National Film Registry in 2005

1987
Fatal Attraction

Overview

Genre: Drama/Thriller
Duration: 119 min
Color: Color (Technicolor)
Country: USA
MPAA Rating: R
Studio: Paramount Pictures

Married New York attorney Dan Gallagher gets more than he bargained for when he has a brief affair with a business associate. While Dan considers his encounter with editor Alex Forrest a one-time fling, she has different ideas. As he tries to get on with his life and shield his indiscretion from his family, she refuses to let him go. When she starts calling and showing up at inappropriate places and times, it's clear that this is one woman who won't take "no" for an answer. Glenn Close truly made a name for herself as psychotic sex object Alex. A cautionary thriller, *Fatal Attraction* continues to scare philandering husbands everywhere straight.

Cast

Michael Douglas: Dan Gallagher
Glenn Close: Alex Forrest
Anne Archer: Beth Gallagher
Ellen Hamilton Latzen: Ellen Gallagher
Stuart Pankin: Jimmy
Ellen Foley: Hildy
Fred Gwynne: Arthur

Behind the Scenes

Director: Adrian Lyne
Writers: James Dearden, Nicholas Meyer (uncredited)
Producers: Stanley R. Jaffe, Sherry Lansing
Film Editor: Michael Kahn
Cinematographer: Howard Atherton
Original Music: Maurice Jarre

Awards

Oscar Nominations: Best Actress, Best Supporting Actress, Best Director, Best Film Editing, Best Picture, Best Writing—Adapted Screenplay

Trivia

• Glenn Close kept the knife she used in the film. It now hangs in her kitchen.
• The score, composed by Maurice Jarre, doesn't start playing until half an hour into the film.

1986
Ferris Bueller's Day Off

Overview

Genre: Comedy
Duration: 102 min
Color: Color
Country: USA
MPAA Rating: PG-13
Studio: Paramount Pictures

If taking it easy were an art form, Ferris Bueller would be Michelangelo. A revered master at cutting class and playing hooky, Ferris decides to take yet another day off as the school year winds down. Joining him on his leisurely expedition is his girlfriend Sloane and best friend Cameron. Together, the truant trio take off for Chicago in Cameron's dad's Ferrari, on a mission to pack as much fun into one day as possible. Bueller's chicanery, however, hasn't gone unnoticed by dean of students Ed Rooney, who is hell-bent on bringing down Ferris once and for all. But, on such a perfect day, Ferris Bueller isn't about to let anyone or anything spoil his good time.

Cast

Matthew Broderick: Ferris Bueller
Alan Ruck: Cameron Frye
Mia Sara: Sloane Peterson
Jeffrey Jones: Ed Rooney
Jennifer Grey: Jeanie Bueller
Cindy Pickett: Katie Bueller
Lyman Ward: Tom Bueller

Behind the Scenes

Director: John Hughes
Writer: John Hughes
Producers: John Hughes, Tom Jacobson
Executive Producer: Michael Chinich
Cinematographer: Tak Fujimoto
Original Music: Arthur Baker, Ira Newborn, John Robie

Awards

Golden Globe Nomination: Best Performance by an Actor in a Motion Picture—Comedy/Musical

Trivia

• It was too expensive to rent a Ferrari so Cameron's father's car was duplicated and made out of fiberglass.

1989
Field of Dreams

Overview

Genre: Drama/Sports
Duration: 107 min
Color: Color
Country: USA
MPAA Rating: PG
Studio: Universal
Pictures

When Ray Kinsella hears a voice in his Iowa cornfield, he gets the idea to plow under much of his crop and build a baseball field. Needless to say, this action arouses a bit of head-scratching from the locals as well as his wife and daughter. But this isn't just any baseball field. Before you can say "Shoeless Joe," the ghosts of baseball legends past start visiting Ray's field and playing ball, and it's pretty cool. So, why is the voice still talking to Ray? And what does his field have to do with a reclusive author? As he doggedly pursues the answers to these and other questions, Ray stands to lose his farm and what's left of his sanity.

Cast

Kevin Costner: Ray Kinsella
Amy Madigan: Annie Kinsella
Gaby Hoffman: Karin Kinsella
Ray Liotta: Shoeless Joe Jackson
Timothy Busfield: Mark
James Earl Jones: Terence "Terry" Mann
Burt Lancaster: Dr. Archibald "Moonlight" Graham
Frank Whaley: Archie Graham

Behind the Scenes

Director: Phil Alden Robinson
Writers: W.P. Kinsella (book), Phil Alden Robinson (screenplay)
Producers: Lawrence Gordon, Charles Gordon
Executive Producer: Brian E. Frankish
Film Editor: Ian Crafford
Cinematographer: John Lindley
Original Music: James Horner

Trivia

• Ben Affleck and Matt Damon, still unknowns at the time, were among the thousands of extras at the Fenway Park scene. When Affleck worked with director Phil Alden Robinson over 10 years later on *The Sum of All Fears*, Affleck said, "Nice working with you again," and Robinson had no idea what he was talking about.

Awards

Oscar Nominations: Best Music, Best Picture, Best Writing—Adapted Screenplay

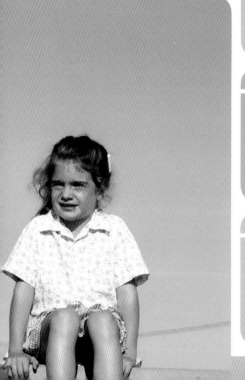

1999
Fight Club

Overview

Genre: Drama/Action
Duration: 139 min
Color: Color
Country: USA
MPAA Rating: R
Studio: Fox 2000
Pictures/Regency
Enterprises

"The first rule of fight club is: you do not talk about fight club" became the famous line from this thriller that disappointed at the box office but soon shot to cult classic status. Edward Norton plays the narrator, a nameless drone who suffers from insomnia. He finds a temporary fix in support groups for ailments he doesn't have, but his sanity crumbles when a woman, Marla, starts faking her way into the same meetings. Then he meets the bold and destructive Tyler Durden, who helps him discover a new therapy: fist fights. He and Tyler start a "Fight Club" for like minded men, but soon the clubs spread around the country, and under Tyler's leadership, spin out of control.

Cast

Edward Norton: The Narrator
Brad Pitt: Tyler Durden
Helena Bonham Carter: Marla Singer
Meat Loaf: Robert "Bob" Paulson
Zach Grenier: Richard Chesler
Richmond Arquette: Intern
David Andrews: Thomas
George Maguire: Group leader

Behind the Scenes

Director: David Fincher
Writers: Chuck Palahniuk (novel), Jim Uhls (screenplay)
Producers: Ross Grayson Bell, Céan Chaffin, Art Linson
Executive Producer: Arnon Milchan
Original Music: Dust Brothers: John King and Michael Simpson

Trivia

• When a member of Fight Club sprays the priest with a hose, the camera shakes for a moment because the cameraman could not stop himself from laughing.

Awards

Oscar Nominations: Best Effects—Sound

1988
A Fish Called Wanda

Overview

Genre: Comedy/Crime
Duration: 108 min
Color: Color
Country: USA
MPAA Rating: R
Studio: MGM/United Artists

It's England versus America all over again as a quartet of jewel thieves turn on each other. When beautiful Wanda and her dimwitted boyfriend Otto team up with British counterparts George and Ken for a jewel heist, it doesn't take long for them to try to double-cross their hosts. As George cools his heels in jail, Wanda tries to pry the location of the stolen gems from his attorney Archie Leach. Meanwhile Ken must try to bump off a witness while also contending with Otto's strong-arm tactics. A hilarious caper movie, *A Fish Called Wanda* has a distinctive Monty Python silliness to it, thanks to co-writer and star John Cleese and Michael Palin's ridiculous stutter-prone Ken.

Cast

John Cleese: Archie Leach
Jamie Lee Curtis: Wanda Gershwitz
Kevin Kline: Otto
Michael Palin: Ken Pile
Maria Aitken: Wendy
Tom Georgeson: George Thomason
Patricia Hayes: Mrs. Coady

Behind the Scenes

Director: Charles Crichton, John Cleese (uncredited)
Writers: John Cleese and Charles Crichton
Producer: Michael Shamberg
Executive Producers: Steve Abbott, John Cleese
Original Music: John Du Prez

Awards

Oscar Winners: Best Supporting Actor
Oscar Nominations: Best Director, Best Writing

Trivia

• Archie Leach recites the poem "Molitva" (1839) by Mikhail Lermontov (1814–1841) in Russian for Wanda Gershwitz.
• The fish Kevin Kline eats are made of gelatin.

The 40 Year Old Virgin

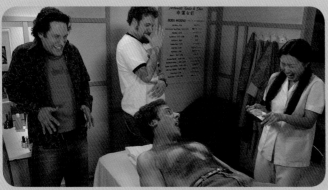

Overview

Genre: Comedy/ Romance
Duration: 116 min
Color: Color
Country: USA
MPAA Rating: R
Studio: Universal Pictures

This 2005 film, which became the breakout hit of the summer, helped propel writer/director/producer Judd Apatow into the mainstream as the next "king of comedy," and redefined co-writer and star Steve Carrell as a leading man. Carrell plays Andy Stitzer, the nice but nerdy action figure collector and stock supervisor at "Smart Tech," who accidentally lets slip to his younger coworkers that he has never "done the deed," and worse still, has given up on trying. Andy's newfound friends (who are slightly clueless themselves) concoct several schemes to help him get a girl, but hit a snag when he starts dating Trish, a mother of two who wants to wait 20 dates before their relationship becomes physical.

Cast

Steve Carell: Andy Stitzer
Catherine Keener: Trish
Paul Rudd: David
Romany Malco: Jay
Seth Rogen: Cal
Elizabeth Banks: Beth
Leslie Mann: Nicky
Jane Lynch: Paula

Behind the Scenes

Director: Judd Apatow
Writers: Judd Apatow, Steve Carell
Producers: Judd Apatow, Shauna Robertson, Clayton Townsend
Executive Producer: Steve Carell, Jon Poll
Original Music: Lyle Workman
Cinematographer: Jack N. Green

Trivia

• The scene where Andy (Steve Carell) gets his chest hair waxed was not fake. Carell had told the director, "It has to be real. It won't be as funny if it's mocked up or if it's special effect. You have to see that this is really happening."

Awards

Writers Guild of America: Best Original Screenplay

1994
Forrest Gump

Overview

Genre: Comedy/
Drama
Duration: 142 min
Color: Color
Country: USA
MPAA Rating: PG-13
Studio: Paramount
Pictures

Waiting for a city bus, Forrest Gump offers a chocolate to a lady sitting beside him and strikes up a conversation: so begins the life story of a boy destined to be different. Clinging to the advice of his best friend Jenny, Forrest runs through his life, from college football to the United States army, even across the country. As he recounts his experiences, three decades of history pass by. In that time, Forrest learns the ins and outs of a changing society and makes many friends along the way. But he always keeps Jenny in his heart. In his own simple way, Forrest touches the lives of those around him without even trying.

Cast

Tom Hanks: Forrest Gump
Robin Wright Penn: Jenny Curran
Gary Sinise: Lieutenant Dan Taylor
Mykelti Williamson: Private Benjamin
Buford "Bubba" Blue
Sally Field: Mrs. Gump
Michael C. Humphreys: Forrest (young)

Behind the Scenes

Director: Robert Zemeckis
Writer: Winston Groom (novel), Eric Roth
(screenplay)
Producers: Wendy Finerman, Steve Starkey,
Steve Tisch
Film Editor: Arthur Schmidt
Cinematographer: Don Burgess

Awards

Oscar Winners: Best Actor, Best Director,
Best Effects—Visual, Best Film Editing, Best
Picture, Best Writing—Adapted Screenplay

Trivia

• Tom Hanks agreed to star in the film only on
the condition that all the events were histori-
cally accurate.

1931
Frankenstein

Overview

Genre: Horror/Drama
Duration: 71 min
Color: Black and White
Country: USA
MPAA Rating: Not Rated
Studio: Universal Pictures

A highly unorthodox experiment results in a scientist creating something out of his control. Dr. Henry Frankenstein and his assistant Fritz skulk around at night in search of organs and parts they will use to bring a dead body back to life. Unbeknownst to the doctor, Fritz brings him the brain of a criminal to use in his creation. Using charges of lightning to reanimate the body, the experiment is a success. But what Dr. Frankenstein now has on his hands is a hulking monster with a damaged brain struggling to understand its very existence. *Frankenstein* still delivers its share of chills and includes the one and only Boris Karloff as the monster.

Cast

Colin Clive: Dr. Henry Frankenstein
Mae Clarke: Elizabeth
John Boles: Victor Moritz
Boris Karloff: The Monster
Edward Van Sloan: Dr. Waldman
Frederick Kerr: Baron Frankenstein
Dwight Frye: Fritz

Behind the Scenes

Director: James Whale
Writers: Mary Shelley (novel), Peggy Webling (play), Francis Edward Faragoh and Garrett Fort (screenplay)
Producer: Carl Laemmle Jr.
Film Editor: Clarence Kolster
Cinematographer: Arthur Edeson

Awards

Added to National Film Registry in 1991

Trivia

• This film, not Shelley's novel, is the source for the idea that lightning was used to bring the monster to life.

1971
The French Connection

Overview

Genre: Action/Crime
Duration: 104 min
Color: Color
Country: USA
MPAA Rating: R
Studio: Twentieth Century Fox

Tough New York narcotics detective Jimmy "Popeye" Doyle and his partner Buddy Russo are the scourge of the city's dope peddlers, using any means necessary to make a bust. After they start tailing a suspicious character named Sal, they slowly start connecting the pieces to a puzzle that could lead to a huge shipment of heroin coming in from France. As more layers and players in the deal are revealed, Popeye pursues his quarry with singular focus and determination. A wild and reckless car chase under an elevated subway perfectly illustrates Doyle's win-at-all-costs approach and reveals the flawed human being behind the great cop.

Cast

Gene Hackman: Jimmy Doyle
Fernando Rey: Alain Charnier
Roy Scheider: Detective Buddy Russo
Tony Lo Bianco: Sal Boca
Marcel Bozzuffi: Pierre Nicoli
Frederic De Pasquale: Devereaux
Bill Hickman: Mulderig
Ann Rebbot: Marie Charnier

Behind the Scenes

Director: William Friedkin
Writers: Robin Moore (book), Ernest Tidyman (screenplay)
Producer: Philip D'Antoni
Executive Producer: G. David Schine
Film Editor: Jerry Greenberg
Cinematographer: Owen Roizman
Original Music: Don Ellis

Trivia

• The real detectives (Eddie Egan and Sonny Grosso) on whom the characters are based make a cameo as the detectives' supervisors.
• The car crash during the famous chase sequence was unplanned. The man whose car was hit was unaware of the filming, and the crash was ultimately left in the film for its realism.

Awards

Oscar Winners: Best Actor, Best Director, Best Film Editing, Best Picture, Best Writing—Adapted Screenplay
Oscar Nominations: Best Supporting Actor, Best Cinematography, Best Sound

1990
The Freshman

Overview

Genre: Comedy/Crime
Duration: 102 min
Color: Color (Technicolor)
Country: USA
MPAA Rating: PG
Studio: TriStar Pictures

About to begin his freshman year as a film student at NYU, Clark Kellogg is in New York for a matter of minutes before he has all of his money and belongings stolen. While pleading his case to his narcissistic faculty advisor Arthur Fleeber, Clark spies the man who robbed him. Having already lost the money and many of Clark's belongings, the crook tries to make good by getting the kid a job working for his Uncle Carmine, a "legitimate businessman." After reluctantly accepting the job, Clark soon finds himself mixed up with crime families, federal agents, endangered species, and something called "The Gourmet Club." Who knew college was so dangerous?

Cast

Marlon Brando: Carmine Sabatini (Jimmy the Toucan)
Matthew Broderick: Clark Kellogg
Bruno Kirby: Victor Ray
Penelope Ann Miller: Tina Sabatini
Maximilian Schell: Larry London
Frank Whaley: Steve Bushak
Jon Polito: Agent Chuck Greenwald
Paul Benedict: Arthur Fleeber

Behind the Scenes

Director: Andrew Bergman
Writer: Andrew Bergman
Producer: Mike Lobell
Film Editor: Barry Malkin
Cinematographer: William A. Fraker
Original Music: David Newman

Trivia

• The character of Carmine Sabatini, played by Marlon Brando, is supposed to be based on his portrayal of Don Vito Corleone in *The Godfather*. Don Vito is arguably Brando's most famous role.
• After filming, Marlon Brando thought this movie would be a colossal bomb. He later changed his tune.
• The name on Clark Kellogg's phony Italian passport—Rodolfo Lassparri—is the name of the villain in the Marx Brothers comedy *A Night at the Opera*.

1953
From Here to Eternity

Overview

Genre: Drama
Duration: 118 min
Color: Black and White
Country: USA
MPAA Rating: Not Rated
Studio: Columbia Pictures

In the days leading up to the Japanese attack on Pearl Harbor, American servicemen in Hawaii grapple with their demons. Burt Lancaster leads the all-star cast as Sgt. Milton Warden, a man in love with a superior officer's wife. Montgomery Clift is headstrong Private Robert E. Lee Prewitt who refuses to bow to pressure to join the company boxing team. And Frank Sinatra earned an Oscar for his portrayal of Private Angelo Maggio, who has made an enemy of stockade sergeant Fatso Judson. All of the drama, including the famous beach scene between Lancaster and Deborah Kerr, focuses on individual stories soon to be lost to the war.

Cast

Burt Lancaster: Sergeant Milton Warden
Deborah Kerr: Karen Holmes
Donna Reed: Alma "Lorene" Burke
Frank Sinatra: Private Angelo Maggio
Montgomery Clift: Private Robert E. Lee "Prew" Prewitt
Philip Ober: Captain Dana "Dynamite" Holmes
Harry Bellaver: Private Mazzioli
Ernest Borgnine: Sergeant James R. Judson

Behind the Scenes

Director: Fred Zinnemann
Writers: James Jones (novel), Daniel Taradash (screenplay)
Producer: Buddy Adler
Film Editor: William A. Lyon
Cinematographer: Burnett Guffey
Original Music: George Duning

Trivia

• Deborah Kerr and Burt Lancaster were meant to be standing in their now-famous scene on the beach at Oahu's Halona Cove.

Awards

Oscar Winners: Best Supporting Actor, Best Supporting Actress, Best Cinematography, Best Director, Best Film Editing, Best Sound, Best Writing, Best Picture
Oscar Nominations: Best Actor, Best Actor, Best Actress, Best Costume Design, Best Music

1982
Gandhi

Overview

Genre: Drama/
Biography
Duration: 188 min
Color: Color
Country: UK/India
MPAA Rating: PG
Studio: Indo-British
Films/International Film
Investors/Goldcrest
Films International

The fascinating life of Indian leader Mohandas Gandhi is explored in this biographical epic directed by Sir Richard Attenborough. Ben Kingsley won an Oscar for his spot-on portrayal of the man who fought for India's independence while maintaining his spiritual center. The story kicks off with Gandhi's early days as a young lawyer fighting for Indian rights in South Africa and follows all the way through his campaign of non-violent protest against the British empire and then to the religious unrest that threatened to tear India apart. So compelling is *Gandhi* that it's easy to forget that it is all based on true events.

Cast

Ben Kingsley: Mohandas Karamchand Gandhi
Candice Bergen: Margaret Bourke-White
Edward Fox: General Reginald Dyer
John Gielgud: Lord Irwin
John Mills: Lord Chelmsford
Martin Sheen: Vince Walker
Athol Fugard: General Jan Christiaan Smuts
Saeed Jaffrey: Sardar Valabhhai Patel

Behind the Scenes

Director: Richard Attenborough
Writer: John Briley
Producers: Richard Attenborough, Rani Dube
Executive Producer: Michael Stanley-Evans
Cinematographers: Ronnie Taylor, Billy Williams
Original Music: Ravi Shankar

Trivia

• 300,000 extras were used for the funeral sequence, but fewer than 100,000 received any payment. The sequence was shot on the 33rd anniversary of Gandhi's funeral to lend credibility and realism to the scene, and 11 camera crews filmed a total of over 20,000 feet of film, which became a mere 125 seconds in the final cut.

Awards

Oscar Winners: Best Actor, Best Art Direction, Best Cinematography, Best Costume Design, Best Director, Best Film Editing, Best Picture, Best Writing
Oscar Nominations: Best Makeup, Best Music, Best Sound

1944
Gaslight

Overview

Genre: Drama/ Mystery
Duration: 114 min
Color: Black and White
Country: USA
MPAA Rating: Not Rated
Studio: Metro-Goldwyn-Mayer (MGM)

After teenager Paula discovers her aunt—world-renowned opera singer Alice Alquist—strangled to death in their London home, Paula runs off to Italy to escape the bad memories and pursue voice training. Ten years later, Paula Alquist marries a pianist she's known for only two weeks and moves back to the London townhouse, which she has inherited. There, the gaslights go down un-expectedly, footsteps echo in the attic, and her husband insists that she has moved household items without remembering. Getting more and more isolated and unhinged, Paula fears that she is losing her mind, and her husband Gregory Anton supports this notion.

Cast

Charles Boyer: Gregory Anton
Ingrid Bergman: Paula Alquist Anton
Joseph Cotten: Brian Cameron
Dame May Whitty: Miss Bessie Thwaites
Angela Lansbury: Nancy Oliver
Barbara Everest: Elizabeth Tompkins

Behind the Scenes

Director: George Cukor
Writers: Patrick Hamilton (play), John Van Druten, Walter Reisch, and John L. Balderston (screenplay)
Producer: Arthur Hornblow Jr.
Film Editor: Ralph E. Winters
Cinematographer: Joseph Ruttenberg

Awards

Oscar Winners: Best Actress, Best Art Direction

Trivia

• When the film was first released, MGM attempted to destroy all prints of the earlier version of this film, also called *Gaslight*, which had been released only 4 years earlier.

1927
The General

Overview

Genre: Comedy/Action
Duration: 75 min
Color: Black and White (Sepiatone)
Country: USA
MPAA Rating: Not Rated
Studio: United Artists

Widely praised as Buster Keaton's best film, *The General* stars the silent film great as Johnny Gray, an engineer who longs to enlist in the Confederate army. When Johnny is turned down for service because of his value to the Confederacy as an engineer, his girlfriend Annabelle Lee is ashamed. Some time later Union spies manage to steal Johnny's locomotive, The General, and take with it Annabelle Lee, who is onboard. Johnny springs into action, chasing down the engine by whatever means available, determined to get back the two things he loves more than anything else. As with so much of Keaton's work, his incredible stunts alone make *The General* a must-see.

Cast

Buster Keaton: Johnny Gray
Marion Mack: Annabelle Lee
Charles Henry Smith: Mr. Lee (Annabelle's father)
Frank Barnes: Annabelle's brother
Glen Cavender: Union Captain Anderson (chief spy)

Behind the Scenes

Directors: Clyde Bruckman, Buster Keaton
Writers: Clyde Bruckman, Buster Keaton
Producers: Buster Keaton, Joseph M. Schenck
Executive Producer: Joseph M. Schenck
Cinematographers: Dev Jennings, Bert Haines

Awards

Added to National Film Registry in 1989

Trivia

• Filming the scene in which the train The Texas crashes through the bridge cost more than any other shot in the entire silent movie era.

1990
Ghost

Overview

Genre: Drama/ Mystery
Duration: 128 min
Color: Color
Country: USA
MPAA Rating: PG-13
Studio: Paramount Pictures

Is true love really eternal? If you aren't a believer, this film may just change your mind. Sam and Molly are a young couple living in New York and very much in love. After an unexpected and violent death, Sam is trapped in a world between the living and the dead where he attempts to find his killer and warn Molly that her life too may be in danger. He meets a con artist psychic named Oda Mae Brown who, unbeknownst to even herself, has the power to communicate with the dead. Oda Mae acts as Sam's conduit to the living and helps him to contact Molly and seek out his killer. Whether or not Sam succeeds may depend on how strong his love is.

Cast

Patrick Swayze: Sam Wheat
Demi Moore: Molly Jensen
Whoopi Goldberg: Oda Mae Brown
Tony Goldwyn: Carl Bruner
Rick Aviles: Willie Lopez
Vincent Schiavelli: Subway ghost
Susan Breslau: Susan

Behind the Scenes

Director: Jerry Zucker
Writers: Bruce Joel Rubin, Peter Barsocchini
Producers: Lisa Weinstein, Howard W. Koch
Executive Producer: Steven-Charles Jaffe
Film Editor: Walter Murch
Cinematographer: Adam Greenberg
Original Music: Maurice Jarre

Awards

Oscar Winners: Best Supporting Actress, Best Writing
Oscar Nominations: Best Film Editing, Best Music, Best Picture

Trivia

• The sounds made by the frightening "shadow demons" are actually a recording of babies crying, played back at a low speed.

1984
Ghostbusters

Overview

Genre: Comedy/Sci-Fi
Duration: 105 min
Color: Color
Country: USA
MPAA Rating: PG
Studio: Columbia Pictures

When three parapsychology professors, Peter Venkman, Ray Stantz, and Egon Spengler, get fired from their teaching positions, they start a paranormal investigation service called the Ghostbusters and hire Winston Zeddmore. As the foursome begins their foray into the world of supernatural sleuthing, they discover that not only is there a spike in activity in New York City but one of their clients, Dana Barrett, lives in a paranormal hotspot. Before long, the guys are in high demand and nabbing ghosts and slimy apparitions all over the place, but a much more menacing force may be living right inside Dana's apartment. With the Big Apple teetering on the brink of destruction, who they gonna call?

Cast

Bill Murray: Dr. Peter Venkman
Dan Aykroyd: Dr. Raymond Stantz
Sigourney Weaver: Dana Barrett
Harold Ramis: Dr. Egon Spengler
Rick Moranis: Louis Tully
Annie Potts: Janine Melnitz
William Atherton: Walter Peck
Ernie Hudson: Winston Zeddmore

Behind the Scenes

Director: Ivan Reitman
Writers: Dan Aykroyd, Harold Ramis, Peter Torokvei
Producer: Ivan Reitman
Executive Producer: Bernie Brillstein
Cinematographers: Laszlo Kovacs, Herb Wagreitch
Original Music: Elmer Bernstein

Trivia

• The marshmallow goo was shaving cream. More than fifty gallons were poured on Walter Peck, just about knocking him to the ground.

Awards

Oscar Nominations: Best Effects—Visual, Best Music—Original Song

1946
Gilda

Overview

Genre: Drama/Thriller
Duration: 110 min
Color: Black and White
Country: USA
MPAA Rating: Not Rated
Studio: Columbia Pictures

After casino owner Ballin Mundson saves gambler Johnny Farrell's life, he hires him as his right-hand man. But when Mundson returns from a trip with a beautiful new wife, Johnny is shocked to see that it's his ex-flame Gilda. Things get even more awkward when Johnny is asked to keep an eye on the flirtatious new bride. With Ballin working on some shady deals involving tungsten, Gilda freely throws herself at men in Johnny's presence, and you can cut the tension with a knife. It's anybody's guess how this whole dysfunctional triangle will play out. The only sure thing is that Gilda is as smoldering as the South American setting and she shows no signs of cooling off.

Cast

Rita Hayworth: Gilda Mundson
Glenn Ford: Johnny Farrell
George Macready: Ballin Mundson
Joseph Calleia: Detective Maurice Obregon
Steven Geray: Uncle Pio
Joe Sawyer: Casey
Gerald Mohr: Capt. Delgado

Behind the Scenes

Director: Charles Vidor
Writers: E.A. Ellington (story), Marion Parsonnet and Joe Eisinger (screenplay)
Producer: Virginia Van Upp
Film Editor: Charles Nelson
Cinematographer: Rudolph Maté
Original Music: Hugo Friedhofer (uncredited)

Trivia

• Johnny Farrell's baby picture is actually a photo of Glenn Ford's son Peter.

Trivia

• When Gilda slaps Johnny hard across the face, Rita Hayworth actually broke two of Glenn Ford's teeth. He took it like a pro and finished the scene.

2000
Gladiator

Overview

Genre: Action/Adventure

Duration: 155 min

Color: Color (Technicolor)

Country: UK/USA

MPAA Rating: R

Studio: DreamWorks SKG/Universal Pictures

A once powerful general and the desired successor to the emperor of Rome, Maximus is betrayed by the son of the late emperor and sentenced to death. He escapes, but is unable to save his family from his would-be fate. Caught and sold into slavery, Maximus is trained to become a gladiator, who fights without fear and with only one goal: to avenge the murder of his family. As he quickly ascends to one of the most feared warriors in the battle arena, Maximus is called to Rome where he will finally get the chance to lay eyes on the corrupt and cowardly Emperor Commodus and perhaps exorcise his demons once and for all.

Cast

Russell Crowe: Maximus
Joaquin Phoenix: Commodus
Connie Nielsen: Lucilla
Oliver Reed: Proximo
Richard Harris: Marcus Aurelius
Derek Jacobi: Gracchus
Djimon Hounsou: Juba
David Schofield: Falco
John Shrapnel: Gaius

Behind the Scenes

Director: Ridley Scott
Writers: David Franzoni (story and screenplay), John Logan, William Nicholson (screenplay)
Producers: Douglas Wick, David Franzoni, Branko Lustig
Executive Producers: Laurie MacDonald, Walter F. Parkes, Ridley Scott (uncredited)
Cinematographer: John Mathieson

Trivia

• Oliver Reed, who plays Proximo, died with three weeks remaining in principal photography. Rather than replace him, director Ridley Scott had the remainder of the script rewritten to include less of Reed, and a stand-in with a 3D CGI mask was used for his remaining scenes.

Awards

Oscar Winners: : Best Actor, Best Costume Design, Best Effects—Visual, Best Picture, Best Sound
Oscar Nominations: Best Supporting Actor, Best Art Direction, Best Cinematography, Best Director, Best Editing, Best Music, Best Writing

1992
Glengarry Glen Ross

Overview

Genre: Drama
Duration: 100 min
Color: Color
Country: USA
MPAA Rating: R
Studio: New Line Cinema

No one knows better than David Mamet that story is character—and he's got them in spades here. Just listen to Mamet's metronomic patter chewed up and spit out like a bitter cocktail olive by some of the best in the business. Al Pacino is Ricky Roma, the quintessential big fish in a small pond—an office where shady real estate is hawked and agents either sell it to a sucker or go to die. You can smell the formaldehyde on Jack Lemmon, who plays Shelley "The Machine" Levene, a former rainman mired in a serious 0-fer-a-decade slump. There isn't a stinker performance in the mix—Baldwin . . . Arkin . . . Harris . . . Spacey. All walking misery in pleated gabardine. And all in top form.

Cast

Al Pacino: Ricky Roma
Jack Lemmon: Shelley Levene
Alec Baldwin: Blake
Alan Arkin: George Aaronow
Ed Harris: Dave Moss
Kevin Spacey: John Williamson
Jonathan Pryce: James Lingk
Bruce Altman: Larry Spannel
Jude Ciccolella: Detective

Behind the Scenes

Director: James Foley
Writer: David Mamet (play and screenplay)
Producers: Jerry Tokofsky, Stanley R. Zupnik
Executive Producer: Joesph M. Caracciolo Jr.
Cinematographer: Juan Ruiz Anchia
Film Editor: Howard Smith
Original Music: James Newton Howard

Trivia

• Veteran actor Jack Lemmon referred to his co-stars as the best ensemble he had ever worked with.
• Six members of this cast have been nominated for Academy Awards for acting, four of which were winners.

Awards

Oscar Nominations: Best Supporting Actor

1972
The Godfather

Overview

Genre: Drama/Crime
Duration: 175 min
Color: Color (Technicolor)
Country: United States
MPAA Rating: R
Studio: Paramount Pictures

B ased on Mario Puzo's 1969 novel, *The Godfather* follows the story of the Corleones, a New York mafia family led by aging patriarch "Don" Vito. When youngest son Michael returns from World War II, he is determined not to get involved in the "family business," but all of that changes when a rival crime syndicate threatens those closest to him. As Michael gets sucked into this violent world, he finds that the price one pays for loyalty is often as steep as that of betrayal. Brilliantly directed by Francis Ford Coppola and featuring a cast of Hollywood heavyweights including Marlon Brando, Al Pacino, and Robert Duvall, *The Godfather* is the film against which all other crime dramas are measured.

Cast

Marlon Brando: "Don" Vito Corleone
Al Pacino: Michael Corleone
James Caan: Santino "Sonny" Corleone
Richard S. Castellano: Peter Clemenza
Robert Duvall: Tom Hagan
Diane Keaton: Kay Adams
John Cazale: Fredo Corleone

Behind the Scenes

Director: Francis Ford Coppola
Writers: Mario Puzo (novel), Mario Puzo and Francis Ford Coppola (screenplay)
Producer: Albert S. Ruddy
Film Editors: Marc Laub, William H. Reynolds, Murray Solomon, Peter Zinner
Cinematographer: Gordon Willis
Original Music: Nino Rota

Trivia

• During the rehearsals of the bedroom scene, a false horse's head was used, but in the actual filming, a real horse's head was used. The head had been procured from a dog food factory.

Awards

Oscar Winners: Best Actor, Best Picture, Best Writing—Adapted Screenplay
Oscar Nominations: Best Supporting Actor, Best Supporting Actor, Best Supporting Actor, Best Costume Design, Best Director, Best Film Editing, Best Music, Best Sound

1974
The Godfather Part II

Overview

Genre: Drama/Crime
Duration: 200 min
Color: Color
Country: USA
MPAA Rating: R
Studio: Paramount
Pictures

The Corleone family saga continues with what many consider the best Godfather movie of the bunch. Michael is now fully in control of the family as it expands operations into Nevada and Cuba. Becoming increasingly isolated and paranoid, he is leery of his enemies as well as his allies, and even his own family. A great addition to this chapter is the parallel story of Vito Corleone's beginnings, first as a youngster in Sicily and then his early days in New York. Robert De Niro portrays young Vito, just one of many stellar performances here along with John Cazale as Michael's brother Fredo and Lee Strasberg as Hyman Roth. *The Godfather II* is arguably the best sequel ever.

Cast

Al Pacino: "Don" Michael Corleone
Robert Duvall: Tom Hagen
Diane Keaton: Kay Corleone
Robert De Niro: Vito Corleone
John Cazale: Fredo Corleone
Talia Shire: Connie Corleone
Lee Strasberg: Hyman Roth
Michael V. Gazzo: Frankie Pentangeli
Richard Bright: Al Beri

Behind the Scenes

Director: Francis Ford Coppola
Writers: Mario Puzo (novel and screenplay), Francis Ford Coppola (screenplay)
Producer: Francis Ford Coppola
Film Editors: Barry Malkin, Richard Marks, Peter Zinner
Cinematographer: Gordon Willis
Original Music: Nino Rota

Trivia

• Marlon Brando and Robert De Niro are the only actors to have won Oscars for playing the same character: Vito Corleone.
• Robert De Niro lived extensively in Sicily to prepare for his role.

Awards

Oscar Winners: Best Supporting Actor, Best Art Direction, Best Director, Best Music, Best Picture, Best Writing—Adapted Screenplay
Oscar Nominations: Best Actor, Best Supporting Actor, Best Supporting Actress, Best Costume Design

1954
Godzilla

Overview

Genre: Horror/Sci-Fi
Duration: 80 min
Color: Black and White
Country: Japan
MPAA Rating: Not Rated
Studio: Toho Company

After several Japanese boats sink off of the fishing community of Odo Island, local villagers believe it is the work of a giant prehistoric monster known as Godzilla. And boy are they right. After folks on Odo get a glimpse of the 164-foot behemoth, they know better than to fight it. Meanwhile, scientists in Tokyo surmise that Godzilla is a mutant dinosaur that has been awakened by atomic fallout. But, rather than run for their lives, much of Tokyo sticks around to see if they can kill, capture, or at least contain the beast. Later reedited and dubbed for American audiences, the original *Godzilla* is still a potent indictment of the atomic age and a highly entertaining film.

Cast

Takashi Shimura: Dr. Kyohei Yamane-hakase
Akira Takarada: Hideto Ogata
Momoko Kôchi: Emiko Yamane
Akihiko Hirata: Dr. Daisuke Serizawa-hakase
Fuyuki Murakami: Professor Tanabe
Ren Yamamoto: Masaji
Toyoaki Suzuki: Shinkichi

Behind the Scenes

Director: Ishiro Honda
Writer: Shigeru Kayama (story), Ishiro Honda and Takeo Murata (screenplay)
Producer: Tomoyuki Tanaka
Film Editor: Kazuji Taira
Cinematographer: Masao Tamai
Original Music: Akira Ifukube

Trivia

• Godzilla was initially going to be an octopus, which probably would have saved Tokyo quite a bit of damage!

Trivia

• Godzilla's roar was achieved by dragging a resin-coated leather glove up and down a contrabass and distorting the sound recording.

1964
Goldfinger

Overview

Genre: Action/Adventure
Duration: 110 min
Color: Color (Technicolor)
Country: UK
MPAA Rating: PG
Studio: Eon Productions/United Artists

The third film in the popular James Bond series sees debonair Agent 007 going up against Auric Goldfinger, a ruthless smuggler bent on knocking over Fort Knox. This time around, Bond is armed with an assortment of helpful gadgets designed to get him out of various precarious situations. And he'll need every one of them because not only is Goldfinger capable of killing men in creative fashions but his Asian henchman Oddjob is absolutely lethal with a bowler hat that can take a man's head off. There are also women to contend with, and in this movie there's Pussy Galore. If 007 can't foil Goldfinger's fiendish plot in time, he just may end up as a gold-plated corpse.

Cast

Sean Connery: James Bond
Honor Blackman: Pussy Galore
Gert Fröbe: Auric Goldfinger
Shirley Eaton: Jill Masterson
Tania Mallet: Tilly Masterson
Harold Sakata: Oddjob
Bernard Lee: M

Behind the Scenes

Director: Guy Hamilton
Writers: Ian Fleming (novel), Paul Dehn and Richard Maibaum (screenplay)
Producers: Albert R. Broccoli, Harry Saltzman
Film Editor: Peter R. Hunt
Cinematographer: Ted Moore

Awards

Oscar Winners: Best Effects—Sound

Trivia

• Honor Blackman (Pussy Galore) was thirty-seven at the time of filming, making her the oldest Bond girl.

1939
Gone with the Wind

Overview

Genre: Drama/ Romance
Duration: 226 min
Color: Color (Technicolor)
Country: United States
MPAA Rating: G
Studio: Selznick International Pictures

A sprawling American epic set around the time of the Civil War, *Gone with the Wind* features one of the screen's most memorable female protagonists in Scarlett O'Hara. The film follows Scarlett from her carefree days as a self-centered teenager living on her beloved Georgia plantation through her adulthood as a strong-willed Southern belle. Along the way she contends with unrequited love, marriage, the ravages of war, personal tragedy, and Rhett Butler, a brash Charleston bachelor and the one man who can give her all she's ever wanted—if she'll let him. Not surprisingly, the film dominated the 1939 Academy Awards, winning 8 Oscars, including Best Picture.

Cast

Vivien Leigh: Scarlett O'Hara
Clark Gable: Rhett Butler
Leslie Howard: Ashley Wilkes
Olivia de Havilland: Melanie Hamilton
Hattie McDaniel: Mammy
Harry Davenport: Dr. Meade
Thomas Mitchell: Gerald O'Hara

Behind the Scenes

Director: Victor Fleming
Writers: Margaret Mitchell (novel) and Sidney Howard (screenplay)
Producer: David O. Selznick
Film Editors: Hal Kern, James Newcom
Cinematographers: Ernest Haller, Lee Garmes (uncredited)

Awards

Oscar Winners: Best Actress, Best Supporting Actress, Best Art Direction, Best Cinematography, Best Director, Best Film Editing, Best Writing, Best Picture

Trivia

• The first film in color to win Best Picture, *Gone with the Wind* would be the top grossing movie of all time if box office receipts were adjusted for inflation.

1966
The Good, the Bad, and the Ugly

Overview

Genre: Action/Western
Duration: 161 min
Color: Color (Technicolor)
Country: Italy
MPAA Rating:
Studio: Produzioni Europee Associate/United Artists

Master of the "spaghetti western," Sergio Leone directs this incredibly entertaining tale of greed, deception, and violence during the American Civil War. Clint Eastwood stars as Blondie, a lone gunslinger who is portrayed as the "good" guy as compared to Lee Van Cleef's "bad" bounty hunter Angel Eyes and Eli Wallach's "ugly" Mexican bandito Tuco. All three men are on the trail of a huge stash of buried gold and each will stop at nothing to make sure their competitors don't get to it first. Under the blazing southwestern sun, the trio will engage in a battle of wills, wits, and trigger fingers. Complementing Leone's always steady direction is a fantastic score by the incomparable Ennio Morricone.

Cast

Eli Wallach: Tuco
Clint Eastwood: Blondie
Lee Van Cleef: Sentenza/Angel Eyes
Aldo Giuffre: Union Captain
Luigi Pistilli: Father Pablo Ramirez
Rada Rassimov: Maria
Enzo Petito: Storekeeper
Claudio Scarchilli: Bounty Hunter
John Bartha: Sheriff

Behind the Scenes

Director: Sergio Leone
Writers: Luciano Vincenzoni and Sergio Leone (story and screenplay), Agenore Incrocci and Furio Scarpelli (screenplay)
Producer: Alberto Grimaldi
Film Editors: Eugene Alabiso, Nino Baragli
Cinematographer: Tonino Delli Colli
Original Music: Ennio Morricone

Trivia

• Sergio Leone spoke little English and Eli Wallach spoke minimal Italian, so the two spoke to each other in French during filming.
• Clint Eastwood sported the same weather-beaten poncho in three different movies.
• The first ten minutes of the movie features no dialogue at all.

1997
Good Will Hunting

Overview

Genre: Drama
Duration: 126 min
Color: Color
Country: USA
MPAA Rating: R
Studio: Miramax Films

When Will Hunting—a poor, orphaned, uneducated janitor at MIT—solves a highly advanced math problem left on a chalkboard by Professor Gerald Lambeau, he is taken under the professor's wing. Lambeau offers to tutor Will if he sees a psychologist to placate his erratic behavior. As his sessions with psychologist Sean Maguire progress, Will is pulled in different directions: Lambeau wants to push Will to fulfill his vast potential in math, while Sean wants Will to take things at his own pace, to avoid pressuring the troubled young man. Meanwhile, Will strikes up a fragile romance with a girl named Skylar. Soon he will have to make a decision that will shape the rest of his life.

Cast

Robin Williams: Sean Maguire
Matt Damon: Will Hunting
Ben Affleck: Chuckie Sullivan
Stellan Skarsgård: Professor Gerald Lambeau
Minnie Driver: Skylar
Casey Affleck: Morgan O'Mally
Cole Hauser: Billy McBride

Behind the Scenes

Director: Gus Van Sant
Writers: Matt Damon, Ben Affleck
Producers: Lawrence Bender
Executive Producers: Su Armstrong, Jonathan Gordan, Bob Weinstein, Harvey Weinstein
Film Editor: Pietro Scalia
Cinematographer: Jean-Yves Escoffier
Original Music: Danny Elfman

Trivia

• The mathematical equations seen in the opening credits are called Fourier analysis, which approximates functions by sines and cosines.
• *Good Will Hunting* became the highest grossing film in Miramax history until *Chicago* (2002).

Awards

Oscar Winners: Best Supporting Actor, Best Writing
Oscar Nominations: Best Actor, Best Supporting Actress, Best Director, Best Film Editing, Best Music, Best Music—Original Song, Best Picture

1990
Goodfellas

Overview

Genre: Drama/Crime
Duration: 146 min
Color: Color (Technicolor)
Country: USA
MPAA Rating: R
Studio: Warner Bros. Pictures

Growing up in Brooklyn, Henry Hill idolizes the gangsters that populate his neighborhood. Starting as a runner for these "good fellas" Henry eventually makes a name for himself when he gets caught by the cops and doesn't rat on his friends. From this moment on he's as good as one of the family and quickly comes to realize that crime *does* pay. Working under one of his idols, Jimmy Conway, Henry also teams up with scary hothead Tommy DeVito, as they participate in some lucrative scores. The dark flipside of these associations is violence and paranoia. And as his life spirals out of control, it's almost impossible for Henry to tell his friends from his enemies.

Cast

Robert De Niro: James "Jimmy" Conway
Ray Liotta: Henry Hill
Joe Pesci: Tommy DeVito
Lorraine Bracco: Karen Hill
Paul Sorvino: Paul Cicero
Frank Sivero: Frankie Carbone
Tony Darrow: Sonny Bunz

Behind the Scenes

Director: Martin Scorsese
Writers: Nicholas Pileggi (book and screenplay), Martin Scorsese (screenplay)
Producer: Irwin Winkler
Executive Producer: Barbara De Fina
Film Editor: Thelma Schoonmaker
Cinematographer: Michael Ballhaus

Awards

Oscar Winners: Best Supporting Actor
Oscar Nominations: Best Supporting Actress, Best Director, Best Film Editing, Best Picture, Best Writing—Adapted Screenplay

Trivia

• The actual Henry Hill was so proud of the film that, though he was in the Witness Protection Program, he revealed his identity. The government removed him almost immediately.

1967
The Graduate

Overview

Genre: Drama/
Romance
Duration: 105 min
Color: Color (Tech-
nicolor)
Country: USA
MPAA Rating: PG
Studio: Embassy
Pictures/Lawrence
Turman Inc.

Mike Nichols copped a Best Director Oscar for this film which looked at, among other things, the generational disconnect of the '60s. Dustin Hoffman stars as Benjamin Braddock, a recent college graduate with no plans toward the future. His rudderless existence is turned upside down when he starts having an affair with his father's business partner's wife, Mrs. Robinson. To complicate things further, Benjamin falls for Mrs. Robinson's beautiful daughter Elaine. Dramatic elements blend beautifully with screwball comedy in this coming-of-age story. Tying all of the action together is a memorable soundtrack featuring '60s stalwarts Simon and Garfunkel.

Cast

Dustin Hoffman: Benjamin Braddock
Anne Bancroft: Mrs. Robinson
Katharine Ross: Elaine Robinson
William Daniels: Mr. Braddock
Murray Hamilton: Mr. Robinson
Elizabeth Wilson: Mrs. Braddock
Buck Henry: Room clerk
Brian Avery: Carl Smith

Behind the Scenes

Director: Mike Nichols
Writers: Charles Webb (novel), Calder Willingham and Buck Henry (screenplay)
Producer: Lawrence Turman
Executive Producer: Joseph E. Levine
Film Editor: Sam O'Steen
Cinematographer: Robert Surtees

Trivia

• Anne Bancroft was only eight years older than her on-screen daughter Katharine Ross and just six years Benjamin's senior.
• Simon and Garfunkel contributed to the film's soundtrack, and their song "Mrs. Robinson" (formerly "Mrs. Roosevelt") became a number one hit.

Awards

Oscar Winners: Best Director
Oscar Nominations: Best Actor, Best Actress, Best Supporting Actress, Best Cinematography, Best Picture, Best Writing—Adapted Screenplay

1937
Grand Illusion

Overview

Genre: Drama/War
Duration: 114 min
Color: Black and White
Country: France
MPAA Rating: Not Rated
Studio: R.A.C. (Réalisation d'art cinématographique)

During a World War I reconnaissance mission, Captain de Boeldieu and Lieutenant Maréchel are shot down in their plane by German aristocrat Captain von Rauffenstein. Their gracious conqueror invites the officers to lunch during which de Boeldieu and Rauffenstein, both aristocrats, discover they have mutual acquaintances. After attempts at escaping various camps are thwarted, the two Frenchmen are installed in the impenetrable Camp Wintersborn, commanded by a battle-scarred von Rauffenstein. A third prisoner, Rosenthal, collaborates with them on a plan to finally escape once and for all.

Cast

Jean Gabin: Lieutenant Maréchal
Pierre Fresnay: Captain de Boeldieu
Dita Parlo: Elsa
Marcel Dalip: Lieutenant Rosenthal
Erich von Stroheim: Captain von Rauffenstein
Julein Carette: Cartier

Behind the Scenes

Director: Jean Renoir
Writers: Jean Renoir (story and screenplay), Charles Spaak (screenplay)
Producers: Frank Rollmer, Albert Pinkovitch (uncredited)
Film Editors: Marthe Huguet, Marguerite Renoir

Awards

Oscar Nominations: Best Picture

Trivia

• This was the first foreign language film to be nominated for the Academy Award for Best Picture.

1940
The Grapes of Wrath

Overview

Genre: Drama
Duration: 128 min
Color: Black and White
Country: USA
MPAA Rating: Not Rated
Studio: Twentieth Century Fox

Director John Ford brings John Steinbeck's stark depiction of Depression-era Dust Bowl devastation to the big screen in this memorable drama. Henry Fonda stars as everyman Tom Joad who returns to his Oklahoma home only to find that the family farm has all but dried up and blown away. Seeking greener pastures, the Joad family sets off for California despite reports of continued hardships and overcrowding out west. Along their journey the Joads encounter others, some starving, some working for slave wages, and all desperate. *The Grapes of Wrath* is as much about the human condition as it is a poignant snapshot of American history.

Cast

Henry Fonda: Tom Joad
Jane Darwell: Ma Joad
John Carradine: Casey
Charley Grapewin: Grandpa
Dorris Bowdon: Rosasharn
Russell Simpson: Pa Joad
Oz Whitehead: Al

Behind the Scenes

Director: John Ford
Writers: John Steinbeck (novel), Nunnally Johnson (screenplay)
Producers: Nunnally Johnson, Darryl F. Zanuck
Film Editor: Robert L. Simpson
Cinematographer: Gregg Toland
Original Music: Alfred Newman

Awards

Oscar Winners: Best Supporting Actress, Best Director
Oscar Nominations: Best Actor, Best Film Editing, Best Picture, Best Sound, Best Writing

Trivia

• In keeping with the mood of the film, director John Ford banned makeup and perfume from the set.

1978
Grease

Overview

Genre: Musical/ Romance
Duration: 110 min
Color: Color (Metrocolor)
Country: USA
MPAA Rating: PG
Studio: Paramount Pictures

John Travolta stars as Danny Zuko, a too-cool-for-school greaser who falls for an uptight Australian "good" girl named Sandy over summer vacation. Unexpectedly re-united at the beginning of their senior year at Rydell High, Danny struggles to maintain his image while wanting to rekindle his romance with Sandy. Their unlikely courtship plays out to an array of show-stopping musical numbers featuring song book favorites such as "Summer Nights," "Greased Lightning," and "You're the One That I Want." Don't let the fact that the entire cast looks closer to retirement age than high school bother you; for sheer entertainment *Grease* is the word.

Cast

John Travolta: Danny Zuko
Olivia Newton-John: Sandy Olsson
Stockard Channing: Betty Rizzo
Jeff Conaway: Kenickie
Barry Pearl: Doody
Michael Tucci: Sonny
Kelly Ward: Putzie
Didi Conn: Frenchy

Behind the Scenes

Director: Randal Kleiser
Writers: Jim Jacobs and Warren Casey (musical), Allan Carr (adaptation), Bronte Woodard (screenplay)
Producer: Allan Carr, Robert Stigwood
Cinematographer: Bill Butler

Trivia

• Stockard Channing, who plays Betty Rizzo, said that the hickeys on her character are real, and that actor Jeff Conaway, who played Kenickie, happily applied them.

Awards

Oscar Nomination: Best Music—Original Song

1963
The Great Escape

Overview

Genre: Action/ Adventure
Duration: 172 min
Color: Color
Country: USA
MPAA Rating: Not Rated
Studio: United Artists

Based on a true story, *The Great Escape* follows the adventures of a group of Allied prisoners of war as they plot to break out of their high-security camp. After constructing what they feel is an escape-proof stalag, the Germans decide to fill it with their most problematic prisoners. The all-star assemblage of troublemakers includes Steve McQueen as "The Cooler King," Richard Attenborough as "Big X," and James Garner as "The Scrounger," among others. Additional experts in forging, intelligence, and tunnel digging round out the group. Perhaps putting all of the wiliest POWs in the same camp wasn't such a great idea after all.

Cast

Steve McQueen: Captain Hilts
James Garner: Flight Lieutenant Hendley
Richard Attenborough: Squadron Leader Roger Bartlett
James Donald: Group Captain Ramsey
Charles Bronson: Flight Lieutenant Danny Velinski
James Coburn: Flying Officer Louis Sedgwick

Behind the Scenes

Director: John Sturges
Writers: Paul Brickhill (book), James Clavell and W.E. Burnett (screenplay)
Producers: John Sturges, James Clavell (uncredited)
Film Editor: Ferris Webster
Cinematographer: Daniel L. Fapp
Original Music: Elmer Bernstein

Trivia

• Steve McQueen breaks character briefly during the Fourth of July scene. Startled by Jud Taylor (Goff), who threw in the line, "No taxation without representation," McQueen mouths "What?" before continuing with the scene.

Awards

Oscar Nomination: Best Film Editing

1993
Groundhog Day

Overview

Genre: Comedy
Duration: 103 min
Color: Color
Country: USA
MPAA Rating: PG
Studio: Columbia
Pictures

A movie for anyone who's ever wished for a second chance, *Groundhog Day* bestows that gift on Pennsylvanian weatherman Phil Connors—but the experience quickly becomes a curse when Phil is forced to relive the same day over and over again. February 2nd is Groundhog Day, when people look to the furry creature for news about the length of the winter season. But for Phil, reporting live from Punxsutawney, Pennsylvania, that day is the only period of time he'll ever see again. And although nothing around him changes, the self-centered, bitter Phil begins to see the world—in particular his co-worker Rita—in a fresh new light.

Cast

Bill Murray: Phil Connors
Andie MacDowell: Rita
Chris Elliott: Larry
Stephen Tobolowsky: Ned Ryerson
Brian Doyle-Murray: Buster Green
Marita Geraghty: Nancy Taylor
Angela Paton: Mrs. Lancaster
Rick Ducommun: Gus

Behind the Scenes

Director: Harold Ramis
Writers: Danny Rubin (story and screenplay), Harold Ramis (screenplay)
Producers: Trevor Albert, Harold Ramis
Executive Producer: C.O. Erickson
Film Editor: Pembroke J. Herring
Cinematographer: John Bailey
Original Music: George Fenton

Trivia

• The groundhog bit Bill Murray twice during the film shoot.
• Harold Ramis needed to give very little scene direction to star Bill Murray, who would simply ask his director, "Good Phil or bad Phil?"

Awards

BAFTA Winner: Best Screenplay—Original
Added to National Film Registry in 2006

1939
Gunga Din

Overview

Genre: Drama/ Adventure
Duration: 117 min
Color: Black and White
Country: USA
MPAA Rating: Not Rated
Studio: RKO Radio Pictures

In British-occupied India three soldiers see their friendship put to the test by a prospective marriage while also facing a dangerous enemy. Sergeants Cutter, MacChesney, and Ballantine have a great life in Her Majesty's service until Ballantine announces that he plans to marry. As they figure out how to keep their friend in the army, Cutter takes off on his own treasure-hunting mission with humble water boy Gunga Din. There is indeed treasure, but it is located in the temple of the Thugees, a fanatical group of killers bent on getting rid of the British. When the other two men come to help Cutter, they find themselves outnumbered. It may be up to Gunga Din to save the day.

Cast

Cary Grant: Sergeant Archibald Cutter
Victor McLaglen: Sergeant "Mac" MacChesney
Douglas Fairbanks Jr.: Sergeant Thomas "Tommy" Ballantine
Sam Jaffe: Gunga Din
Eduardo Ciannelli: Guru
Joan Fontaine: Emaline "Emmy" Stebbins
Montagu Love: Colonel Weed

Behind the Scenes

Director: George Stevens
Writer: Rudyard Kipling (poem), Ben Hecht (story and play), Charles MacArthur (story), William Faulkner, Fred Guiol, and Joel Sayre (screenplay)
Producer: George Stevens
Film Editors: Henry Berman, John Lockert
Cinematographer: Joseph H. August

Trivia

• The battle between the Thuggees and the British Indian army was added late in production because RKO Radio Pictures thought the movie would benefit from the action.
• Sergeant Cutter's first name is Archibald, which was also Cary Grant's true given name.

Awards

Oscar Nominations: Best Cinematography

1978
Halloween

Overview

Genre: Horror/Thriller
Duration: 91 min
Color: Color (Metrocolor)
Country: USA
MPAA Rating: R
Studio: Compass International Pictures/ Falcon International Productions

Halloween 1963: Six-year-old Michael Myers brutally killed his older sister Judith. For 15 years he's rotted away at the Smith's Grove Sanitarium, but just one day before Halloween, he escapes. Dr. Loomis, who has worked with Michael all these years, suspects he intends to return to his hometown of Haddonfield, Illinois. Loomis tries to warn the sheriff and save the town from the return of this personification of evil. Though it has all the trappings of your classic slasher flicks— blood, gore, and fornicating teens—*Halloween* just seems to be a little scarier than the rest. Director John Carpenter's incessant synthesizer score definitely helps ratchet up the creepy quotient.

Cast

Donald Pleasence: Dr. Sam Loomis
Jamie Lee Curtis: Laurie Strode
Nancy Loomis: Annie Brackett
P.J. Soles: Lynda van der Klok
Charles Cyphers: Sheriff Leigh Brackett
Kyle Richards: Lindsey Wallace
Brian Andrews: Tommy Doyle

Behind the Scenes

Director: John Carpenter
Writers: John Carpenter, Debra Hill
Producers: Debra Hill, John Carpenter (uncredited)
Executive Producers: Irwin Yablans, Moustaffa Akkad
Cinematographer: Dean Cundey

Awards

Added to National Film Registry in 2006

Trivia

• This film was produced independently, and shot on a budget of only $300,000. It went on to become the highest-grossing independent movie made to that day.

1971
Harold and Maude

Overview

Genre: Comedy/Romance
Duration: 91 min
Color: Color (Technicolor)
Country: USA
MPAA Rating: PG
Studio: Paramount Pictures

Harold, a troubled young man whose main diversion is faking suicide, and Maude, an energetic 79-year-old with a light heart and cheerful philosophy, are cinematic proof of the old axiom that "opposites attract." Pushing well beyond society norms, the unlikely pair encounter each other at strangers' funerals, which each attends for their own reasons. They proceed to form a partnership as engaged as it as unusual, as sweet as it is troubling. A darkly comic and truly touching love story, Maude slowly draws Harold out of his macabre entertainments and restrictive world and teaches him, as well as anyone willing to listen, how best to love life.

Cast

Ruth Gordon: Maude
Bud Cort: Harold Parker Chasen
Vivian Pickles: Mrs. Chasen
Cyril Cusack: Glaucus
Charles Tyner: Uncle Victor (Ball)
Ellen Geer: Sunshine Doré
Eric Christmas: Priest

Behind the Scenes

Director: Hal Ashby
Writer: Colin Higgins
Producers: Colin Higgins and Charles Mulvehill
Executive Producer: Mildred Lewis
Cinematographer: John A. Alonzo
Original Music: Cat Stevens

Awards

Golden Globe Nominations: Best Actor in Musical/Comedy, Best Actress in Musical/Comedy

Trivia

• The film features many songs by Cat Stevens, including two that he composed specifically for the movie, "Don't Be Shy" and "If You Want to Sing Out, Sing Out."

1950
Harvey

Overview

Genre: Comedy
Duration: 104 min
Color: Black and White
Country: USA
MPAA Rating: Not Rated
Studio: Universal International Pictures

Jimmy Stewart stars as Elwood P. Dowd, one of the most agreeable gentlemen you'd ever want to meet. But with Elwood comes Harvey, who just so happens to be a six-foot-tall invisible rabbit. Now, most folks find Elwood and Harvey wonderful company—especially the gang at Charlie's Bar—but his long-suffering sister Veta and her daughter Myrtle May would prefer to keep Elwood and his imaginary friend away from their society functions. When Veta finally decides to have Elwood committed to a sanitarium, it is she who gets mistakenly locked up. As hospital staffers try to avoid a lawsuit, Elwood and Harvey may just make believers of them yet.

Cast

James Stewart: Elwood P. Dowd
Josephine Hull: Veta Louise Simmons
Peggy Dow: Miss Kelly
Charles Drake: Dr. Sanderson
Cecil Kellaway: Dr. Chumley
Victoria Horne: Myrtle Mae Simmons
Jesse White: Marvin Wilson

Behind the Scenes

Director: Henry Koster
Writers: Oscar Brodney, Mary Chase (play and screenplay)
Producer: John Beck
Film Editor: Ralph Dawson
Cinematographer: William H. Daniels
Original Music: Frank Skinner

Awards

Oscar Winner: Best Supporting Actress
Oscar Nomination: Best Actor

Trivia

• It is insinuated throughout the film that Elwood, played by James Stewart, is an alchoholic. Yet Elwood is only seen taking a single drink during the course of the movie.

1978
Heaven Can Wait

Overview

Genre: Comedy/ Fantasy
Duration: 101 min
Color: Color
Country: USA
MPAA Rating: PG
Studio: Paramount Pictures

Joe Pendleton is on his way to becoming starting quarterback with the Los Angeles Rams when an overzealous angel pulls him out of an accident before it happens. Stuck between heaven and Earth Joe pleads his case to Mr. Jordan, the man in charge, who confirms that Joe is indeed not due to die for many more years. The task now at hand is finding Joe a replacement body so that he can return to Earth. After looking at several possibilities, he may have just found a match in soon-to-be-dead wealthy industrialist Leo Farnsworth. As Farnsworth, Joe meets a beautiful activist, but he still can't figure out how he's going to quarterback the Rams to the Super Bowl.

Cast

Warren Beatty: Joe Pendleton
Julie Christie: Betty Logan
James Mason: Mr. Jordan
Jack Warden: Max Corkle
Charles Grodin: Tony Abbott
Dyan Cannon: Julia Farnsworth
Buck Henry: The escort
Vincent Gardenia: Detective Lieutenant Krim
Joseph Maher: Sisk

Behind the Scenes

Directors: Warren Beatty, Buck Henry
Writers: Harry Segall (play), Warren Beatty and Elaine May (screenplay), Robert Towne (uncredited)
Producers: Warren Beatty, Buck Henry
Executive Producers: Hawk Koch, Charles H. Maguire
Cinematographer: William A. Fraker

Trivia

• This film featured a Rams-Steelers Super Bowl. Coincidentally, after it was released, the following year's Super Bowl was in fact between the Rams and the Steelers.

Awards

Oscar Winners: Best Art Direction
Oscar Nominations: Best Actor, Best Supporting Actor, Best Supporting Actress, Best Cinematography, Best Director, Best Music, Best Picture, Best Writing—Adapted Screenplay

1952
High Noon

Overview

Genre: Drama/Western
Duration: 85 min
Color: Black and White
Country: USA
MPAA Rating: Not Rated
Studio: United Artists

When the clock strikes 12, trouble is coming to the town of Hadleyville and it's up to Marshal Will Kane to do something about it. Only moments after getting married and resigning his position, Kane finds out that Frank Miller, a man he once arrested for murder, will be on the noon train and gunning for him. On top of this, Miller's gang has already arrived and an unfair fight seems almost certain. As Kane canvases the town for potential deputies he finds both volunteers and friends scarce. Leaving town with his new bride is an option, but a man can't run forever.

Cast

Gary Cooper: Marshal Will Kane
Grace Kelly: Amy Fowler Kane
Thomas Mitchell: Mayor Jonas Henderson
Lloyd Bridges: Deputy Marshal Harvey Pell
Katy Jurado: Helen Ramirez
Otto Kruger: Judge Percy Mettrick
Lon Chaney Jr.: Martin Howe

Behind the Scenes

Director: Fred Zinnemann
Writers: John W. Cunningham (story), Carl Foreman (screenplay)
Producers: Carl Foreman and Stanley Kramer
Film Editor: Elmo Williams
Cinematographer: Floyd Crosby
Original Music: Dimitri Tiomkin

Awards

Oscar Winners: Best Actor, Best Film Editing, Best Music—Original Song, Best Music

Trivia

• This story of a lone man facing a murderous gang was seen as an allegory for Hollywood's failure to stand up for individuals during the McCarthy hearings.

1986
Hoosiers

Overview

Genre: Drama/Sports
Duration: 114 min
Color: Color
Country: USA
MPAA Rating: PG
Studio: Orion Pictures

Inspired by true events, *Hoosiers* is the story of the Hickory Huskies high school basketball team and their improbable run toward the Indiana state finals. New head coach Norman Dale quickly realizes that Hickory isn't keen on change and finds himself at odds with parents, teachers, and players alike. Unbowed, Dale names the town drunk as his assistant coach and helps him realize his full potential and reconnect with his son. When the team starts winning, they also start to win the support of their town. With the Huskies and their coach peaking at the right time, they just may have what it takes to make it to the state championship game.

Cast

Gene Hackman: Coach Norman Dale
Barbara Hershey: Myra Fleener
Dennis Hopper: Shooter
Sheb Wooley: Cletus Summers
Fern Persons: Opal Fleener
Chelcie Ross: George
Robert Swan: Rollin
Michael O'Guinne: Rooster

Behind the Scenes

Director: David Anspaugh
Writer: Angelo Pizzo
Producers: Carter Dehaven III, Angelo Pizzo
Executive Producers: John Daly, Derek Gibson
Film Editor: C. Timothy O'Meara
Cinematographer: Fred Murphy
Original Music: Jerry Goldsmith

Trivia

• Dennis Hopper (who played Shooter) asked for a ten-second advance warning before filming the scene when Shooter stumbles drunkenly onto the court in the middle of the game. He used this notice to spin in circles and make himself dizzy so that his walk would appear realistic.

Awards

Oscar Nominations: Best Supporting Actor, Best Music

1987
Hope and Glory

Overview

Genre: Comedy/Drama
Duration: 113 min
Color: Color (Technicolor)
Country: UK
MPAA Rating: PG-13
Studio: Columbia Pictures

Loosely based on writer/director John Boorman's own experiences, this account of a young boy growing up in England during World War II won numerous awards, with good reason. As seen through the fanciful eyes of Billy Rowan, the war is both a harsh reality and a great adventure. While the women left behind worry about their men, the German blitz, and their children, Billy and his friends become the kings of their rubble-strewn streets. Even when disaster strikes, family takes center stage and what's remembered are those same familiar faces and how some kept a stiff upper lip, some cried, and all still managed to keep their senses of humor.

Cast

Sebastian Rice-Edwards: Bill Rowan
Geraldine Muir: Sue Rowan
Sarah Miles: Grace Rowan
David Hayman: Clive Rowan
Sammi Davis: Dawn Rowan
Derrick O'Connor: Mac
Susan Woolridge: Molly

Behind the Scenes

Director: John Boorman
Writer: John Boorman
Producer: John Boorman
Executive Producers: Jake Eberts, Edgar F. Gross
Cinematographer: Philippe Rousselot
Original Music: Peter Martin

Awards

Oscar Nominations: Best Art Direction, Best Cinematography, Best Director, Best Picture, Best Writing

Trivia

• The "news reel" footage of the battles between the Royal Air Force and the Luftwaffe is actually from the film *Battle of Britain*, made in 1969.

1948
I Remember Mama

Overview

Genre: Drama
Duration: 134 min
Color: Black and White
Country: USA
MPAA Rating: Not Rated
Studio: RKO Radio Pictures

Every immigrant family that ever landed on American shores has a tale to tell, and the Hansons are no exception. Having grown up in San Francisco in the early 1900s, oldest daughter Katrin Hanson tells the story of her Norwegian family and their unique experiences as they settled into their new country. At the center of it all is Mama, who holds everything together in the face of money problems, health issues, and death. Irene Dunne delivers a heartwarming performance as a mother so kind and smart and caring that she'll make yours look like a war criminal by comparison. Also look out for Oskar Homolka, who steals every scene he's in as blustery Uncle Chris.

Cast

Irene Dunne: Martha "Mama" Hanson
Barbara Bel Geddes: Katrin Hanson
Oskar Homolka: Uncle Chris Halverson
Philip Dorn: Lars "Papa" Hanson
Peggy McIntyre: Christine Hanson
June Hedin: Dagmar Hanson
Steve Brown: Nels Hanson

Behind the Scenes

Director: George Stevens
Writers: Kathryn Forbes (novel), John Van Druten (play), DeWitt Bodeen (screenplay)
Producer: Harriet Parsons
Executive Producer: George Stevens
Cinematographer: Nicholas Masuraca
Original Music: Roy Webb

Awards

Oscar Nominations: Best Supporting Actor, Best Actress, Best Supporting Actress, Best Supporting Actress, Best Cinematography

Trivia

• Oskar Homolka was the only member of the cast who played his role on Broadway as well as in the film.

1967
In the Heat of the Night

Overview

Genre: Drama/Mystery
Duration: 109 min
Color: Color (DeLuxe)
Country: USA
MPAA Rating: Not Rated
Studio: United Artists

When a black police detective from Philadelphia is mistakenly picked up as a murder suspect in a small Mississippi town, he sticks around to help with the case. On the recommendation of his superiors, Detective Virgil Tibbs joins forces with bigoted police chief Bill Gillespie to try to uncover who killed a wealthy factory owner. Both men bring prejudices to the table, Gillespie has little use for Northern intellectuals and Tibbs is already leery of a town and sheriff so quick to collar an innocent black man. Once they get past their general dislikes for each other, they realize that the only way they will be able to solve this murder is to stop seeing it through colored glasses.

Cast

Sidney Poitier: Detective Virgil Tibbs
Rod Steiger: Police Chief Bill Gillespie
Warren Oates: Officer Sam Wood
Lee Grant: Mrs. Leslie Colbert
James Patterson: Purdy
Larry Gates: Eric Endicott
William Schallert: Mayor Webb Schubert

Behind the Scenes

Director: Norman Jewison
Writers: John Ball (novel), Stirling Silliphant (screenplay)
Producer: Walter Mirisch
Film Editor: Hal Ashby
Cinematographer: Haskell Wexler
Original Music: Quincy Jones

Awards

Oscar Winners: Best Actor, Best Film Editing, Best Picture, Best Sound, Best Writing—Adapted Screenplay

Trivia

• The dialogue in the scene at Gillespie's house was almost entirely improvised by Sydney Poitier and Rod Steiger.

Let us ALL be Alert
We don't want ANYONE!

1934
It Happened One Night

Overview

Genre: Comedy/
Romance
Duration: 105 min
Color: Black and
White
Country: USA
MPAA Rating: Not
Rated
Studio: Columbia
Pictures

The sparks fly between Clark Gable and Claudette Colbert in Frank Capra's delightful road comedy. Ellie Andrews escapes from her millionaire father's yacht when he threatens to get her marriage to a playboy annulled. On the run, Ellie boards a bus to New York containing brash reporter Peter Warne who has just been fired from his paper. Soon Peter discovers Ellie's true identity and promises to help her in exchange for her story. The road back is not easy though as the unlikely pair deals with stolen bags, torrential rains, hired detectives, and differing hitchhiking approaches. The bigger question remains, will they survive each other?

Cast

Clark Gable: Peter Warne
Claudette Colbert: Ellie Andrews
Walter Connolly: Alexander Andrews
Roscoe Karns: Oscar Shapeley
Jameson Thomas: King Westley
Alan Hale: Danker
Arthur Hoyt: Zeke

Behind the Scenes

Director: Frank Capra
Writers: Samuel Hopkins Adams (story),
Robert Riskin (screenplay)
Producer: Frank Capra
Film Editor: Gene Havlick
Cinematographer: Joseph Walker
Original Music: George Leybourne

Awards

Oscar Winners: Best Actor, Best Actress,
Best Director, Best Picture, Best Writing—
Adapted Screenplay

Trivia

• Claudette Colbert refused to undress while
shooting so Frank Capra came up with the
"walls of Jericho" idea of hanging a sheet for
privacy.

1934
It's a Gift

Overview

Genre: Comedy
Duration: 73 min
Color: Black and White
Country: USA
MPAA Rating: Not Rated
Studio: Paramount Productions

There should be no argument; this is W.C. Fields' funniest film. The plot is classic Fields: he's Harold Bissonette, a bumbling grocery store owner with a shrewish wife and insufferable children. When he comes into some money, he decides to give up his business and buy an orange grove in California. But, as with most of his movies, the flimsy storyline merely sets up some of the most insanely funny comic bits ever filmed. Just try not to bust a gut when a blind man enters Bissonette's store and practically destroys it or when a loudmouthed insurance salesman disturbs his sleep looking for someone named Karl LaFong. You'll want to watch certain scenes several times.

Cast

W.C. Fields: Harold Bissonette
Kathleen Howard: Amelia Bissonette
Jean Rouverol: Mildred Bissonette
Julian Madison: John Durston
Tommy Bupp: Norman Bissonette
Baby LeRoy: Baby Elwood Dunk
Tammany Young: Everett Ricks

Behind the Scenes

Director: Norman Z. McLeod
Writers: Charles Bogle (story), J.P. McEvoy (play), Jack Cunningham and W.C. Fields (screenplay)
Producer: William Le Baron
Cinematographer: Henry Sharp

Trivia

• Fields actually lived in a house on the location of the infamous orange grove.

Trivia

• Actor Chill Wills made his onscreen debut in this film as an uncredited "campfire singer."

1963
It's a Mad, Mad, Mad, Mad World

Overview

Genre: Comedy/
Adventure
Duration: 182 min
Color: Color
(Technicolor)
Country: USA
MPAA Rating: G
Studio: Stanley
Kramer Productions/
United Artists

After an old thief crashes his car, he reveals to a group of motorists where he stashed $350,000 right before figuratively and literally kicking the bucket. From this point on, it's every man and woman for themselves as the greedy group takes off in search of the buried loot. Along the way, others join the frantic fray, and all are beset with numerous roadblocks en route to the fortune. This zany chase features a who's who of American comedy with names like Sid Caesar, Milton Berle, Phil Silvers, and Jonathan Winters, among others, supplying the laughs. Add Spencer Tracy into the mix as a beleaguered police captain—as well as several surprising cameos—and you're in for the ride of your life.

Cast

Spencer Tracy: Captain C.G. Culpepper
Milton Berle: J. Russell Finch
Sid Caesar: Melville Crump
Buddy Hackett: Benjy Benjamin
Ethel Merman: Mrs. Marcus
Mickey Rooney: Ding "Dingy" Bell
Dick Shawn: Sylvester Marcus
Phil Silvers: Otto Meyer
Jonathan Winters: Lennie Pike

Behind the Scenes

Director: Stanley Kramer
Writers: William Rose, Tania Rose
Producer: Stanley Kramer
Film Editors: Gene Fowler Jr., Robert Jones, Frederic Knudtson
Cinematographer: Ernest Laszlo
Original Music: Ernest Gold

Trivia

• This film was Jonathan Winters's onscreen debut, and Leo Gorcey's first film appearance since leaving the Bowery Boys series nearly 10 years before.
• This film was so long it required two scripts for all the actors. One contained all the dialogue, and the other described all the action.

Awards

Oscar Winner: Best Effects—Sound
Oscar Nominations: Best Cinematography, Best Film Editing, Best Music—Original Song, Best Music, Best Sound

1946
It's a Wonderful Life

Overview

Genre: Comedy/Drama
Duration: 132 min
Color: Black and White
Country: USA
MPAA Rating: Not Rated
Studio: RKO Radio Pictures

Frank Capra's timeless Christmas classic stars Jimmy Stewart as George Bailey, a man at the end of his rope who gets to see what life would be like in his hometown had he never been born. It's Christmas Eve and George's Uncle Billy has misplaced a large sum of money that stands to ruin the family business and throw the entire town of Bedford Falls into the greedy clutches of local miser Henry Potter. As George contemplates taking his own life, he is visited by a guardian angel who ventures to show George just how big a role he's played in the lives of others. *It's a Wonderful Life* is a surefire cure for even the most difficult cases of "Bah, humbug!"

Cast

James Stewart: George Bailey
Donna Reed: Mary Hatch Bailey
Lionel Barrymore: Henry F. Potter
Thomas Mitchell: Uncle Billy Bailey
Henry Travers: Clarence
Beulah Bondi: Mrs. Bailey
Frank Faylen: Ernie Bishop

Behind the Scenes

Director: Frank Capra
Writers: Philip Van Doren Stern (story), Frances Goodrich, Albert Hackett, and Frank Capra (screenplay)
Producer: Frank Capra
Film Editor: William Hornbeck
Original Music: Dimitri Tiomkin

Awards

Oscar Nominations: Best Actor, Best Director, Best Film Editing, Best Picture, Best Sound

Trivia

• The scene on the bridge between George and Clarence was actually shot in 90-degree heat, which is why Jimmy Stewart is perspiring so profusely.

1975
Jaws

Overview

Genre: Horror/Thriller
Duration: 124 min
Color: Color
(Technicolor)
Country: USA
MPAA Rating: PG
Studio: Universal
Pictures

Something in the water is feeding on beach goers in a quiet vacation town. When a great white shark devours a swimmer off Amity Island, it's up to Police Chief Martin Brody to find the shark without panicking the tourists. After the predator devours another swimmer, the town hires grizzled old salt Captain Quint to hunt it down. Quint's mates on this spine-tingling voyage are landlubber Brody and hotshot marine biologist Matt Hooper. As they troll the waters hunting for this mammoth killer, it becomes clear that it will take every ounce of strength and courage they have… and perhaps a bigger boat.

Cast

Roy Scheider: Police Chief Martin Brody
Robert Shaw: Quint
Richard Dreyfuss: Matt Hooper
Lorraine Gary: Ellen Brody
Murray Hamilton: Mayor Larry Vaughn
Carl Gottlieb: Ben Meadows
Jeffrey Kramer: Deputy Leonard "Lenny" Hendricks
Susan Backlinie: Christine "Chrissie" Watkins

Behind the Scenes

Director: Steven Spielberg
Writers: Peter Benchley (novel and screenplay), Carl Gottlieb (screenplay)
Producers: David Brown and Richard D. Zanuck
Film Editor: Verna Fields
Cinematographer: Bill Butler
Original Music: John Williams

Trivia

• The scene of Roy Scheider trapped in the sinking *Orca* was a difficult shot to film and took many takes. Roy Scheider had no faith in the effects crew to rescue him in case of an emergency, so he stashed axes and hatchets around the cabin.

Awards

Oscar Winners: Best Film Editing, Best Music, Best Sound
Oscar Nominations: Best Picture

1979
The Jerk

Overview

Genre: Comedy
Duration: 94 min
Color: Color (Technicolor)
Country: USA
MPAA Rating: R
Studio: Universal Pictures

Steve Martin stars as Navin Johnson, the slow-witted adopted white son of a poor black family in Mississippi. As he strikes out on his own, Navin's first hitchhiking attempt only gets him as far as the end of the fence in front of his house. From there he lands a job at a filling station where he matches wits with criminals, invents a useful gadget for eyeglasses, and dodges a crazed killer. Eventually he lands with a carnival where he discovers his "special purpose" and finds true love. Martin is at the height of his comedic powers here, wielding a full arsenal of inspired idiocy. *The Jerk* is every bit as funny and silly as its title suggests.

Cast

Steve Martin: Navin R. Johnson
Bernadette Peters: Marie Kimble Johnson
Catlin Adams: Patty Bernstein
Mabel King: Mother
Richard Ward: Father
Dick Anthony Williams: Taj Jonson
Bill Macy: Stan Fox

Behind the Scenes

Director: Carl Reiner
Writers: Steve Martin and Carl Gottlieb (story and screenplay)
Producers: William E. McEuen and David V. Picker
Cinematographer: Victor J. Kemper
Original Music: Jack Elliott

Trivia

• Bill Murray shot a cameo for the movie that ended up on the cutting room floor.

Trivia

• The original title intended for this film was *Easy Money*.

1996
Jerry Maguire

Overview

Genre: Comedy/
Romance
Duration: 139 min
Color: Color
Country: USA
MPAA Rating: R
Studio: Gracie Films/
TriStar Pictures

After hotshot sports agent Jerry Maguire has a crisis of conscience that leads to his firing, he sets out to start a new company with a new vision for the future of the industry. It all starts with a mission statement, a partner (single mother Dorothy Boyd), and a client (football player Rod Tidwell): not exactly the strongest foundation for a new business. But, as the mission statement becomes reality, the partner a lover, and the client a friend, Jerry begins to become the person he always wanted to be. After months of trying to build up his small company, Jerry Maguire's personal and professional fortunes may all rest on one game, one moment, and one person—himself.

Cast

Tom Cruise: Jerry Maguire
Cuba Gooding Jr.: Rod Tidwell
Renée Zellweger: Dorothy Boyd
Kelly Preston: Avery Bishop
Jerry O'Connell: Frank Cushman
Jay Mohr: Bob Sugar
Bonnie Hunt: Laurel Boyd
Regina King: Marcee Tidwell

Behind the Scenes

Director: Cameron Crowe
Writer: Cameron Crowe
Producers: James L. Brooks, Cameron Crowe, Laurence Mark, Richard Sakai
Executive Producer: Bridget Johnson
Cinematographer: Janusz Kaminski
Original Music: Nancy Wilson

Trivia

• The scene of Jerry and Ray talking in the living room for the first time was improvised.
• *Rolling Stone* magazine publisher Jann Wenner appears as Scully. Wenner was once Cameron Crowe's boss.

Awards

Oscar Winner: Best Supporting Actor
Oscar Nominations: Best Actor, Best Film Editing, Best Picture, Best Writing

2007
Juno

Overview

Genre: Comedy/Romance
Duration: 96 min
Color: Color
Country: USA
MPAA Rating: PG-13
Studio: Fox Search-light

Juno MacGuff, a wisecracking no-nonsense sixteen-year-old, becomes pregnant after a one-time sexual encounter with her awkward but sweet best friend Paulie Bleeker. When she can't go through with an abortion, she decides to give the baby up for adoption. With the help of her parents, who have reluctantly joined her effort, and her friend Leah, Juno decides upon a seemingly perfect couple—Vanessa and Mark Loring. She becomes fast friends with Mark, but is slightly put off by the anxious Vanessa. As her pregnancy progresses, Juno struggles to come to terms with the Lorings' changing relationship and her own feelings for Paulie.

Cast

Ellen Page: Juno MacGuff
Michael Cera: Paulie Bleeker
Jennifer Garner: Vanessa Loring
Jason Bateman: Mark Loring
Allison Janney: Bren MacGuff
J.K. Simmons: Mac MacGuff
Olivia Thirlby: Leah

Behind the Scenes

Director: Jason Reitman
Writer: Diablo Cody
Producers: Lianne Halfon, John Malkovich, Mason Novick, Russell Smith
Executive Producers: Joseph Drake, Dan Dubiecki, Nathan Kahane
Cinematographer: Eric Steelberg

Awards

Oscar Winner: Best Writing
Oscar Nominations: Best Director, Best Picture, Best Actress

Trivia

• Juno's ridiculous hambruger phone is the property of screenwriter Diablo Cody.

1993
Jurassic Park

Overview

Genre: Sci-Fi/ Adventure
Duration: 127 min
Color: Color
Country: USA
MPAA Rating: PG-13
Studio: Universal Pictures

Everybody loves dinosaurs—until they try to eat you. The most unique theme park in the world, featuring dinosaurs created through the wonders of imaginative biology, becomes a nightmarish prison when prototype systems fail, a tropical storm crashes on the island-park, and the main attractions break free to walk the Earth once again, after a hiatus of about 65 million years. With the laws of evolution suddenly turned on their head, the group of humans trapped on the island must adapt quickly—or become extinct. With a full complement of stars, including Sam Neil, Jeff Goldblum, and Richard Attenborough, Steven Spielberg's sci-fi thriller is sure to please, and terrify.

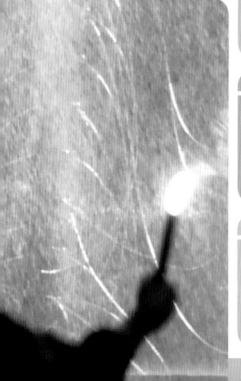

Cast

Sam Neill: Dr. Alan Grant
Laura Dern: Dr. Ellie Sattler
Jeff Goldblum: Ian Malcolm
Richard Attenborough: John Hammond
Bob Peck: Robert Muldoon
Martin Ferrero: Donald Gennaro
Joseph Mazzello: Tim Murphy
Ariana Richards: Lex Murphy
Samuel L. Jackson: Ray Arnold

Behind the Scenes

Director: Steven Spielberg
Writers: Michael Crichton (novel and screenplay), David Koepp (screenplay)
Producers: Kathleen Kennedy, Gerald R. Molen
Film Editor: Michael Kahn
Cinematographer: Dean Cundey
Original Music: John Williams

Trivia

• After fierce competition from other studios, Universal bought the movie rights to *Jurassic Park* before Michael Crichton's book was even published.

Awards

Oscar Winners: Best Effects—Sound, Best Effects—Visual, Best Sound

1984
The Karate Kid

Overview

Genre: Family/Sports
Duration: 126 min
Color: Color
Country: USA
MPAA Rating: PG
Studio: Columbia Tristar/Motion Picture Group

When Daniel Larusso moved from New Jersey to California, he never imagined the troubles that would await him. After meeting the enchanting Ali, Daniel finds himself in the middle of an ongoing fight with her ex-boyfriend and a group of boys from the local karate school. When Daniel discovers that the handyman from his apartment complex, Mr. Miyagi, is also a karate master, he convinces Mr. Miyagi to teach him karate. Daniel must learn to harness his skills and trust his instincts—and Mr. Miyagi's unconventional teaching methods—as the tournament gets closer, rivalries grow bigger, and the risks become higher.

Cast

Ralph Macchio: Daniel Larusso
Pat Morita: Mr. Kesuke Miyagi
Elisabeth Shue: Ali Mills
Martin Kove: John Kreese
Randee Heller: Lucille Larusso
William Zabka: Johnny Lawrence
Ron Thomas: Bobby Brown

Behind the Scenes

Director: John G. Avildsen
Writer: Robert Mark Kamen
Producer: Jerry Weintraub
Executive Producer: R.J. Louis
Film Editors: Walt Mulconery, Bud Smith, John G. Avildsen
Cinematographer: James Crabe

Awards

Oscar Nominations: Best Supporting Actor

Trivia

• *The Karate Kid* was named after a character in D.C. Comics' "Legion of Super-Heroes." The comic book publisher granted the producers permission to use the name.

1984
The Killing Fields

Overview

Genre: Drama/War
Duration: 141 min
Color: Color
Country: UK
MPAA Rating: R
Studio: Enigma
Productions/Goldcrest
Films International/
International Film
Investors/Warner Bros.

A brutally honest account of the Cambodian civil war and resulting Pol Pot regime, *The Killing Fields* tells the tragic story as seen through the eyes of *New York Times* journalist Sydney Schanberg and his friend and interpreter Dith Pran. On one side you have Schanberg, who is in the country for the story, and on the other you have Pran, a Cambodian citizen who is himself a journalist but is also living through this horror. As the realities of the Khmer Rouge government begin to set in, Pran's family is evacuated but he stays behind to tell an even sadder tale. Haing S. Ngor, a Cambodian refugee himself—and non-actor—won the Oscar for his portrayal of Dith Pran.

Cast

Sam Waterson: Sydney Schanberg
Haing S. Ngor: Dith Pran
John Malkovich: Alan "Al" Rockoff
Julian Sands: John Swain
Craig T. Nelson: Major Reeves
Spalding Gray: United States consul
Athol Fugard: Dr. Sundesval

Behind the Scenes

Director: Roland Joffé
Writer: Bruce Robinson
Producers: David Puttnam, Roland Joffé
Film Editor: Jim Clark
Cinematographer: Chris Menges
Original Music: Mike Oldfield

Awards

Oscar Winners: Best Supporting Actor, Best Cinematography, Best Film Editing
Oscar Nominations: Best Actor, Best Director, Best Picture, Best Adapted Screenplay

Trivia

• With his Best Supporting Actor win, Haing S. Ngor became the first Southeast Asian to win an Academy Award for acting.

1933
King Kong

Overview

Genre: Sci-Fi/Thriller
Duration: 100 min
Color: Black and White
Country: USA
MPAA Rating: Not Rated
Studio: RKO Radio Pictures

After flamboyant filmmaker Carl Denham casts unknown Ann Darrow to star in his next adventure film, the entire crew sets sail for a mysterious island. Once there, they encounter restless natives, dinosaurs, and the dominating presence of a giant ape called Kong. Ann soon finds herself in harm's way when she's kidnapped by the natives and offered up as a gift to Kong. Though she's eventually freed from the ape's clutches, no one is safe from Denham, who plans to bring Kong back to New York and exhibit him as "The Eighth Wonder of the World." Only compared to human greed can the terrible ape pale in comparison.

Cast

Fay Wray: Ann Darrow
Robert Armstrong: Carl Denham
Bruce Cabot: John "Jack" Driscoll
Frank Reicher: Captain Englehorn
Sam Hardy: Charles Weston
Noble Johnson: Skull Island nation leader
Steve Clemente: Witch King

Behind the Scenes

Directors: Merian C. Cooper, Ernest B. Schoedsack
Writers: Merian C. Cooper and Edgar Wallace (story), James Ashmore Creelman and Ruth Rose (screenplay)
Producers: Marien C. Cooper and Ernest B. Schoedsack

Awards

Added to National Film Registry in 1990

Trivia

• King Kong was only 19 feet tall during the island scenes; he became 25 feet tall when filmed for the New York City scenes.

1947
Kiss of Death

Overview

Genre: Drama/Crime
Duration: 98 min
Color: Black and White
Country: USA
MPAA Rating: Not Rated
Studio: Twentieth Century Fox

Forget about the pale 1995 remake; check out a young Richard Widmark stealing the show as cackling psychopath Tommy Udo in this film noir classic. Victor Mature stars as Nick Bianco, a thief whose wife killed herself when he was in prison. When Nick finds out that some of his former cohorts may have been responsible for her death, he works out a deal with the DA to get paroled and get the goods on crazed killer Tommy Udo. But ratting on Udo is dangerous business, and Nick still has his kids and new wife to think about. In *Kiss of Death,* Widmark made the most of his first big break, creating one of the silver screen's most memorable villains.

Cast

Victor Mature: Nick Bianco
Brian Donlevy: Louis D'Angelo
Coleen Gray: Nettie Cavallo
Richard Widmark: Tommy Udo
Taylor Holmes: Earl Howser
Howard Smith: Warden
Karl Malden: Sergeant William Cullen

Behind the Scenes

Director: Henry Hathaway
Writers: Eleazar Lipsky (story), Ben Hecht and Charles Lederer (screenplay)
Producer: Fred Kohlmar
Film Editor: J. Watson Webb Jr.
Cinematographer: Nobert Brodine
Original Music: David Buttolph

Awards

Oscar Nominations: Best Supporting Actor, Best Writing

Trivia

• This film featured the onscreen debuts of Richard Widmark, Susan Cabot, and Jesse White.

1979
Kramer vs. Kramer

Overview

Genre: Drama
Duration: 105 min
Color: Color (Technicolor)
Country: USA
MPAA Rating: PG
Studio: Columbia TriStar

When Joanna Kramer leaves her workaholic husband Ted, it's because he's unwilling to cut back his business hours and rarely spends time with her or their young son Billy. With Joanna gone, Ted must now learn to care for Billy on his own and put his career on the backburner. Though the transition is tough and even laughable at times, he gradually becomes more competent as a housekeeper, caretaker, and, most importantly, a father. And when Joanna returns seeking custody of the boy, Ted won't give him up without a fight. Kramer vs. Kramer grabbed the Best Picture Oscar for 1979 as well as the attention of struggling married couples everywhere.

Cast

Dustin Hoffman: Ted Kramer
Meryl Streep: Joanna Kramer
Jane Alexander: Margaret Phelps
Justin Henry: Billy Kramer
Howard Duff: John Shaunessy
George Coe: Jim O'Connor
JoBeth Williams: Phyllis Bernard

Behind the Scenes

Director: Robert Benton
Writers: Avery Corman (novel), Robert Benton (screenplay)
Producer: Stanley R. Jaffe
Film Editor: Jerry Greenberg
Cinematographer: Néstor Almendros

Awards

Oscar Winners: Best Actor, Best Supporting Actress, Best Director, Best Picture, Best Writing—Adapted Screenplay

Trivia

• Dustin Hoffman contributed extensively to the dialogue of the film, having just gone through a divorce himself.

1954
La Strada

Overview

Genre: Drama
Duration: 115 min
Color: Black and White
Country: Italy
MPAA Rating: Not Rated
Studio: Ponti-De Laurentiis Cinematografica

Federico Fellini's famous circus picture follows a tragic love triangle. When her mother sells young Gelsomina to Zampanò—a gypsy carnival strongman who travels from town to town—she becomes his simple yet faithful sidekick, performing as a clown and trumpeter. Tired of his physical and emotional abuse, Gelsomina finds temporary escape in the sight of Il Matto, a high-wire equilibrist. Il Matto charms Gelsomina and gives her a sense of self-worth she had previously lacked. Though she has feelings for the aerialist, Gelsomina stays loyal to Zampanò. But this is no fairytale, and the strongman's temper gets the better of him yet again.

Cast

Anthony Quinn: Zampano
Giulietta Masina: Gelsomina
Richard Basehart: Il Matto
Aldo Silvani: Signor Giraffa
Marcella Rovena: La Vedova
Livia Venturini: La Suorina

Behind the Scenes

Director: Federico Fellini
Writers: Federico Fellini, Tullio Pinelli, Ennio Flaiano
Producers: Dino De Laurentiis, Carlo Ponti
Film Editor: Leo Cattozzo
Cinematographer: Otello Martelli
Original Music: Nino Rota

Awards

Oscar Winner: Best Foreign Language Filim
Oscar Nomination: Best Writing

Trivia

• This movie was the winner of the first ever Academy Award for Best Foreign Language Film.

1955
Lady and the Tramp

Overview

Genre: Family/Musical
Duration: 75 min
Color: Color (Technicolor)
Country: USA
MPAA Rating: G
Studio: Walt Disney Productions

Lady, a cocker spaniel who was a Christmas gift from Jim Dear to his wife Darling, feels jilted when she is ignored in the face of the impending birth of Darling's first baby. When Aunt Sarah arrives with her crafty Siamese cats Si and Am and wreaks havoc on Lady's pampered life, Lady escapes and meets the streetwise stray Tramp, who shows her the joys of a life of freedom. Various encounters with the ever-dangerous dogcatcher and a climactic fight to save Darling's baby provide the adventure while Lady and Tramp are joined by friends Jock and Trusty in this love story that also explores the importance of loyalty and friendship.

Cast

Barbara Luddy: Lady (voice)
Larry Roberts: Tramp (voice)
Peggy Lee: Darling/Si/Am/Peg (voice)
Bill Thompson: Jock/Bulldog in Pound/Policeman at Zoo/Dachsie/Joe (voice)
Bill Baucom: Trusty (voice)
Stan Freberg: Beaver (voice)

Behind the Scenes

Directors: Clyde Geronimi, Wilfred Jackson, Hamilton Luske
Writers: Ward Greene (story), Erdman Penner, Joe Rinaldi, Ralph Wright, and Don DaGradi (screenplay)
Producer: Walt Disney
Original Music: Oliver Wallace

Awards

BAFTA Nominations: Best Animated Film

Trivia

• The film was the first feature-length animated movie to be shot in widescreen, and Disney's first fully original animated story.

1971
The Last Picture Show

Overview

Genre: Drama
Duration: 118 min
Color: Black and White
Country: USA
MPAA Rating: R
Studio: Columbia Pictures

A wind-swept one-horse town, Anarene, Texas, is home to Sonny Crawford and Duane Jackson, best friends and high school seniors facing an uncertain future. The two spend most of their time at the pool hall or movie theater, both run by town sage Sam the Lion. Duane's girlfriend Jacy Farrow is the prettiest girl in town and her cold, alcoholic mother warns her not to waste such beauty on Duane. Sonny, meanwhile, is having an affair with the lonely wife of his basketball coach. The town itself seems to be slowly dying. While Duane scuffles to find a toe hold somewhere and Jacy searches for a wealthier beau, it's Sonny who seems destined to give the eulogy for Anarene.

Cast

Timothy Bottoms: Sonny Crawford
Jeff Bridges: Duane Jackson
Cybill Shepard: Jacy Farrow
Ben Johnson: Sam the Lion
Cloris Leachman: Ruth Popper
Ellen Burstyn: Lois Farrow
Randy Quaid: Lester Marlow

Behind the Scenes

Director: Peter Bogdanovich
Writers: Larry McMurtry (novel and screenplay), Peter Bogdanovich (screenplay)
Producers: Stephen J. Friedman
Executive Producer: Bert Schneider
Film Editor: Donn Cambern
Cinematographer: Robert Surtees

Awards

Oscar Winners: Best Supporting Actor, Best Supporting Actress

Trivia

• This film was shot entirely on location in Archer City, Texas, which was the hometown of writer Larry McMurtry and the basis for his fictional Anarene.

1962
Lawrence of Arabia

Overview

Genre: Drama
Duration: 222 min
Color: Color (Technicolor)
Country: UK
MPAA Rating: PG
Studio: Horizon Pictures/Columbia Pictures

An epic movie if ever there was one, *Lawrence of Arabia* stars Peter O'Toole as the charasmatic title character, a bored British officer who seeks adventure in the desert during the First World War. Lawrence manages to convince his superiors to allow him to make his desert journey so that he can possibly assist in forming a coalition among fractious Arab tribes against their common enemy, the Turkish. Once there, Lawrence experiences success beyond his wildest imagination and is lionized for his vision and leadership. Clad in the flowing robes and headdress of an Arab leader, Lawrence has grand plans that rest in his palms as precariously as grains of sand.

Cast

Peter O'Toole: T.E. Lawrence
Alec Guinness: Prince Feisal
Anthony Quinn: Auda abu Tayi
Jack Hawkins: General Lord Edmund Allenby
Omar Sharif: Sherif Ali ibn el Kharish
José Ferrer: Turkish Bey
Anthony Quayle: Colonel Harry Brighton
Claude Rains: Mr. Dryden

Behind the Scenes

Director: David Lean
Writers: T.E. Lawrence (writings), Robert Bolt and Michael Wilson (screenplay)
Producers: David Lean, Sam Spiegel
Film Editor: Anne V. Coates
Cinematographer: Freddie Young
Original Music: Maurice Jarre

Trivia

• The film's production was moved to Spain, but shooting was halted for three months because writer Robert Bolt had been jailed for participation in a nuclear disarmament demonstration.

Awards

Oscar Winners: Best Art Direction, Best Cinematography, Best Director, Best Film Editing, Best Music, Best Picture, Best Sound
Oscar Nominations: Best Actor, Best Supporting Actor, Best Writing

2006
Little Miss Sunshine

Overview

Genre: Comedy/Drama
Duration: 101 min
Color: Color
Country: USA
MPAA Rating: R
Studio: Big Beach Films/Fox Searchlight

Olive Hoover is an unconventional beauty pageant contestant and the youngest in a highly dysfunctional family. When she is invited to the Little Miss Sunshine pageant finals in California as a replacement, the entire family embarks on a tragicomic road trip in an old yellow VW bus. Dealing with emotional and physical roadblocks along the way, their journey inflicts new wounds even as it is healing others. *Little Miss Sunshine* is a hilarious but grounded look at American culture and family life that is both uplifting and heartbreaking by turns, and a powerful testament to the importance of family.

Cast

Abigail Breslin: Olive Hoover
Greg Kinnear: Richard Hoover
Paul Dano: Dwayne Hoover
Alan Arkin: Grandpa Edwin Hoover
Toni Collette: Sheryl Hoover
Steve Carell: Frank Ginsberg
Jill Talley: Cindy

Behind the Scenes

Directors: Valerie Faris, Jonathan Dayton
Writer: Michael Arndt
Producers: Albert Berger, David T. Friendly, Peter Saraf, Marc Turtletaub, Ron Yerxa
Executive Producers: Michael Beugg, Jeb Brody
Cinematographer: Tim Suhrstedt

Awards

Oscar Winners: Best Supporting Actor, Best Writing
Oscar Nominations: Best Picture, Best Supporting Actress

Trivia

• The beauty pageant girls were veterans of the circuit. They wore their costumes, including hair and makeup, and performed their usual talent routines.

1983
Local Hero

Overview

Genre: Comedy/Drama
Duration: 111 min
Color: Color
Country: UK
MPAA Rating: PG
Studio: Enigma Productions/Goldcrest Films International/Warner Bros.

When a large Texas oil company decides to build a refinery near a small Scottish village, they send one of their men to negotiate the purchase of the land. Despite having no Scottish ancestry to speak of, Mac MacIntyre is sent to Scotland based on the sound of his name. Once there, he encounters an assortment of quirky villagers including Gordon Urquhart, who doubles as both an innkeeper and the town's chief negotiator. When word gets out about the prospective sale, the locals smell money mixed in with the sea air. As he goes about hammering out a fair deal with Gordon, Mac starts falling in love with the village and its people.

Cast

Peter Riegert: Mac MacIntyre
Burt Lancaster: Felix Happer
Fulton Mackay: Ben
Denis Lawson: Gordon Urquhart
Norman Chancer: Moritz
Peter Capaldi: Danny Oldsen
Rikki Fulton: Geddes

Behind the Scenes

Director: Bill Forsyth
Writer: Bill Forsyth
Producer: David Puttnam
Film Editor: Michael Bradsell
Cinematographer: Chris Menges
Original Music: Mark Knopfler

Awards

BAFTA Winner: Best Direction
BAFTA Nominations: Best Cinematography, Best Editing, Best Film, Best Score, Best Screenplay—Original, Best Supporting Actor

Trivia

• The village and the beach were not near each other but were on opposite coasts of Scotland. The production team built a cardboard church on the beach to link the two settings.

2003 The Lord of the Rings: The Return of the King

Overview

Genre: Drama/Fantasy
Duration: 200 min
Color: Color
Country: USA
MPAA Rating: PG-13
Studio: New Line Cinema/WingNut Films

The third installment of director Peter Jackson's award-winning adaptation of the classic fantasy trilogy by J.R.R. Tolkien, *The Return of the King* returns to the land of Middle Earth for the final confrontation between an unlikely band of heroes and the evil power of Sauron, lord of the land of Mordor. Consciously evoking the ancient epics of early medieval northern Europe, *The Return of the King* is the heroic saga of the modern age, reaching a climax not on the battlefield but in an internal battle of wills, with the diminutive hobbit Frodo wrestling with the insidious power of Sauron's One Ring. Either he or it must be destroyed . . . and with him will stand or fall all of Middle Earth.

Cast

Elijah Wood: Frodo Baggins
Sean Astin: Samwise Gamgee
Cate Blanchett: Galadriel
Orlando Bloom: Legolas
Andy Serkis: Gollum/Sméagol
Ian McKellen: Gandalf
Viggo Mortensen: Aragorn
John Rhys-Davies: Gimli
Bernard Hill: King Théoden

Behind the Scenes

Director: Peter Jackson
Writers: J.R.R. Tolkien (novel), Fran Walsh, Philippa Boyens, and Peter Jackson (screenplay)
Producers: Peter Jackson, Barrie M. Osborne, Fran Walsh
Executive Producers: Michael Lynne, Mark Ordesky, Robert Shaye, Bob Weinstein, Harvey Weinstein

Trivia

• This film made an astronomical 1408% profit for New Line Cinema off their initial costs.
• The first film of the Lord of the Rings trilogy, *The Fellowship of the Ring*, included 540 computer-generated effects, while the second, *The Two Towers*, had 799. *The Return of the King* took the cake with 1488.

Awards

Oscar Winners: Best Achievement in Sound Mixing, Best Art Direction, Best Costume Design, Best Director, Best Editing, Best Makeup, Best Music, Best Music—Original Song, Best Picture, Best Visual Effects, Best Writing—Adapted Screenplay

1985
Lost in America

Overview

Genre: Comedy
Duration: 91 min
Color: Color
(Technicolor)
Country: USA
MPAA Rating: R
Studio: Warner Bros.
Pictures

Taking a page out of the script from *Easy Rider*, a disillusioned yuppie and his wife decide to drop out of society and see America—but from a Winnebago rather than a motorcycle. After David Howard is passed over for a promotion at his ad agency, he quits his job and convinces his wife Linda to do likewise so that they can hit the open road and find themselves. But David's idyllic itinerary hits a few snags along the way. And when the couple's financial nest egg all but vanishes, their dreams begin to dry up in the hot desert air. *Lost in America* is classic Albert Brooks; his darkest moments are almost always his funniest.

Cast

Albert Brooks: David Howard
Julie Hagerty: Linda Howard
Garry Marshall: Desert Inn casino manager
Art Frankel: Employment agent
Sylvia Farrel: Sylvia
Maggie Roswell: Patty
Hans Wagner: Hans
Michael Greene: Paul Dunn

Behind the Scenes

Director: Albert Brooks
Writers: Albert Brooks, Monica Johnson
Producer: Marty Katz
Executive Producer: Herb Nanas
Film Editor: David Finfer
Cinematographer: Eric Saarinen
Original Music: Arthur B. Rubinstein

Trivia

• In his autobiography, Garry Marshall, who plays the casino manager, describes how frustrated he became when Albert Brooks made him do many takes of their scene together. Once he saw the film, however, he understood that Brooks had purposely done this to make his frustration show through.

Awards

National Society of Film Critics Winner: Best Screenplay

2003
Lost in Translation

Overview

Genre: Comedy/
Romance
Duration: 102 min
Color: Color
Country: USA/Japan
MPAA Rating: R
Studio: Focus Features

Bill Murray stars as Bob Harris, an American actor on the downside of his career who is in Japan doing advertisements for a whiskey company. At his hotel Bob meets a young woman named Charlotte who has been spending a lot of time alone while her photographer husband travels to various assignments. Bob's midlife crisis and Charlotte's crisis of confidence mesh perfectly. Though they are miserable alone, they fare much better when they join forces and try to navigate the complexities of their foreign environment. A bittersweet May-December friendship blossoms between the two in the neon lights of downtown Tokyo.

Cast

Scarlett Johansson: Charlotte
Bill Murray: Bob Harris
Akiko Takeshita: Ms. Kawasaki
Giovanni Ribisi: John
Anna Faris: Kelly
Fumihiro Hayashi: Charlie
Hiroko Kawasaki: Hiroko

Behind the Scenes

Director: Sofia Coppola
Writer: Sofia Coppola
Producers: Sofia Coppola, Ross Katz
Executive Producers: Francis Ford Coppola, Fred Roos
Film Editor: Sarah Flack
Cinematographer: Lance Acord

Trivia

• Sofia Coppola wrote the lead, Bob Harris, specifically for Bill Murray, and she said that if he had turned it down, she wouldn't have done the movie. Luckily, Murray responded to the hundreds of messages Coppola left on his automated voice mailbox—which he uses rather than an agent—and eventually took the role.

Awards

Oscar Winners: Best Writing—Original Screenplay
Oscar Nominations: Best Actor, Best Director, Best Picture

1945
The Lost Weekend

Overview

Genre: Drama
Duration: 101 min
Color: Black and White
Country: USA
MPAA Rating: Not Rated
Studio: Paramount Pictures

Kudos to Billy Wilder for writing and directing (a double Oscar win) the first serious Hollywood film to address the pink elephant in the room—the perils of alcoholism. The film follows the five-day bender of tortured alcoholic and failed writer Don Birnam (played masterfully by Ray Milland), whose harrowing descent into blackoutville plays out like a booze-fueled nightmare. Not only is the film revolutionary for tackling this taboo subject, but it also helped pave the way for other serious celluloid characterizations of addiction. Though later films gamely tackled similar subject matter, *The Lost Weekend* remains the one that's good to the last destructive drop.

Cast

Ray Milland: Don Birnam
Jane Wyman: Helen St. James
Phillip Terry: Wick Birman
Howard Da Silva: Nat
Doris Dowling: Gloria
Frank Faylen: "Bim" Nolan
Mary Young: Mrs. Deveridge

Behind the Scenes

Director: Billy Wilder
Writers: Charles R. Jackson (novel), Billy Wilder and Charles Brackett (screenplay)
Producer: Charles Brackett
Film Editor: Doane Harrison
Cinematographer: John F. Seitz
Original Music: Miklos Rozsa

Awards

Oscar Winners: Best Actor, Best Director, Best Picture, Best Screenplay
Oscar Nominations: Best Cinematography, Best Film Editing, Best Music

Trivia

• Writer/director Billy Wilder claimed that the liquor industry offered Paramount $5 million if the studio would agree not to release the film.

1931
M

Overview

Genre: Drama/Thriller
Duration: 120 min
Color: Black and White
Country: Germany
MPAA Rating: Not Rated
Studio: Nero-Film AG

In 1930, the tranquil city of Berlin is shattered by a series of child murders. Parents live in fear as the anonymous menace preys on his young victims. Elsie Beckman becomes victim number nine, paying for the gift of a balloon (a lure from the murderer) with her life. The police have been active, interviewing suspects, collecting clues, and organizing raids. Law enforcement has cracked down so much that the criminal element has difficulty going about its daily routine. Underworld boss Schränker comes up with a scheme to enlist beggars to watch every child on the street, in order to catch the murderer and give him a taste of their own justice.

Cast

Peter Lorre: Franz Becker
Ellen Widmann: Madame Becker
Inge Landgut: Elsie Becker
Otto Wernicke: Inspector Karl Lohmann
Theodor Loos: Commissioner Groeber
Gustaf Gründgens: The Safebreaker

Behind the Scenes

Director: Fritz Lang
Writers: Thea von Harbou and Fritz Lang
Producer: Seymour Nebenzal
Cinematographer: Fritz Arno Wagner

Trivia

• The movie was banned in Germany in July 1934.
• Both director Fritz Lang and star Peter Lorre left Germany as the Nazis came into power.

Trivia

• Peter Lorre's whistling was actually dubbed by director Fritz Lang.

1941
The Maltese Falcon

Overview

Genre: Drama/Crime
Duration: 101 min
Color: Black and White
Country: USA
MPAA Rating: Not Rated
Studio: Warner Bros. Pictures

The private eye movie against which all others are measured, *The Maltese Falcon* marked John Huston's directorial debut and stars Humphrey Bogart as no-nonsense San Francisco detective Sam Spade. After a mysterious woman asks for help finding her sister, Spade soon finds himself caught up in the middle of a double-homicide and in the company of an unscrupulous bunch of characters all in search of a rare statue. This movie has everything you could want from a film noir, including double-crosses, murder, and a fantastic femme fatale potrayed by Mary Astor. Adding to the intrigue are a colorful assortment of characters played by the likes of Sydney Greenstreet and the always excellent Peter Lorre.

Cast

Humphrey Bogart: Sam Spade
Mary Astor: Brigid O'Shaughnessy
Gladys George: Iva Archer
Peter Lorre: Joel Cairo
Barton MacLane: Detective Lieutenant Dundy
Lee Patrick: Effie Perine
Sydney Greenstreet: Kasper Gutman
Ward Bond: Detective Tom Polhaus

Behind the Scenes

Director: John Huston
Writers: Dashiell Hammett (novel), John Huston (screenplay)
Executive Producer: Hal B. Wallis
Film Editor: Tom Richards
Cinematographer: Arthur Edeson
Original Music: Adolph Deutsch

Trivia

• Humphrey Bogart dropped the "Maltese falcon" during the shooting so two falcons had to be used. The original prop is in the Warner Brothers Studios movie museum.

Awards

Oscar Nominations: Best Supporting Actor, Best Picture, Best Writing

1962
The Man Who Shot Liberty Valance

Overview

Genre: Drama/ Western
Duration: 123 min
Color: Black and White
Country: USA
MPAA Rating: Not Rated
Studio: Paramount Pictures

John Ford is in oh-so-familiar territory here directing this story of a U.S. senator who, upon returning to his old western stomping grounds, sits down with a reporter to set the record straight about his past. Through flashbacks we learn that Senator Stoddard started out as a fish-out-water lawyer in this rough frontier town and ran afoul of a notorious outlaw. If not for the intervention of his friend Tom Doniphon, he probably never would have survived, married his wife, and been the man that he is today. Along with Jimmy Stewart and John Wayne playing to type as the do-gooder lawyer and rough rancher, Lee Marvin's mad dog Liberty Valance truly stands out.

Cast

John Wayne: Tom Doniphon
James Stewart: Ransom Stoddard
Vera Miles: Hallie Stoddard
Lee Marvin: Liberty Valance
Edmond O'Brien: Dutton Peabody
Andy Devine: Marshal Link Appleyard
Ken Murray: Doc Willoughby

Behind the Scenes

Director: John Ford
Writers: Dorothy M. Johnson (story), Willis Goldbeck and James Warner Bellah (screenplay)
Producers: Willis Goldbeck, John Ford (uncredited)
Film Editor: Otho Lovering

Awards

Oscar Nominations: Best Costume Design

Trivia

• Liberty Valance plays what is known as the "Dead Man's Poker," aces and eights, before his shootout with Ransom Stoddard.

1962
The Manchurian Candidate

Overview

Genre: Drama/Thriller
Duration: 126 min
Color: Black and
White
Country: USA
MPAA Rating: PG-13
Studio: United Artists

When a U.S. Army platoon is taken hostage during the Korean War, something mysterious happens to them while in captivity. Upon returning to the United States, Sergeant Raymond Shaw, the son of an ambitious mother, is given the Congressional Medal of Honor and is lauded by men who never particularly liked him. One of those men, Captain Bennett Marco, has been having feverish nightmares and he slowly begins to remember what really happened in that POW camp. Was Shaw truly a hero or is there some larger conspiracy at work here? *The Manchurian Candidate* is a taut political thriller that will keep you riveted to the very end.

Cast

Frank Sinatra: Major Bennett Marco
Laurence Harvey: Raymond Shaw
Janet Leigh: Eugenie Rose Chaney
Angela Lansbury: Mrs. Iselin
Henry Silva: Chunjin
James Gregory: Senator John Yerkes Iselin
John McGiver: Senator Thomas Jordan

Behind the Scenes

Director: John Frankenheimer
Writers: Richard Condon (novel), George Axelrod (screenplay)
Producers: George Axelrod, John Frankenheimer
Executive Producer: Howard W. Koch
Cinematographer: Lionel Lindon

Awards

Oscar Nominations: Best Supporting Actress, Best Film Editing

Trivia

• The blurriness in the well-known shot where Bennett Marco gives the deck of cards containing all queens to Raymond Shaw was actually inadvertent.

1979
Manhattan

Overview

Genre: Comedy/Romance
Duration: 96 min
Color: Black and White
Country: USA
MPAA Rating: R
Studio: United Artists

Woody Allen's gorgeous black and white valentine to New York City follows the relationship foibles of middle-aged television writer Isaac Davis. Dating a young high school student with an old soul, Isaac knows his romance with Tracy can't last forever. By chance he runs into his best friend's mistress, and Isaac now finds himself attracted to the more age-appropriate woman. As he struggles with his feelings for both women and the disappointments of an uninspiring job, Isaac learns that his ex-wife is writing a book about their failed marriage. With problems like these it's comforting to know that he'll always have his one true love—Manhattan.

Cast

Woody Allen: Isaac Davis
Diane Keaton: Mary Wilkie
Michael Murphy: Yale Pollack
Mariel Hemingway: Tracy
Meryl Streep: Jill Davis
Anne Byrne: Emily Pollack
Karen Ludwig: Connie

Behind the Scenes

Director: Woody Allen
Writers: Woody Allen, Marshall Brickman
Producer: Charles H. Joffe
Executive Producers: Robert Greenhut, Jack Rollins (uncredited)
Film Editor: Susan E. Morse
Cinematographer: Gordon Willis

Awards

Oscar Nominations: Best Supporting Actress, Best Writing

Trivia

• There is a clause in the studio's licensing contract of this film which stipulates that *Manhattan* must always be shown in widescreen in any airing or home release.

1964
Mary Poppins

Overview

Genre: Family/Musical
Duration: 139 min
Color: Color (Technicolor)
Country: USA
MPAA Rating: G
Studio: Walt Disney Productions

When yet another one of their nannies quits, the Banks family is startled by the magical replacement who appears on their doorstep just days later. Not your typical child care professional, Mary Poppins has the ability to fly with an umbrella, travel up the stairway banister, and a seemingly endless bag of tricks that capture the imagination of young Jane and Michael. As she takes the children on a series of song and dance adventures, she also teaches them about life. But when their buttoned-down banker father catches wind of these unconventional methods, Mary may just have to teach him a thing or two as well.

Cast

Julie Andrews: Mary Poppins
Dick Van Dyke: Bert/Mr. Dawes Sr.
David Tomlinson: Mr. Banks
Glynis Johns: Mrs. Banks
Hermione Baddeley: Ellen
Karen Dotrice: Jane Banks
Matthew Garber: Michael Banks

Behind the Scenes

Director: Robert Stevenson
Writers: P.L. Travers (book), Bill Walsh and Don DaGradi (screenplay)
Producers: Walt Disney, Bill Walsh
Film Editor: Cotton Warburton
Cinematographer: Edward Colman

Awards

Oscar Winners: Best Actress, Best Effects, Best Film Editing, Best Music—Original Song, Best Music

Trivia

• This is the first Disney film and the only film produced by Walt Disney himself to be nominated for the Best Picture Academy Award.

1970
M*A*S*H

Overview

Genre: Comedy/Drama
Duration: 116 min
Color: Color (DeLuxe)
Country: USA
MPAA Rating: R
Studio: Twentieth Century Fox

The Korean War serves as the backdrop for this black comedy about the colorful members of a mobile army surgical hospital. Top-notch surgeons Hawkeye Pierce and Trapper John McIntyre are unconvential, to say the least. Serving close to the front lines, these two rely on such things as football, practical jokes, and plenty of martinis to help get them through the carnage they see. They also are not too keen on authority, and jump at the chance to expose people like Majors Frank Burns and Margaret "Hot Lips" Houlihan as hypocrites. Though war and bloodshed are tough targets for humor, director Robert Altman hit the bullseye with M*A*S*H.

Cast

Donald Sutherland: Captain Benjamin Franklin "Hawkeye" Pierce
Elliott Gould: Captain John Francis Xavier "Trapper John" McIntyre
Sally Kellerman: Major Margaret "Hot Lips" Houlihan
Robert Duvall: Major Frank Burns

Behind the Scenes

Director: Robert Altman
Writers: Richard Hooker and W.C. Heinz (novel), Ring Lardner Jr. (screenplay)
Producer: Ingo Preminger
Film Editor: Danford B. Greene
Cinematographer: Harold E. Stine
Original Music: Johnny Mandel

Awards

Oscar Winner: Best Writing—Adapted Screenplay

Trivia

• Robert Altman's 14-year-old son Mike Altman wrote the theme song's lyrics, and made more money through royalties than his father had been paid to direct the film.

1999
The Matrix

Overview

Genre: Action/Sci-Fi
Duration: 136 min
Color: Color
Country: USA
MPAA Rating: R
Studio: Warner Bros.
Pictures

A malevolent hacker named Neo, known as lowly programmer Thomas Anderson by day, is plagued by a feeling that reality isn't what it seems. He searches for Morpheus, a man branded as a terrorist, who may hold the key to Neo's ultimate question: "What is the Matrix?" But when Morpheus contacts Neo and warns him that he can only be *shown* the Matrix, Neo may not be prepared for the real world in which he will soon awaken. Shortly, Neo and Morpheus's band of followers will face the ultimate battle: fighting for the very survival of the human race. Heart-pounding action sequences and revolutionary special effects couple with a thought-provoking script to create an instant classic.

Cast

Keanu Reeves: Neo
Laurence Fishburne: Morpheus
Carrie-Anne Moss: Trinity
Hugo Weaving: Agent Smith
Gloria Foster: Oracle
Joe Pantoliano: Cypher
Marcus Chong: Tank
Julian Arahanga: Apoc

Behind the Scenes

Directors: Andy Wachowski, Larry Wachowski
Writers: Andy Wachowski, Larry Wachowski
Producer: Joel Silver
Executive Producers: Bruce Berman, Dan Cracchiolo, Andrew Mason, Barrie M. Osborne, Erwin Stoff, Andy Wachowski, Larry Wachowski
Film Editor: Zach Staenberg
Cinematographer: Bill Pope

Trivia

• Before production, the principal actors had to spend four months with martial arts experts to learn the fight moves.

Awards

Oscar Winners: Best Editing, Best Effects—Sound, Best Effects—Visual, Best Sound

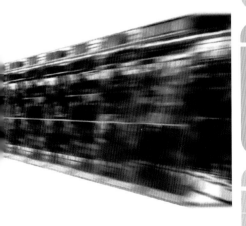

2000
Memento

Overview

Genre: Drama/Mystery
Duration: 113 min
Color: Black and White, Color
Country: USA
MPAA Rating: R
Studio: Team Todd/ I Remember Productions/Summit Entertainment

A sordid tale of murder and revenge, *Memento* follows insurance investigator Leonard Shelby as he tries to find the man that raped and killed his wife. Injured in the attack on his wife, Leonard suffers from a rare form of amnesia that keeps him from forming any new memories. He does, however, recollect everything up until his wife's death at the hands of a John G. He also recalls a former client who had the same condition he is learning to cope with. As each new day presents a blank slate, Leonard finds himself in the company of people he's not sure he can trust. As he gets closer to finding John G., will Leonard remember who he is long enough to seek his revenge?

Cast

Guy Pearce: Leonard
Carrie-Anne Moss: Natalie
Joe Pantoliano: Teddy Gammell
Mark Boone Junior: Burt
Russ Fega: Waiter
Jorja Fox: Leonard's Wife
Stephen Tobolowsky: Sammy
Harriet Sansom Harris: Mrs. Jankis

Behind the Scenes

Director: Christopher Nolan
Writers: Jonathan Nolan (story), Christopher Nolan (screenplay)
Producers: Jennifer Todd and Suzanne Todd
Executive Producer: Aaron Ryder
Film Editor: Dody Dorn
Cinematographer: Wally Pfister
Original Music: David Julyan

Trivia

• Though the first scene is played entirely backwards, all but one sound effect is played forward as normal. The only sound that plays backwards is Teddy (Joe Pantoliano) screaming, "No!"
• Christopher Nolan based his screenplay on his brother's short story, but the screenplay is still called "original" because the film came out before the story was published.

Awards

Oscar Nominations: Best Editing, Best Writing

1997
Men in Black

Overview

Genre: Comedy/Sci-Fi
Duration: 98 min
Color: Color
Country: USA
MPAA Rating: PG-13
Studio: Columbia Tristar-Motion Picture Group

Agent K, a veteran member of a secret agency that regulates the movements of aliens on Earth, finds himself in need of a new partner and recruits the wisecracking NYPD cop James Edwards. Sporting sharp suits and sunglasses that earn them the moniker "Men in Black," they are on the hunt for an intergalactic terrorist, or Bug, that landed illegally to find a source of power known as "the Galaxy." The Bug doesn't care who it destroys in its path, even if he involves a planet whose government is willing to destroy Earth just to keep it from its quarry. Agent K and the newly renamed Agent J must race against time to stop the Bug before Earth is destroyed.

Cast

Tommy Lee Jones: Agent K
Will Smith: James Edwards (Agent J)
Linda Fiorentino: Dr. Laurel Weaver
Vincent D'Onofrio: Edgar
Rip Torn: Chief Zed
Tony Shalhoub: Jack Jeebs

Behind the Scenes

Director: Barry Sonnenfeld
Writers: Lowell Cunningham (comic), Ed Solomon (screenplay)
Producers: Laurie MacDonald, Walter F. Parkes
Executive Producer: Steven Spielberg
Original Music: Danny Elfman

Awards

Oscar Winner: Best Makeup
Oscar Nominations: Best Art Direction, Best Music

Trivia

• When the alien ship flies over New York's Shea Stadium, the player who loses his concentration and gets hit with a fly ball is Bernard Gilkey.

1969
Midnight Cowboy

Overview

Genre: Drama
Duration: 113 min
Color: Black and White, Color (DeLuxe)
Country: USA
MPAA Rating: R
Studio: United Artists

Jon Voight stars as Joe Buck, a young stud from Texas who comes to New York looking to parlay his good looks into a regular gig as a hustler. He soon finds out that life in the city is not as glamorous or lucrative as he imagined. Facing an uncertain future, Joe makes the acquaintance of an odd small-time con man named Ratso Rizzo. Together, Joe and Ratso form a business partnership that eventually evolves into an unlikely friendship. Living in Ratso's condemned apartment, these two lost souls cling to each other and weather their rough existence. Rated X for its sexual content, *Midnight Cowboy* still drew big audiences and won the Oscar for Best Picture.

Cast

Dustin Hoffman: Enrico Salvatore "Ratso" Rizzo
John Voight: Joe Buck
Sylvia Miles: Cass
John McGiver: Mr. O'Daniel
Brenda Vaccaro: Shirley
Barnard Hughes: Towny

Behind the Scenes

Director: John Schlesinger
Writers: James Leo Herlihy (novel) and Waldo Salt (screenplay)
Producer: Jerome Hellman
Film Editor: Hugh A. Robertson
Cinematographer: Adam Holender
Original Music: John Barry

Awards

Oscar Winners: Best Director, Best Picture, Best Writing—Adapted Screenplay
Oscar Nominations: Best Actor, Best Supporting Actress, Best Film Editing

Trivia

• *Midnight Cowboy* is still the only X-rated film to win the Academy Award for Best Picture.

1988
Midnight Run

Overview

Genre: Comedy/Action
Duration: 128 min
Color: Color
Country: USA
MPAA Rating: R
Studio: Universal Pictures

Robert DeNiro stars as Jack Walsh, an ex-cop turned bounty hunter who has been hired to find a bail-jumping embezzler and bring him back to Los Angeles. By Walsh's standards this should be a pretty uneventful assignment, but after tracking down Jonathan Mardukas he finds that his prisoner is more trouble than he bargained for. Along with the FBI and another bumbling bounty hunter, Mardukas is also being sought by the man he stole $15 million from, mob boss Jimmy Serrano. As if all of this weren't bad enough, Mardukas's constant talking is really starting to grate on Walsh. Whether either of these two makes it back to L.A. in one piece remains to be seen.

Cast

Robert De Niro: Jack Walsh
Charles Grodin: Jonathan Mardukas
Yaphet Kotto: FBI Agent Alonzo Mosely
John Ashton: Marvin Dorfler
Dennis Farina: Jimmy Serrano
Joe Pantoliano: Eddie Moscone
Richard Foronjy: Tony Darvo

Behind the Scenes

Director: Martin Brest
Writer: George Gallo
Producer: Martin Brest
Executive Producer: William S. Gilmore
Film Editors: Chris Lebenzon, Michael Tronick, Billy Weber
Original Music: Danny Elfman

Awards

Golden Globe Nominations: Best Motion Picture—Comedy/Musical, Best Performance by an Actor—Comedy/Musical

Trivia

• John Ashton, who played Marvin Dorfler, said that Robert De Niro was so into his part that De Niro really did slug him during the fight scene on the train.

1947
Miracle on 34th Street

Overview

Genre: Family/Drama
Duration: 96 min
Color: Black and White
Country: USA
MPAA Rating: Not Rated
Studio: Twentieth Century Fox

The Macy's Day Parade: the highlight of the holiday season in New York City. But when a last-minute replacement for Santa Claus must be found, Macy's store supervisor Doris Walker finds herself with more Christmas spirit than she asked for. The replacement calls himself Kris Kringle and seems to believe that he is actually Santa Claus. Worse yet, he threatens the cynicism of Walker's own daughter who, following in her mother's footsteps, professes herself unwilling to believe untruths. Brought to court by a humorless psychiatrist, Mr. Kringle must prove that he is who he claims to be—but he may have better luck proving that faith is the greatest miracle of all.

Cast

Maureen O'Hara: Doris Walker
John Payne: Fred Gailey
Edmund Gwenn: Kris Kringle
Gene Lockhart: Judge Henry X. Harper
Natalie Wood: Susan Walker
Porter Hall: Granville Sawyer
William Frawley: Charlie Halloran

Behind the Scenes

Director: George Seaton
Writers: Valentine Davis (story), George Seaton (screenplay)
Producer: William Perlberg
Film Editor: Robert L. Simpson
Cinematographers: Lloyd Ahern, Charles G. Clarke

Awards

Oscar Winners: Best Supporting Actor, Best Writing—Original Story, Best Writing—Screenplay
Oscar Nomination: Best Picture

Trivia

• Natalie Wood was just eight years old when she made this film, but it was her third credited film appearance.

1989
Mississippi Burning

Overview

Genre: Drama/Crime
Duration: 127 min
Color: Color
Country: USA
MPAA Rating: R
Studio: Orion Pictures

In 1964 Mississippi, the Klan rules the night, using violence—including firebombing and murder—to further its agenda. Knowing Southerner Rupert Anderson and straight-arrow Northerner Alan Ward, two FBI agents with very different personalities, arrive in Mississippi to investigate the disappearance of three civil rights workers. Through unconventional interrogation methods, the investigators discover that the missing men have been killed in cold blood and where the bodies have been hidden. The movie is loosely based on the 1964 Klan murders of Michael Schwerner, Andrew Goodman, and James Chaney in Philadelphia, Mississippi.

Cast

Gene Hackman: Agent Rupert Anderson
Willem Dafoe: Agent Alan Ward
Frances McDormand: Mrs. Pell
Brad Dourif: Deputy Clinton Pell
R. Lee Ermey: Mayor Tilman
Stephen Tobolowsky: Clayton Townley
Michael Rooker: Frank Bailey

Behind the Scenes

Director: Alan Parker
Writers: Chris Gerolmo, Alan Parker
Producers: Robert F. Colesberry, Frederick Zollo
Film Editor: Gerry Hambling
Cinematographer: Peter Biziou
Original Music: Trevor Jones

Awards

Oscar Winner: Best Cinematography
Oscar Nominations: Best Actor, Best Supporting Actress, Best Director, Best Film Editing, Best Picture, Best Sound

Trivia

• The courthouse used for interior shots of the sheriff's office and courtroom was so dilapidated that the cast and crew had to dodge falling debris as they filmed.

1955
Mister Roberts

Overview

Genre: Comedy/
Drama
Duration: 123 min
Color: Color
(Warnercolor)
Country: USA
MPAA Rating: Not
Rated
Studio: Warner Bros.

Doug Roberts is a U.S. naval officer aboard a cargo ship during World War II. While Doug likes his crewmates well enough, he'd really rather be on a fighting ship somewhere in the middle of the Pacific. Every week he requests a transfer, but the ship's blowhard captain won't allow it. On top of this, Captain Morton seems to enjoy crushing the spirit of his men whenever he gets the chance. Though he may never see any live combat, Doug isn't going to let Captain Morton keep letting the men down without putting up a fight. Henry Fonda's at his earnest best here as Mr. Roberts, and Jack Lemmon nabbed an Oscar for his hilarious portrayal of Ensign Pulver.

Cast

Henry Fonda: Lieutenant Douglas A. "Doug"
Roberts
James Cagney: Captain Morton
William Powell: Lieutenant "Doc"
Jack Lemmon: Ensign Frank Thurlowe Pulver
Ward Bond: Chief Petty Officer Dowdy
Philip Carey: Mannion

Behind the Scenes

Directors: John Ford, Mervyn LeRoy, Joshua
Logan (uncredited)
Writers: Thomas Heggen (novel and play),
Joshua Logan (play and screenplay), Frank S.
Nugent (screenplay)
Producer: Leland Hayward
Film Editor: Jack Murray

Awards

Oscar Winner: Best Supporting Actor
Oscar Nomination: Best Picture, Best
Sound

Trivia

• This was William Powell's final film.

1975
Monty Python and the Holy Grail

Overview

Genre: Comedy/Adventure
Duration: 89 min
Color: Color
Country: UK
MPAA Rating: PG
Studio: Michael White Productions/Python Pictures

An irreverent romp through the most famous quest of England's most famous legendary king, *Monty Python and the Holy Grail* creatively addresses its subject with casual attention to time period, plot consistency, and character development. The result: a nonstop medley of hilarious scenes. An appropriate lack of historical sense, anachronistic Marxism, the odd musical number, and a recurring theme of rabbits round out (or maybe completely distort) this madcap summary of British mythology. The most beloved of Monty Python's films, *Holy Grail* is anything but holy—but is sure to please nevertheless.

Cast

Graham Chapman: King Arthur/Hiccuping guard/others
John Cleese: Tim/Newt/Sir Lancelot/others
Eric Idle: Maynard/Concord/Sir Robin/others
Terry Gilliam: Patsy/others
Terry Jones: Sir Bedamere/others
Michael Palin: Sir Galahad/Dennis/others

Behind the Scenes

Director: Terry Gilliam, Terry Jones
Writers: Graham Chapman, John Cleese, Eric Idle, Terry Gilliam, Terry Jones, Michael Palin
Producers: Mark Forstater, Michael White
Cinematographer: Terry Bedford
Original Music: De Wolfe, Neil Innes

Trivia

• An early version of the script set the Grail and its discovery in Harrods department store in London.

Trivia

• Some of the funding for *Monty Python and the Holy Grail* came from British bands Pink Floyd and Led Zeppelin.

1987
Moonstruck

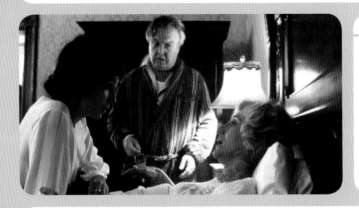

Overview

Genre: Comedy/Romance
Duration: 102 min
Color: Color (Technicolor)
Country: USA
MPAA Rating: PG
Studio: Metro-Goldwyn-Mayer

Ah the perils of love. When widowed Loretta Castorini decides to swear off real love and instead agrees to marry "safe bet" mama's boy Johnny Cammareri, she thinks that her life is set. But her sense of a secure future is short-lived when she meets and falls for her fiancé's hot-tempered brother Ronny. Swept up in an impossibly difficult situation, Loretta must soon decide between practicality and passion. Set in New York, this delightful romantic comedy follows a terrific ensemble cast as they navigate life's romantic triumphs and foibles. *Moonstruck* reminds us that love is not always perfect and sometimes family is all we have.

Cast

Cher: Loretta Castorini
Nicolas Cage: Ronny Cammareri
Vincent Gardenia: Cosmo Castorini
Olympia Dukakis: Rose Castorini
Danny Aiello: Johnny Cammareri
Julie Bovasso: Rita Cappomaggi
John Mahoney: Perry

Behind the Scenes

Director: Norman Jewison
Writer: John Patrick Shanley
Producers: Patrick Palmer, Norman Jewison
Film Editor: Lou Lombardo
Cinematographer: David Watkin

Awards

Oscar Winners: Best Actress, Best Supporting Actress, Best Writing
Oscar Nominations: Best Supporting Actor, Best Director, Best Picture

Trivia

• Like most movies, *Moonstruck* was shot out of sequnce so Cher's hair occasionally shows no strands of gray, even before the scene where she has it colored.

1939
Mr. Smith Goes to Washington

Overview

Genre: Drama
Duration: 129 min
Color: Black and White
Country: USA
MPAA Rating: Not Rated
Studio: Columbia Pictures Corporation

After Senator Sam Foley dies, the state political machine scrambles to find a warm body to serve in the interim. They eventually find their man in the form of Jefferson Smith, the likable leader of the Boy Rangers. Upon reaching Washington, Mr. Smith's naiveté is fodder for a wisecracking press corps. He considers packing it in but is reinvigorated when he starts working on a bill that will help his Boy Rangers. In his earnestness to get his bill passed he unexpectedly runs afoul of the very men who appointed him senator. Mr. Smith will soon find out whether one honest man is any match for a corrupt system.

Cast

James Stewart: Jefferson Smith
Claude Rains: Senator Joseph Paine
Edward Arnold: Jim Taylor
Guy Kibbee: Governor Hubert "Happy" Hopper
Thomas Mitchell: Diz Moore
Eugene Pallette: Chick McGann
Jean Arthur: Clarissa Saunders

Behind the Scenes

Director: Frank Capra
Writers: Lewis R. Foster (story and screenplay), Sidney Buchman (screenplay)
Producer: Frank Capra
Film Editors: Al Clark, Gene Havlick
Cinematographer: Joseph Walker
Original Music: Dimitri Tiomkin

Awards

Oscar Winners: Best Writing—Original Story

Trivia

- James Stewart drank bicarbonate of soda to make his throat dry and voice hoarse for the famous filibuster scene.

1979
The Muppet Movie

Overview

Genre: Family/Comedy
Duration: 98 min
Color: Color
(Eastmancolor)
Country: UK/USA
MPAA Rating: G
Studio: Henson
Associates (HA)

When Kermit the Frog runs into a harried Hollywood agent in his swamp, he catches the acting bug and decides to head for California. On his way to Tinseltown, Kermit makes friends with a lousy comedian, Fozzie Bear, a wild band of musicians known as Dr. Teeth and Electric Mayhem, a beauty queen named Ms. Piggy, and others. As Kermit and his pals make their way west, he is also forced to confront fast-food entrepreneur Doc Hopper, who wants Kermit to do commercials for his fried frogs' legs chain. Filled with great songs, unexpected cameos, and plenty of laughs, *The Muppet Movie* is one cross-country trip worth making.

Cast

Jim Henson: Kermit the Frog/Rowlf/Dr. Teeth/Waldorf
Frank Oz: Miss Piggy/Fozzie Bear/Animal/Sam the Eagle
Jerry Nelson: Floyd Pepper/Robin the Frog/Crazy Harry/Lew Zealand

Behind the Scenes

Director: James Frawley
Writers: Jack Burns, Jerry Juhl
Producer: Jim Henson
Executive Producer: Martin Starger
Film Editor: Christopher Greenbury
Cinematographer: Isidore Mankofsky
Original Music: Paul Williams

Awards

Oscar Nominations: Best Music—Original Song, Best Music—Original Song Score and Its Adaptation

Trivia

• The plot of this film is meant to mirror Jim Henson's rise to fame.

1986
Murphy's Romance

Overview

Genre: Comedy/Romance
Duration: 107 min
Color: Color (Metrocolor)
Country: USA
MPAA Rating: PG-13
Studio: Columbia TriStar-Motion Picture Group

Recently divorced Emma Moriarity and her young son Jake just moved to a small town in Arizona looking to open a boarding ranch for horses. With very little money and no friends to speak of, Emma makes the acquaintance of Murphy Jones, the town pharmacist. Over time Murphy and Emma become good friends, but the single mom and the widower remain just that, friends. Nevertheless, the chemistry between the older gentleman and the younger woman is undeniable. But when Emma's immature ex shows up on her doorstep, it looks like three's a crowd. Yet, when it comes to Emma Moriarity, wild horses couldn't drag Murphy away.

Cast

Sally Field: Emma Moriarty
James Garner: Murphy Jones
Brian Kerwin: Bobby Jack Moriarty
Corey Haim: Jake Moriarty
Dennis Burkley: Freeman Coverly
Georgann Johnson: Margaret
Dortha Duckworth: Bessie

Behind the Scenes

Director: Martin Ritt
Writers: Max Schott (book), Harriet Frank Jr. and Irving Ravetch
Producer: Laura Ziskin
Executive Producer: Martin Ritt
Film Editor: Sidney Levin
Cinematographer: William A. Fraker

Awards

Oscar Nominations: Best Actor, Best Cinematography

Trivia

• Sally Field wanted James Garner to star opposite her and had to fight the studio to cast him, because he was viewed at the time as primarily a television actor.

1935
Mutiny on the Bounty

Overview

Genre: Drama/Adventure
Duration: 132 min
Color: Black and White
Country: USA
MPAA Rating: Not Rated
Studio: Metro-Goldwyn-Mayer (MGM)

Midshipman Roger Byam joins first mate Fletcher Christian and the crew of the HMS *Bounty* as they set sail for Tahiti under callous Captain William Bligh. The good Captain quickly shows his men that this is no pleasure cruise, as he rules by fear and dishes out more punishment than he does food. The ship makes it to its destination but not before many of the crew, including Byam, feel the Captain's sadistic wrath. The island paradise provides a welcome respite, but on the journey home many of the crew have had all they can stand. Loosely based on the historical event, *Mutiny on the Bounty* provides plenty of high seas drama.

Cast

Charles Laughton: Captain William Bligh
Clark Gable: Fletcher Christian
Franchot Tone: Roger Byam
Herbert Mundin: Smith
Eddie Quillan: Ellison
Donald Crisp: Burkitt
Henry Stephenson: Sir Joseph Banks

Behind the Scenes

Director: Frank Lloyd
Writers: Charles Nordhoff and James Norman Hall (novel), Talbot Jennings, Jules Furthman, and Carey Wilson (screenplay)
Producer: Irving Thalberg (uncredited)
Film Editor: Margaret Booth
Cinematographer: Arthur Edeson

Awards

Oscar Winners: Best Picture
Oscar Nominations: Best Actor, Best Director, Best Editing, Best Music, Best Writing

Trivia

• Unlike the real-life William Bligh, Charles Laughton, who played Bligh, was terrified of the ocean and experienced violent seasickness for the majority of the filming.

1936
My Man Godfrey

Overview

Genre: Comedy/ Romance
Duration: 94 min
Color: Black and White
Country: USA
MPAA Rating: Not Rated
Studio: Universal Pictures

Godfrey Parke is a so-called "forgotten man" who lives at the city dump. One night two socialites approach him looking for a forgotten man as part of a snobby scavenger hunt. Godfrey wants no part of pushy Cornelia, but agrees to go along with her younger sister Irene, who proceeds to hire him as the family butler. Among the kooky Bullocks, Godfrey stands out as the lone sane person. It's no surprise then when Irene starts falling for him. Still, Cornelia can't stand him so much that perhaps she may have feelings for him too. When one of the Bullock's party guests recognizes Godfrey, it complicates matters further. It's situations like these that make a man long for the city dump.

Cast

William Powell: Godfrey Parke
Carole Lombard: Irene Bullock
Alice Brady: Angelica Bullock
Gail Patrick: Cornelia Bullock
Eugene Pallette: Alexander Bullock
Jean Dixon: Molly
Alan Mowbray: Tommy Gray
Mischa Auer: Carlo
Pat Flaherty: Mike

Behind the Scenes

Director: Gregory La Cava
Writers: Eric Hatch (play and screenplay), Morrie Ryskind and Gregory La Cava (screenplay)
Producer: Gregory La Cava
Executive Producer: Charles R. Rogers
Film Editors: Ted J. Kent, Russell F. Schoengarth
Cinematographer: Ted Tetzlaff

Trivia

• William Powell and Carole Lombard were once married, but they had been divorced for three years by the time they made this film. In fact, Powell declared that Lombard was the only actress right for the part of Irene Bullock.

Awards

Oscar Nominations: Best Actor, Best Supporting Actor, Best Actress, Best Supporting Actress, Best Director, Best Writing

1984
The Natural

Overview

Genre: Drama/Sports
Duration: 134 min
Color: Color (Technicolor)
Country: USA
MPAA Rating: PG
Studio: TriStar Pictures

Baseball player Roy Hobbs could have been the greatest to ever play the game until a scandalous incident sidetracked his career. Years later, Roy is back, hoping to take one last crack with the struggling New York Knights. The problem is, no one on the team believes there's anything left in this aging rookie. But when fate steps in and Hobbs gets his chance, he opens eyes and baseballs alike. As the Knights' fortunes change, Hobbs soon finds himself the target of a curious sportswriter, a slick gambler, and a beautiful blonde. Featuring a stellar cast, beautiful cinematography, and a rousing score, *The Natural* is the baseball movie equivalent of a grand slam.

Cast

Robert Redford: Roy Hobbs
Glenn Close: Iris Gaines
Robert Duvall: Max Mercy
Kim Basinger: Memo Paris
Wilford Brimley: Pop Fisher
Darren McGavin: Gus Sands
Robert Prosky: The Judge

Behind the Scenes

Director: Barry Levinson
Writers: Bernard Malamud (novel), Roger Towne and Phil Dusenberry (screenplay)
Producer: Mark Johnson
Executive Producers: Philip M. Breen, Roger Towne
Film Editor: Stu Linder

Awards

Oscar Nominations: Best Supporting Actress, Best Art Direction, Best Cinematography, Best Music

Trivia

• When Darren McGavin (Gus Sands) was told he would have a lesser billing than the other stars on the film, he elected instead to leave his role uncredited.

1976
Network

Overview

Genre: Drama
Duration: 121 min
Color: Color (Metrocolor)
Country: USA
MPAA Rating: R
Studio: Metro-Goldwyn-Mayer (MGM)/United Artists

If ever there was a movie that foretold the future of television, it's 1976's *Network*. Network executive Max Schumacher has just informed his best friend Howard Beale, the longtime anchor of UBS News, that he is being replaced by someone younger. Blown away by this news, Beale announces on the air that he plans to take his own life on his final broadcast. Instead of following through on his threat, Beale delivers a bizarre on-air rant that inexplicably turns him into a huge TV star. When the network sees the ratings these antics capture, they decide to offer more of the same. This kind of programming can't last forever, can it?

Cast

Faye Dunaway: Diana Christensen
William Holden: Max Schumacher
Peter Finch: Howard Beale
Robert Duvall: Frank Hackett
Wesley Addy: Nelson Chaney
Ned Beatty: Arthur Jensen
Arthur Burghardt: Great Ahmed Kahn

Behind the Scenes

Director: Sidney Lurnet
Writer: Paddy Chayefsky
Producer: Howard Gottfried
Film Editor: Alan Heim
Cinematographer: Owen Roizman
Original Music: Elliot Lawrence

Trivia

• This was only the second film in history to win three Academy Awards for acting.
• All music heard throughout the film comes from commercials and television show theme songs.

Awards

Oscar Winners: Best Actor (posthumous), Best Actress, Best Supporting Actress, Best Writing
Oscar Nominations: Best Actor, Best Supporting Actor, Best Cinematography, Best Director, Best Film Editing, Best Picture

1935
A Night at the Opera

Overview

Genre: Comedy/ Musical
Duration: 96 min
Color: Black and White
Country: USA
MPAA Rating: Not Rated
Studio: Metro-Goldwyn-Mayer (MGM)

When wealthy Mrs. Claypool wants to break into high society circles, she enlists the help of confidence man Otis B. Driftwood. Driftwood encourages her to sponsor an Italian opera tenor to perform for a prestigious New York opera company for a considerable sum. Mistaken identity leads to the wrong Italian tenor being contracted. The Marx Brothers' characters stow away in a too-small ship's cabin to New York. Pursued by the police for illegal entry into the country, Driftwood, Fiorello, and Tomoso work together to give the bad guy (pompous and cruel tenor Rudolfo Lassparri) his comeuppance while reuniting Rosa and Ricardo, two star-crossed lovers, and giving Ricardo a chance to shine during an unforgettable, anarchic opera scene finale.

Cast

Groucho Marx: Otis B. Driftwood
Chico Marx: Fiorello
Harpo Marx: Tomasso
Kitty Carlisle: Rosa Castaldi
Allan Jones: Ricardo Baroni
Walter Woolf King: Rodolfo Lassparri
Sig Ruman: Herbert Gottlieb
Margaret Dumont: Mrs. Claypool

Behind the Scenes

Director: Sam Wood
Writers: James Kevin McGuinness (story), George S. Kaufman and Morrie Ryskind (screenplay)
Producer: Irving Thalberg (uncredited)
Film Editor: William LeVanway
Cinematographer: Merritt B. Gerstad
Original Music: Herbert Stothart

Trivia

• The famous "Stateroom Scene" was originally a tool to get a cheap laugh—Groucho Marx was supposed to be crowded out of the room and change his pants in the corridor. When the Marx brothers did not like the way the scene was working, they scrapped that idea and recorded the current scene, entirely improvised, on the spot.

Awards

Added to National Film Registry in 1993

1955
The Night of the Hunter

Overview

Genre: Drama/Thriller
Duration: 93 min
Color: Black and White
Country: USA
MPAA Rating: Not Rated
Studio: United Artists

Robert Mitchum stars as malevolent preacher Harry Powell, a convict whose idea of God's work is killing defenseless widows for their money. One night while Harry is locked up for car theft, he meets a bank robber named Ben who is soon to be executed. After failing to worm the location of the money from his robbery out of Ben, the good preacher decides it would be best to pay a call on his grieving widow Willa and her two children. He quickly insinuates himself into the lives of the family and their friends. Harry will stop at nothing to find that money, be it by menace or marriage or murder.

Cast

Robert Mitchum: Harry Powell
Shelley Winters: Willa Harper
Lillian Gish: Rachel Cooper
James Gleason: Birdie Steptoe
Evelyn Varden: Icey Spoon
Peter Graves: Ben Harper
Don Beddoe: Walt Spoon

Behind the Scenes

Director: Charles Laughton, Robert Mitchum (uncredited)
Writer: Davis Grubb (novel), James Agee (screenplay), Charles Laughton (uncredited)
Producer: Paul Gregory
Film Editor: Robert Golden
Cinematographer: Stanley Cortez

Awards

Added to National Film Registry in 1992

Trivia

• The scene with the preacher riding a horse far off in the distance was really a midget riding a small pony.

1968
Night of the Living Dead

Overview

Genre: Horror
Duration: 96 min
Color: Black and White
Country: USA
MPAA Rating: Not Rated
Studio: Continental/Image Ten

On a trip to their father's grave in rural Pennsylvania, siblings Johnny and Barbra discover a horror stalking the cemetery. Johnny collapses while Barbra runs off to a nearby farmhouse, where she encounters other people hiding out from flesh-eating zombies. The seven people hiding in the house fend off the ghouls and devise a means of escape. Several mishaps result in the decimation of their ranks as one by one they are killed—some, horribly, returning as zombies themselves. Directed by George A. Romero on a shoestring budget, *Night of the Living Dead* inspired an entire generation of independent horror filmmakers.

Cast

Duane Jones: Ben
Judith O'Dea: Barbra
Karl Hardman: Harry Cooper
Marilyn Eastman: Helen Cooper/Bug-eating zombie
Keith Wayne: Tom
Judith Ridley: Judy

Behind the Scenes

Director: George A. Romero
Writers: John A. Russo, George A. Romero
Producers: Karl Hardman, Russell Streiner
Executive Producer: Anand Bhatt
Film Editor: George A. Romero
Cinematographer: George A. Romero
Original Music: Scott Vladimir Licina

Awards

Added to National Film Registry in 1999

Trivia

• The budget for this film only allowed for minimal affects, such as chocolate syrup being used for blood.

2007
No Country for Old Men

Overview

Genre: Drama/Thriller
Duration: 122 min
Color: Color
Country: USA
MPAA Rating: R
Studio: Paramount Vantage/Miramax Films

Hunting antelope in the Texas wilderness, Llewelyn Moss comes upon a drug deal gone bad, with several bodies, one badly injured man, and a satchel containing $2 million. Rather than reporting the crime scene to the police, Moss takes home a submachine gun, a pistol, and the cash. Unfortunately for Moss, a cold-blooded killer named Anton Chigurh is also on the trail of this money and will stop at nothing to track it down. Bearing witness to the cat and mouse carnage is veteran lawman Ed Tom Bell—the film's moral center—who tries to deflect further damage while questioning the world in which it takes place.

Cast

Tommy Lee Jones: Sheriff Ed Tom Bell
Javier Bardem: Anton Chigurh
Josh Brolin: Llewelyn Moss
Woody Harrrelson: Carson Wells
Kelly Macdonald: Carla Jean Moss
Garret Dillahunt: Deputy Wendell
Tess Harper: Loretta Bell

Behind the Scenes

Directors: Ethan Coen, Joel Coen
Writers: Cormac McCarthy (novel), Ethan Coen and Joel Coen (screenplay)
Producers: Ethan Coen, Joel Coen, Scott Rudin
Executive Producers: Robert Graf, Mark Roybal

Awards

Oscar Winners: Best Director, Best Picture, Best Supporting Actor, Best Writing—Adapted Screenplay

Trivia

• None of the three main characters—Sheriff Bell, Anton Chigurh, and Llewelyn Moss—are ever on screen together. The only character to even talk to all three is Carla Jean Moss.

1979
Norma Rae

Overview

Genre: Drama
Duration: 110 min
Color: Color
Country: USA
MPAA Rating: PG
Studio: Twentieth Century Fox

Sally Field won the Academy Award for her role as Norma Rae Webster, a blue-collar worker in a southern textile mill. Concerned for the health and well-being of her fellow workers and fed up with substandard working conditions, Norma Rae feels inspired to act by Reuben, a union organizer from New York. This causes dissention both at the factory and at home, as her common-law husband grows suspicious of Norma Rae's motives, thinking that she's having an affair with the Northerner. Still Norma Rae sticks to her cause, orchestrating a work stoppage at the mill that forces management to seriously consider the consequences of ignoring the workers' demands for a safer workplace.

Cast

Sally Field: Norma Rae
Beau Bridges: Sonny
Ron Leibman: Reuben
Pat Hingle: Vernon
Barbara Baxley: Leona
Morgan Paull: Wayne Billings
Gail Strickland: Bonnie Mae

Behind the Scenes

Director: Martin Ritt
Writers: Harriet Frank Jr., Irving Ravetch
Producers: Tamara Asseyev, Alexandra Rose
Film Editor: Sidney Levin
Cinematographer: John A. Alonzo
Original Music: David Shire

Awards

Oscar Winners: Best Actress, Best Music—Original Song
Oscar Nominations: Best Picture, Best Writing—Adapted Screenplay

Trivia

• Sally Field took her feisty role to another level when she fractured the rib of an actor playing a policeman during one take.

1959
North by Northwest

Overview

Genre: Drama/Thriller
Duration: 136 min
Color: Color
Country: USA
MPAA Rating: Not Rated
Studio: Metro-Goldwyn-Mayer (MGM)

Cary Grant stars as advertising executive Roger Thornhill, a man who finds himself in the wrong place at the wrong time. While having drinks with business associates at New York's Plaza Hotel, Thornhill is misidentified by two thugs as someone named George Kaplan and removed from the hotel at gunpoint. Thus begins one of the most maddening cases of mistaken identity in movie history. The more Roger tries to clear his name the more deeply he becomes enmeshed in a case involving espionage and murder. Thornhill's odyssey includes trains, planes, and a little bit of mountain climbing. *North by Northwest* is Hitchcock at his best.

Cast

Cary Grant: Roger O. Thornhill
Eva Marie Saint: Eve Kendall
James Mason: Phillip Vandamm
Martin Landau: Leonard
Leo G. Carroll: The Professor
Josephine Hutchinson: Mrs. Townsend
Philip Ober: Lester Townsend

Behind the Scenes

Director: Alfred Hitchcock
Writer: Ernest Lehman
Producers: Alfred Hitchcock and Herbert Coleman
Film Editor: George Tomasini
Cinematographer: Robert Burks
Original Music: Bernard Herrmann

Awards

Oscar Nominations: Best Art Direction, Best Film Editing, Best Writing

Trivia

• Alfred Hitchcock was denied access to film the interior of the UN, so a hidden camera was snuck into the building and the rooms were recreated from that footage.

1968
The Odd Couple

Overview

Genre: Comedy
Duration: 105 min
Color: Color (Technicolor)
Country: English
MPAA Rating: G
Studio: Paramount Pictures

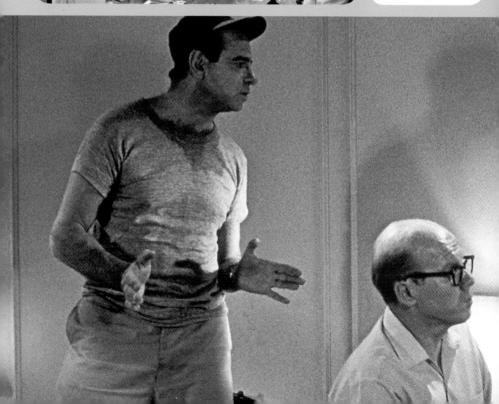

After his wife throws him out of the house, compulsive neat freak Felix Ungar arrives at the apartment of his ultra-sloppy friend, sportswriter Oscar Madison. Concerned over Felix's delicate mental state, Oscar invites Felix to share his apartment. How bad could it be? Before long, Felix's anal cooking and cleaning antics, and maudlin recollections of his marriage, start to grate on Oscar. But this dysfunctional arrangement is a two-way street and Oscar's filthy lifestyle is no picnic for Felix either. When an unstoppable tidying force comes up against an uncleanable object, can anyone possibly win? *The Odd Couple* remains one of the best "buddy comedies" of all time.

Cast

Jack Lemmon: Felix Ungar
Walter Matthau: Oscar Madison
John Fiedler: Vinnie
Herb Edelman: Murray
David Sheiner: Roy
Larry Haines: Speed
Monica Evans: Cecily Pigeon
Carole Shelley: Gwendolyn Pigeon

Behind the Scenes

Director: Gene Saks
Writer: Neil Simon (play and screenplay)
Producer: Howard W. Koch
Film Editor: Frank Bracht
Cinematographer: Robert B. Hauser
Original Music: Neal Hefti

Trivia

• Walter Matthau had played Oscar on Broadway, but he asked the play's author, Neil Simon, if he could play Felix instead. He thought Felix would be more of a challenge, wheareas Oscar was too similar to his own personality, but Simon finally prevailed upon him to play Oscar.

Awards

Oscar Nominations: Best Film Editing, Best Writing—Adapted Screenplay

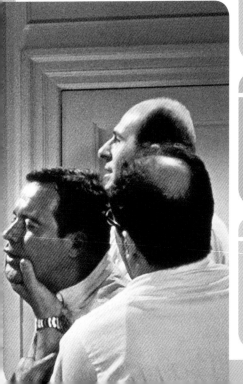

1982
An Officer and a Gentleman

Overview

Genre: Drama/ Romance
Duration: 124 min
Color: Color (Metrocolor)
Country: USA
MPAA Rating: R
Studio: Lorimar Film Entertainment/Para- mount

Zack Mayo is a Navy Flight School student with a bad attitude and checkered past. A troubled loner, Mayo feels that he can only rely on himself. This firm belief is called into question by his no-excuses Sergeant who pushes him to the edge and a local girl who opens his eyes to the possibilities of love and loyalty. As Sergeant Foley tests Mayo's drive, ability, and stamina, he forces him to recognize that life is not a solitary sport. A film about camaraderie, love, and never giving up, *An Officer and a Gentleman* also earned Louis Gossett Jr. an Oscar for his performance as Sergeant Foley.

Cast

Richard Gere: Zach Mayo
Debra Winger: Paula Pokrifki
Louis Gossett Jr.: Gunnery Sergeant Emil Foley
David Keith: Sid Worley
Robert Loggia: Byron Mayo
Lisa Blount: Lynette Pomeroy
Lisa Eilbacher: Casey Seeger

Behind the Scenes

Director: Taylor Hackford
Writer: Douglas Day Stewart
Producer: Martin Elfand
Film Editor: Peter Zinner
Cinematographer: Donald E. Thorin
Original Music: Jack Nitzsche

Awards

Oscar Winners: Best Supporting Actor, Best Music—Original Song
Oscar Nominations: Best Actress, Best Film Editing, Best Music

Trivia

• Actor John Travolta and singer John Denver were both offered the role of Zach Mayo, but they both turned it down.

1999
Office Space

Overview

Genre: Comedy
Duration: 89 min
Color: Color
Country: English
MPAA Rating: R
Studio: Twentieth Century Fox

Fed up with his office job at Initech, Peter Gibbons visits a hypnotherapist to help himself relax. Hypnosis leaves him in a blissful, carefree state of mind, and he decides to simply not go to work anymore. Upon returning to work to pick up his address book, he interviews with two "efficiency experts" who ultimately decide to give him a promotion. But when Peter learns that his two best friends are being fired, they come up with a scheme to slowly steal money from Initech. An overbearing boss, a disgruntled low-level employee, and a beautiful waitress all play a part in this hilarious depiction of office life.

Cast

Ron Livingston: Peter Gibbons
Jennifer Aniston: Joanna
David Herman: Michael Bolton
Ajay Naidu: Samir Nagheenanajar
Diedrich Bader: Lawrence
Stephen Root: Milton Waddams
Gary Cole: Bill Lumbergh

Behind the Scenes

Director: Mike Judge
Writer: Mike Judge
Producers: Daniel Rappaport, Michael Rotenberg, Mike Judge (uncredited)
Executive Producer: Guy Riedel
Cinematographer: Tim Suhrstedt
Original Music: John Frizzell

Trivia

• David Herman, who plays Michael Bolton, has an incredibly unsuccessful ventriloquist act that he blames on his dummy Jofus.

Trivia

• The prop department, needing a bright color to show up on the screen, created Milton's red stapler. Swingline started producing red staplers again due to demand after the film.

1968
Oliver!

Overview

Genre: Musical/Drama
Duration: 153 min
Color: Color (Technicolor)
Country: UK
MPAA Rating: G
Studio: Romulus Films/Columbia Pictures

Charles Dickens' street urchin classic gets a musical makeover in this Academy Award–winning film. After he has the nerve to ask for a second helping of gruel, young Oliver Twist gets booted out of his dismal orphanage and is sold to an equally depressing undertaker. But when this new situation proves too much to bear, Oliver runs away to London. There, on the city streets, Oliver meets a lively lad named the Artful Dodger who introduces him to an old thief named Fagin and their den of pickpockets. Filled with memorable musical numbers, *Oliver!* netted five Oscars, including Best Score, Best Director, and Best Picture.

Cast

Ron Moody: Fagin
Shani Wallis: Nancy
Oliver Reed: Bill Sikes
Harry Secombe: Mr. Bumble
Mark Lester: Oliver Twist
Jack Wild: The Artful Dodger
Joseph O'Conor: Mr. Brownlow

Behind the Scenes

Director: Carol Reed
Writers: Charles Dickens (novel), Vernon Harris (screenplay)
Producer: John Woolf
Film Editor: Ralph Kemplen
Cinematographer: Oswald Morris
Original Music: Lionel Bart

Awards

Oscar Winners: Best Art Direction, Best Director, Best Music, Best Picture, Best Sound, Honorary Award for outstanding choreography achievement

Trivia

• Lionel Bart, the composer, was unable to read music. For his entire career, Bart would sing the melodies he wanted to a pianist, who would then transcribe and orchestrate them.

1954
On the Waterfront

Overview

Genre: Drama
Duration: 108 min
Color: Black and White
Country: USA
MPAA Rating: PG
Studio: Columbia Pictures

Marlon Brando stars as down-and-out prizefighter Terry Malloy in Elia Kazan's powerful drama set on the docks of New York and New Jersey. Working as an errand boy, Terry witnesses the murder of a dock worker ordered by corrupt union chief Johnny Friendly. Initially deciding to keep his mouth shut, Terry experiences a crisis of conscience when he meets and falls for the dead man's sister. Will Terry protect his job or risk everything and inform against the mob? *On the Waterfront* is widely thought to be Kazan's response to his own involvement testifying before the House Un-American Activities committee during the 1950s.

Cast

Marlon Brando: Terry Malloy
Karl Malden: Father Barry
Lee J. Cobb: Johnny Friendly
Rod Steiger: Charley "the Gent" Malloy
Pat Henning: Timothy J. "Kayo" Dugan
Eva Marie Saint: Edie Doyle
Leif Erickson: Glover
James Westerfield: Big Mac

Behind the Scenes

Director: Elia Kazan
Writers: Malcolm Johnson (article), Budd Schulberg (story and screenplay)
Producer: Sam Spiegel
Film Editor: Gene Milford
Cinematographer: Boris Kaufman
Original Music: Leonard Bernstein

Trivia

• The film originated from the 1948 murder of a New York dock hiring boss, and Johnny Friendly was based on the crime boss Michael Clemente, a top enforcer for the family that ran the Hoboken docks.

Awards

Oscar Winners: Best Actor, Best Supporting Actress, Best Art Direction, Best Cinematography, Best Director, Best Film Editing, Best Picture, Best Writing
Oscar Nominations: Best Supporting Actor, Best Music

1984
Once Upon A Time in America

Overview

Genre: Drama/Crime
Duration: 229 min
(original), 139 min
(USA)
Color: Color
Country: USA/Italy
MPAA Rating: R
Studio: Warner Bros.
Pictures

Poor young David "Noodles" Aaronson tries to make a life for himself on New York's Lower East Side. He and his gang, Patrick "Patsy" Goldberg, Philip "Cockeye" Stein, and Dominic, first work for local gangster Bugsy, but later switch allegiance to Maximilian "Max" Bercovicz. When Noodles must choose between his dream girl and Max, he chooses Max and gets rewarded with a beating by rival hoods. The gang makes a lot of money from Prohibition and heists, but betrayal, death, prison, and loneliness mar the proceedings. Befitting his storied career, Director Sergio Leone's final movie is an amazing accomplishment in filmmaking. Forget the edited 139-minute version and instead take in the full 229-minute masterpiece.

Cast

Robert De Niro: David "Noodles" Aaronson
James Woods: Maximilian "Max" Bercovicz
Elizabeth McGovern: Deborah Gelly
Tuesday Weld: Carol
Treat Williams: James Conway O'Donnell
James Hayden: Patrick "Patsy" Goldberg
Joe Pesci: Frankie Minaldi

Behind the Scenes

Director: Sergio Leone
Writers: Harry Grey (novel), Leonardo Benvenuti, Piero De Bernardi, Enrico Medioli, Franco Arcalli, Franco Ferrini, Sergio Leone (screenplay)
Producer: Arnon Milchan
Executive Producer: Claudio Mancini
Cinematographer: Tonino Delli Colli
Original Music: Ennio Morricone

Trivia

• Sergio Leone wanted to release the film in two three-hour segments, but the studio would not allow it and asked an editor to drastically shorten the movie.

Awards

Golden Globe Nominations: Best Director, Best Original Score

1968
Once Upon a Time in the West

Overview

Genre: Drama/Western
Duration: 165 min
Color: Color
Country: Italy/USA
MPAA Rating: PG-13
Studio: Finanzia San Marco/Rafran Cinematografica/Paramount Pictures

Playing against type, Henry Fonda stars as villainous Frank, who shoots down anybody who gets in the way of corrupt railroad baron Morton's plan for his transcontinental railway line. Frank murders Brett McBain and his children, but the land is still owned by the new Mrs. McBain, married just a month earlier. Meanwhile, a mysterious stranger known as Harmonica comes searching for Frank. The stranger joins forces with escaped outlaw Cheyenne, blamed for the cold-blooded killing of the McBain Family (for which Frank has framed him), who wants to clear his name. The question remains why everyone wants this seemingly worthless land.

Cast

Henry Fonda: Frank
Claudia Cardinale: Jill McBain
Jason Robards: Cheyenne
Charles Bronson: Harmonica
Gabriele Ferzetti: Morton
Paolo Stoppa: Sam

Behind the Scenes

Director: Sergio Leone
Writers: Dario Argento and Bernardo Bertolucci (story), Sergio Leone (story and screenplay), Sergio Donati (screenplay)
Producer: Fulvio Morsella
Executive Producer: Bino Cicogna
Cinematographer: Tonino Delli Colli

Trivia

Future directors Bernardo Bertolucci and Dario Argento co-wrote the story for this film with Sergio Leone.

Trivia

• Hawaiian Princess Luukialuana (Luana) Kalaeloa played the Indian woman who flees from the train station in the opening scene.

1975
One Flew Over the Cuckoo's Nest

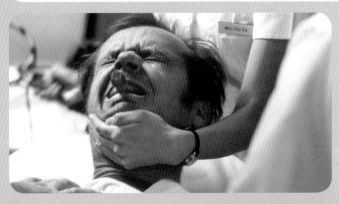

Overview

Genre: Drama
Duration: 133 min
Color: Color
Country: USA
MPAA Rating: R
Studio: United Artists

K en Kesey's novel set in an Oregon insane asylum is seamlessly adapted for the screen in 1975's winner of the Academy Award for Best Picture. Jack Nicholson stars as R.P. McMurphy, a convict feigning insanity in order to get himself out of prison. His plan works all too well and he soon finds himself in the company of a colorful assortment of mental patients. But Mc-Murphy soon finds out that this hospital, with its rules and regulations, is just another prison for his free-spirited ways. Leading his fellow inmates to rebel against authority, in the form of Nurse Ratched, McMurphy's insurrections produce both high comedy and serious consequences.

Cast

Jack Nicholson: R.P. McMurphy
Louise Fletcher: Nurse Mildred Ratched
William Redfield: Dale Harding
Brad Dourif: Billy Bibbit
Will Sampson: Chief Bromden
Dean R. Brooks: Dr. John Spivey
Danny DeVito: Martini
Christopher Lloyd: Taber

Behind the Scenes

Director: Milos Forman
Writers: Ken Kesey (novel), Dale Wasserman (play), Lawrence Hauben and Bo Goldman (screenplay)
Producers: Michael Douglas, Saul Zaentz
Film Editors: Richard Chew, Sheldon Kahn, Lynzee Klingman

Trivia

• The extras and supporting crew members were residents at the Oregon State Mental Hospital.
• The majority of scenes between Jack Nicholson and Dean R. Brooks were improvised.

Awards

Oscar Winners: Best Actor, Best Actress, Best Director, Best Picture, Best Writing—Adapted Screenplay
Oscar Nominations: Best Supporting Actor, Best Cinematography, Best Film Editing, Best Music

1980
Ordinary People

Overview

Genre: Drama
Duration: 124 min
Color: Color
(Technicolor)
Country: USA
MPAA Rating: R
Studio: Paramount
Pictures

The Jarret family are all profoundly depressed and can't seem to get close to each other. Son Conrad, fragile after spending four months in a psychiatric hospital, returns home to a cold mother and a befuddled father who tries to connect with him. Perfectionist mother Beth wants everything to appear normal with no acknowledgment of the grief experienced by all parties. As a condition of his release, Conrad must visit psychiatrist Dr. Tyrone Berger, who helps the boy get in touch with his feelings and understand his relationship to his withholding mother. Conrad also finds romance and companionship with a girl from his school choir.

Cast

Donald Sutherland: Calvin Jarrett
Mary Tyler Moore: Beth Jarrett
Judd Hirsch: Dr. Tyrone C. Berger
Timothy Hutton: Conrad Jarrett
M. Emmett Walsh: Coach Salan
Elizabeth McGovern: Jeannine Pratt
Dinah Manoff: Karen

Behind the Scenes

Director: Robert Redford
Writers: Judith Guest (novel), Alvin Sargent (screenplay), Nancy Dowd (uncredited)
Producer: Ronald L. Schwary
Film Editor: Jeff Kanew
Cinematographer: John Bailey
Original Music: Marvin Hamlisch

Awards

Oscar Winners: Best Supporting Actor, Best Director, Best Picture, Best Writing—Adapted Screenplay

Trivia

• This was the film debut of both Timothy Hutton and Elizabeth McGovern.

1970
The Out of Towners

Overview

Genre: Comedy
Duration: 98 min
Color: Color
Country: USA
MPAA Rating: G
Studio: Paramount Pictures

George and Gwen Kellerman of Dayton, Ohio, are on their way to New York where George has a big job interview. Though they have their itinerary worked out to perfection, their best-laid plans go awry. After their flight gets diverted, these two intrepid souls must contend with lost luggage and a train ride from hell before they even make it to the Big Apple. Once there, their real nightmare begins. From garbage strikes to mistaken identity to muggings, the Kellermans must negotiate a veritable obstacle course of metropolitan land mines. For anyone who has ever had a trip go horribly wrong, *The Out of Towners* will bring back those painfully hilarious memories.

Cast

Jack Lemmon: George Kellerman
Sandy Dennis: Gwen Kellerman
Sandy Baron: Lenny Moyers
Philip Bruns: Officer Meyers
Graham Jarvis: Murray the mugger
Carlos Montalban: Manuel Vargas

Behind the Scenes

Director: Arthur Hiller
Writer: Neil Simon
Producer: Paul Nathan
Film Editor: Fred A. Chulack
Cinematographer: Andrew Laszlo
Original Music: Quincy Jones

Awards

Golden Globe Nominations: Best Actor—Comedy/Musical, Best Actress—Comedy/Musical

Trivia

• Typically, Neil Simon writes plays first and then adapts them; but the number of locations involved in the story convinced him to write *The Out of Towners* directly for the screen.

1942
The Palm Beach Story

Overview

Genre: Comedy/ Romance
Duration: 88 min
Color: Black and White
Country: USA
MPAA Rating: Not Rated
Studio: Paramount Pictures

An often overlooked and underrated screwball comedy, *The Palm Beach Story* centers around Geraldine and Tom Jeffers, a young married couple struggling to make ends meet. When Gerry comes to the realization that she can be of more use to her husband's career as a single woman, she leaves in hopes of meeting someone rich who can help finance his unique project. On her way to the wealthy playground of Palm Beach, Gerry finds herself the guest of a drunken hunting club that buys her passage aboard the train. She eventually meets a well-mannered millionaire who becomes quite smitten with her. Gerry's harebrained plans may just be working, but Tom isn't going to take this whole thing lying down.

Cast

Claudette Colbert: Geraldine "Gerry" Jeffers
Joel McCrea: Tom Jeffers (Captain McGlew)
Mary Astor: The Princess Centimillia
Rudy Vallee: John D. Hackensacker III
Sig Arno: Toto
Robert Warwick: Mr. Hinch, Ale and Quail Club
Arthur Stuart Hull: Mr. Osmond
Torben Meyer: Dr. Kluck

Behind the Scenes

Director: Preston Sturges
Writer: Preston Sturges
Producer: Buddy G. DeSylva (uncredited)
Film Editor: Stuart Gilmore
Cinematographer: Victor Milner
Original Music: Victor Young

Trivia

• This film was Rudy Vallee's first true comedic role, and it quickly earned him a contract from Paramount and an award for Best Actor of 1942 from the National Board of Review.
• Many of the original versions of this film were considered far too inappropriate. Censors at the Hays Office rejected several drafts of the script for being too "sex suggestive." They believed it treated the topics of marriage and divorce too lightly, and found that the character John D. Hackensacker III was too similar to John D. Rockefeller.

1973
Paper Moon

Overview

Genre: Comedy/Drama
Duration: 102 min
Color: Black and White
Country: USA
MPAA Rating: PG
Studio: Paramount Pictures

Yet another black and white gem from director Peter Bogdanovich, this one is set during the depression and follows the exploits of grifter Moses ("Mose") Pray. A charlatan who makes his living selling personalized bibles, Mose attends a funeral where he is asked to take the dead woman's orphaned daughter Addie—who bears a striking resemblance to Moses—to an aunt's house in Missouri. Along the way Mose comes to realize that this little spitfire is every bit the con man that he is . . . if not better. Real-life father and daughter Ryan and Tatum O'Neal bring a great natural chemistry to their roles and, at 10 years old, Tatum became the youngest person to win an Academy Award for her role as Addie.

Cast

Ryan O'Neal: Moses Pray
Tatum O'Neal: Addie Loggins
Madeline Kahn: Trixie Delight
John Hillerman: Deputy Hardin/Jess Hardin
P.J. Johnson: Imogene
Jessie Lee Fulton: Miss Ollie
James N. Harrell: The minister
Lila Waters: The minister's wife

Behind the Scenes

Director: Peter Bogdanovich
Writers: Joe David Brown (novel), Alvin Sargent (screenplay)
Producers: Peter Bogdanovich, Frank Marshall
Film Editor: Verna Fields
Cinematographer: Laszlo Kovacs

Trivia

• Although Tatum O'Neal's award was for a supporting role, hers is widely considered the most substantial role ever nominated as a supporting performance, as she is onscreen for almost the entirety of the film.
• The cigarettes that Tatum O'Neal smokes were made of lettuce and contained no nicotine.

Awards

Oscar Winners: Best Supporting Actress
Oscar Nominations: Best Supporting Actress, Best Sound, Best Writing—Adapted Screenplay

1970
Patton

Overview

Genre: Drama/
Biography
Duration: 170 min
Color: Color
Country: USA
MPAA Rating: PG
Studio: Twentieth
Century Fox

George C. Scott delivers a "command" performance as larger-than-life U.S. General George S. Patton. Starting with his brilliant campaign against Erwin "The Desert Fox" Rommel's German army in North Africa, Patton's military brilliance is evident. But so too is his hubris, as he gets into a "can you top this" contest of conquest with British Field Marshal Bernard Montgomery in Sicily. After slapping a crying soldier in an army hospital, he all but sabotages his entire career and overshadows his many accomplishments. Clearly the characteristics that made him a great leader also made him an impossible person. But that person, flaws and all, makes for fascinating viewing.

Cast

George C. Scott: General George S. Patton Jr.
Karl Malden: General Omar N. Bradley
Stephen Young: Captain Chester B. Hansen
Michael Strong: Brigadier General Hobart Carver
Frank Latimore: Lieutenanent Henry Davenport
Karl Michael Vogler: Field Marshal Erwin Rommel

Behind the Scenes

Director: Franklin J. Schaffner
Writers: Omar N. Bradley and Ladislas Farago (book), Francis Ford Coppola and Edmund H. North (screenplay)
Producer: Frank McCarthy
Film Editor: Hugh S. Fowler
Cinematographer: Fred J. Koenekamp

Trivia

• George C. Scott rejected both his nomination and win of the Academy Award for Best Actor, because he thought that competition between actors was unfair. Producer Frank McCarthy accepted the award on his behalf but returned it to the Academy the day after the ceremony as Scott wanted.

Awards

Oscar Winners: Best Actor, Best Art Direction, Best Director, Best Film Editing, Best Picture, Best Sound, Best Writing
Oscar Nominations: Best Cinematography, Best Effects—Visual, Best Music

1985
Pee-wee's Big Adventure

Overview

Genre: Comedy
Duration: 90 min
Color: Color
(Technicolor)
Country: USA
MPAA Rating: PG
Studio: Warner Bros.
Pictures

Paul Reubens stars as his adolescent alter ego Pee-wee Herman in this comic caper. When Pee-wee's beloved bicycle gets stolen, he takes off on a cross-country odyssey to track it down. Along the way he runs across an assortment of colorful characters including an escaped convict and a strange trucker named Large Marge. While he has little luck in finding his bike, Pee-wee still manages to put on quite a show in a biker bar and play hero to a pet shop full of animals. Directed by Tim Burton, *Pee-wee's Big Adventure* has a fantastic cartoon look to match its subject matter. Already a pop culture icon before the movie, Pee-wee Herman is now also forever linked to the song "Tequila."

Cast

Paul Reubens: Pee-wee Herman
Elizabeth Daily: Dottie
Mark Holton: Francis Buxton
Diane Salinger: Simone
Judd Omen: Mickey
Irving Hellman: Mr. Crowtray
Monte Landis: Mario
Damon Martin: Chip

Behind the Scenes

Director: Tim Burton
Writers: Phil Hartman, Paul Reubens, Michael Varhol
Producers: Richard Gilbert Abramson, Robert Shapiro, Paul Reubens (uncredited)
Executive Producers: William E. McEuen
Cinematographer: Victor J. Kemper
Original Music: Danny Elfman

Trivia

• When Pee-wee first arrives at Warner Bros. Studios, the Batmobile enters on the left side of the screen, behind the blue Warner Bros. sign, and turns left away from the camera.
• Director Tim Burton has a brief cameo as one of the street toughs who set upon Pee-wee.
• As the Alamo tour guide, actress Jan Hooks made up much of her spiel on the spot.

1940
The Philadelphia Story

Overview

Genre: Comedy/ Romance
Duration: 112 min
Color: Black and White
Country: USA
MPAA Rating: Not Rated
Studio: Metro-Goldwyn-Mayer (MGM)

A hilarious romantic comedy, *The Philadelphia Story* centers around the broken marriage of socialite Tracy Lord and her playboy ex-husband C.K. Dexter Haven. A couple of years after their breakup, Tracy is set to marry the well-to-do George Kittridge. As all of this is about to happen, Dexter catches wind of a scandal sheet's plans to publish a smear piece on Tracy's father. Still having a soft spot for his ex, Dexter makes a deal with the magazine to get two of its reporters into Tracy's wedding in exchange for them dropping their other story. Dexter's selfless act may just save the day, or upset the applecart.

Cast

Cary Grant: C.K. Dexter Haven
Katharine Hepburn: Tracy Lord
James Stewart: Macaulay Connor
Ruth Hussey: Elizabeth Imbrie
John Howard: George Kittredge
Roland Young: Uncle Willie
John Halliday: Seth Lord

Behind the Scenes

Director: George Cukor
Writers: Philip Barry (play), Donald Ogden Stewart (screenplay), Waldo Salt (uncredited)
Producer: Joseph L. Mankiewicz
Film Editor: Frank Sullivan
Cinematographer: Joseph Ruttenberg
Original Music: Franz Waxman

Awards

Oscar Winners: Best Actor, Best Writing
Oscar Nominations: Best Director, Best Actress, Best Supporting Actress, Best Picture

Trivia

- Billionaire Howard Hughes bought the film rights to *The Philadelphia Story* and gave them to Katharine Hepburn as a gift.

1959
Pillow Talk

Overview

Genre: Comedy
Duration: 102 min
Color: Color (Eastmancolor)
Country: USA
MPAA Rating: Not Rated
Studio: Universal International Pictures

Due to a shortage of telephone lines, interior decorator career gal Jan Morrow must share her phone line with womanizing Broadway composer Brad Allen. Irked that Brad hogs the phone singing the same "original" love song to each conquest, Jan lambastes Brad, and the two spar continually over the phone. When Brad spots a woman who piques his interest in a club and, recognizing her voice, realizes it's Jan, he concocts an alter ego, wealthy Texan Rex Stetson, to woo her. Jan does fall for Stetson, but eventually learns the truth, and Brad comes to the realization that maybe this woman isn't like all the others.

Cast

Rock Hudson: Brad Allen
Doris Day: Jan Morrow
Tony Randall: Jonathan Forbes
Thelma Ritter: Alma
Nick Adams: Tony Walters
Julia Meade: Marie
Allen Jenkins: Harry

Behind the Scenes

Director: Michael Gordon
Writers: Russell Rouse and Clarence Green (story), Maurice Richlin and Stanly Shapiro (screenplay)
Producers: Ross Hunter, Martin Melcher
Executive Producer: Edward Muhl
Cinematographer: Arthur E. Arling

Awards

Oscar Winners: Best Writing
Oscar Nominations: Best Actress, Best Supporting Actress, Best Art Direction, Best Music

Trivia

• At the end of the film Rock Hudson picks up Doris Day. After many takes, the crew had to devise a harness that hooked over Hudson's shoulders to help him lift her.

The Pink Panther Strikes Again

Overview

Genre: Comedy/Crime
Duration: 103 min
Color: Color
Country: UK and USA
MPAA Rating: PG
Studio: United Artists

Peter Sellers returns for arguably the funniest chapter in the sidesplitting misadventures of French police inspector Jacques Clouseau. In this installment, Clouseau's old boss—former Chief Inspector Dreyfus—has gone irretrievably insane and won't rest until Clouseau is dead. Of course, as Dreyfus already knows, killing the bumbling detective is a lot more difficult than it sounds. But Dreyfus has a backup plan. If he can't do away with Clouseau himself, he'll hold the world hostage with a death ray until someone does it for him. For his fourth time around in this role, Sellers is remarkably fresh and incredibly funny, donning ridiculous disguises and clumsily avoiding one assassination attempt after another.

Cast

Peter Sellers: Chief Inspector Jacques Clouseau
Herbert Lom: Charles Dreyfus
Lesley-Anne Down: Olga Bariosova
Burt Kwouk: Cato Fong
Colin Blakely: Section Director Alec Drummond
Leonard Rossiter: Superintendent Quinlan
André Maranne: Sergeant François Chevalier
(as Andre Maranne)

Behind the Scenes

Director: Blake Edwards
Writers: Blake Edwards, Frank Waldman
Producer: Blake Edwards
Film Editor: Alan Jones
Cinematographer: Harry Waxman
Original Music: Henry Mancini

Trivia

• The "pink panther" is a priceless diamond featured in the first and second Clouseau Pink Panther films. In *The Pink Panther Strikes Again*, there is no mention of the diamond.

Awards

Oscar Nominations: Best Music—Original Song

1940
Pinocchio

Overview

Genre: Family/Musical
Duration: 88 min
Color: Color (Technicolor)
Country: USA
MPAA Rating: G
Studio: Walt Disney Productions

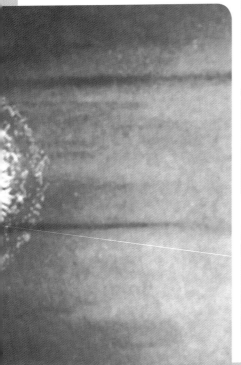

Daring to wish upon a star, lonely wood-carver Geppetto wins the favor of the Blue Fairy, who grants his wish and gives life to Geppetto's marionette, Pinocchio. Warning that he must earn the right to be a real boy, the Blue Fairy leaves Pinocchio in the hands of Jiminy Cricket, an affable character who agrees to act as Pinocchio's conscience. Barely has Pinocchio left Geppetto's loving arms, however, when the world shows its fangs. Captured by the duplicitous Honest John, Pinocchio's real dangers turn out to be his own character flaws. His trials are set in Disney's fantastical world, but his ultimate lesson—that being real depends on strength of character and an open heart—has proven itself universally appealing.

Cast

Mel Blanc: Cleo/Figaro/Gideon (uncredited)
Walter Catlett: Honest John (uncredited)
Frankie Darro: Lampwick (uncredited)
Cliff Edwards: Jiminy Cricket (uncredited)
Dickie Jones: Alexander/Pinocchio (uncredited)
Charles Judels: The Coachman/Stromboli (uncredited)
Christian Rub: Geppetto (uncredited)
Evelyn Venable: The Blue Fairy (uncredited)

Behind the Scenes

Directors: Hamilton Luske, Ben Sharpsteen
Writers: Carlo Collodi (story), Ted Sears, Otto Englander, Webb Smith, William Cottrell, Joseph Sabo, Erdman Penner, Aurelius Battaglia
Producer: Walt Disney
Original Music: Leigh Harline, Paul Smith

Trivia

• When Pinocchio is changed into a real boy, his hands become real human 5-fingered hands, but as a puppet he has 4 fingers and white gloves.
• *Pinocchio* was the first Disney movie available for sale on DVD.

Awards

Oscar Winners: Best Music, Best Music—Original Song

1987
Planes, Trains, and Automobiles

Overview

Genre: Comedy
Duration: 93 min
Color: Color
(Technicolor)
Country: USA
MPAA Rating: R
Studio: Paramount
Pictures

Ad executive Neal Page is desperate to get out of New York and back to Chicago in time to spend Thanksgiving with his family. All he has to do is navigate some holiday traffic, airport delays, and a fellow passenger named Del Griffith. As one thing after another throws these unlikely traveling companions together, disaster and hilarity seem to follow. In fact, the way things are going, these two may not even make it home in time for Christmas. Steve Martin and John Candy prove a powerhouse comedic pairing as uptight Page and the genial but grating Griffith. John Hughes' *Planes, Trains, and Automobiles* serves up plenty of laughs with room left over for a heartwarming dessert.

Cast

Steve Martin: Neal Page
John Candy: Del Griffith
Laila Robins: Susan Page
Michael McKean: State trooper
Kevin Bacon: Taxi racer
Dylan Baker: Owen
Carol Bruce: Joy Page
Olivia Burnette: Marti Page

Behind the Scenes

Director: John Hughes
Writer: John Hughes
Producer: John Hughes
Executive Producers: Michael Chinich, Neil A. Machlis
Cinematographer: Donald Peterman
Original Music: Ira Newborn

Trivia

• In the classic Marathon car rental scene, the f-bomb is dropped some 18 times in around one minute of screen time.
• In one scene where Neal Page calls home, you can hear dialogue from another John Hughes movie—*She's Having a Baby*—on the TV in the background.

1968
Planet of the Apes

Overview

Genre: Sci-Fi/ Adventure
Duration: 112 min
Color: Color
Country: USA
MPAA Rating: G
Studio: Twentieth Century Fox

When three astronauts emerge from hibernation after some 2,000 years in space, they find that their ship has landed on a strange planet somewhat resembling Earth. After scouting around, they soon discover a colony of mute humans living almost like cavemen. They barely have time to process this sight before a group of militant gorillas ride in on horseback, killing one of the men and capturing the other two. When all is said and done, the lone survivor, George Taylor, realizes that he is trapped on a planet ruled by intelligent apes where humans are the un-evolved animals. An all-time sci-fi classic, *Planet of the Apes* will definitely make you think twice about whether we're any better than our thoughtful primate cousins.

Cast

Charlton Heston: George Taylor
Roddy McDowall: Cornelius
Kim Hunter: Zira
Maurice Evans: Dr. Zaius
James Whitmore: President of the Assembly
James Daly: Honorious
Linda Harrison: Nova
Robert Gunner: Landon

Behind the Scenes

Director: Franklin J. Schaffner
Writers: Pierre Boulle (novel), Michael Wilson and Rod Serling (screenplay)
Producer: Arthur P. Jacobs
Film Editor: Hugh S. Fowler
Cinematographer: Leon Shamroy
Original Music: Jerry Goldsmith

Trivia

• Several other productions were delayed because many of Hollywood's top makeup artists were working on this film—80 in all. Their work, especially that of designer John Chambers, garnered one of only two honorary awards for makeup in history (a category for best makeup was created in 1981).

Awards

Oscar Winners: Honorary Award for John Chambers' outstanding makeup achievement in the movie
Oscar Nominations: Best Costume Design, Best Music

1986
Platoon

Overview

Genre: Drama/War
Duration: 120 min
Color: Color
Country: UK/USA
MPAA Rating: R
Studio: Orion Pictures

An inexperienced army soldier gets a crash course in battlefield ethics—or lack thereof—in this gripping war drama. Charlie Sheen stars as Chris Taylor, a young student who volunteers for duty and, upon arriving in Vietnam, soon finds out how untenable the war is. Two very different men lead his platoon. Sergeant Bob Barnes is a battle-scarred killing machine and Sergeant Elias Grodin is a more cerebral leader who understands that his actions affect the lives of many. From rain and heat to raids and firefights, Private Taylor gets the full war experience as the men fight both the enemy and each other.

Cast

Tom Berenger: Sergeant Bob Barnes
Willem Dafoe: Sergeant Elias Grodin
Charlie Sheen: Private Chris Taylor
Forest Whitaker: Big Harold
Francesco Quinn: Rhah
John C. McGinley: Sergeant Red O'Neill
Kevin Dillon: Bunny
Johnny Depp: Private Gator Lerner
Reggie Johnson: Junior Martin

Behind the Scenes

Director: Oliver Stone
Writer: Oliver Stone
Producers: Arnold Kopelson, A. Kitman Ho
Executive Producers: John Daly, Derek Gibson
Film Editor: Claire Simpson
Cinematographer: Robert Richardson
Original Music: Georges Delerue

Trivia

• Johnny Depp, who plays Private Gator Lerner, wrote the name Sherilyn on his helmet for his girlfriend at the time, actress Sherilyn Fenn.
• Before shooting the film, all of the actors were required to participate in a 14-day boot camp, in which they were given military haircuts and deprived of sleep and showers.

Awards

Oscar Winners: Best Director, Best Film Editing, Best Picture, Best Sound
Oscar Nominations: Best Supporting Actor, Best Supporting Actor, Best Cinematography, Best Writing

1982
Poltergeist

Overview

Genre: Horror/Thriller
Duration: 114 min
Color: Color (Metrocolor)
Country: USA
MPAA Rating: PG
Studio: Metro-Goldwyn-Mayer (MGM)

The Freelings are your everyday American family; they live in an average house and lead ordinary lives. One night as everyone is sleeping, five-year-old Carol Anne sits transfixed by the white glow of the family television set and begins talking to the "TV people." This seemingly innocuous incident kicks off a string of unexplainable phenomena. In the beginning these odd events are more curious than anything else, but all of that changes when Carol Anne disappears into an alternate dimension where spirits are holding her captive. Calling in paranormal specialists to help locate their daughter, the Freelings will stop at nothing to get her back.

Cast

Craig T. Nelson: Steve Freeling
JoBeth Williams: Diane Freeling
Beatrice Straight: Dr. Lesh
Dominique Dunne: Dana Freeling
Oliver Robins: Robbie Freeling
Heather O'Rourke: Carol Anne Freeling
Michael McManus: Ben Tuthill

Behind the Scenes

Director: Tobe Hooper
Writers: Steven Spielberg (story and screenplay), Michael Grais and Mark Victor (screenplay)
Producers: Frank Marshall, Steven Spielberg
Cinematographer: Matthew F. Leonetti
Original Music: Jerry Goldsmith

Awards

Oscar Nominations: Best Effects—Sound, Best Effects—Visual, Best Music

Trivia

• Steven Spielberg incorporated two of his own childhood fears—clowns and scary trees—into character Robbie Freeling's nightmare encounters.

1984
The Pope of Greenwich Village

Overview

Genre: Drama/Crime
Duration: 121 min
Color: Color
(Metrocolor)
Country: USA
MPAA Rating: R
Studio: United Artists

Not your usual movie about cops and goombahs, *The Pope of Greenwich Village* is part crime caper, part character study, and all good. Out on the street, Charlie is staring down child support and alimony payments to his ex-wife as well as being that much farther away from owning his own place. His cousin Paulie, meanwhile, is thinking big; he wants to buy a racehorse and just may have stumbled onto the sweetest little score that could be the answer to all of their financial problems. Featuring standout performances by Mickey Rourke, Eric Roberts, Geraldine Page and countless others, *The Pope of Greenwich Village* is a terrific film that never got its due.

Cast

Eric Roberts: Paulie
Mickey Rourke: Charlie
Daryl Hannah: Diane
Geraldine Page: Mrs. Ritter
Kenneth McMillan: Barney
Burt Young: Bed Bug Eddie
Jack Kehoe: Bunky

Behind the Scenes

Director: Stuart Rosenberg
Writer: Vincent Patrick (novel and screenplay)
Producers: Gene Kirkwood, Hawk Koch
Film Editor: Robert Brown
Cinematographer: John Bailey

Awards

Oscar Nominations: Best Supporting Actress

Trivia

• Michael Cimino was originally slated to direct but was replaced by Stuart Rosenberg, who directed *Cool Hand Luke*, among other films.

1990
Pretty Woman

Overview

Genre: Comedy/ Romance
Duration: 119 min
Color: Color
Country: USA
MPAA Rating: R
Studio: Touchstone Pictures

This modern day fairytale follows the unlikely romance of Edward, a high-powered business-man, and Vivian, a beautiful prostitute. The two meet on Edward's business trip to Los Angeles and Vivian agrees to act as his professional "date" for the week. As Edward treats Vivian to the best dinners, the opera, and lavish shopping sprees, she opens his eyes to the simpler things: teaching him how to be himself, let loose, and enjoy life. The more time the two spend together the more they grow to care for one another. But can a relationship between two such opposites ever really work? It's up to these two to see if they can write their own Hollywood ending.

Cast

Richard Gere: Edward Lewis
Julia Roberts: Vivian Ward
Ralph Bellamy: James Morse
Jason Alexander: Philip Stuckey
Laura San Giacomo: Kit De Luca
Alex Hyde-White: David Morse
Hector Elizondo: Barney Thompson

Behind the Scenes

Director: Garry Marshall
Writer: J.F. Lawton
Producers: Arnon Milchan, Steven Reuther
Executive Producer: Laura Ziskin
Film Editors: Raja Gosnell, Priscilla Nedd
Cinematographer: Charles Minsky
Original Music: James Newton Howard

Awards

Oscar Nominations: Best Actress

Trivia

• The necklace that Vivian wears to the opera cost $250,000. A security man from the jeweler was on the set watching after it.

1987
The Princess Bride

Overview

Genre: Family/
Adventure
Duration: 98 min
Color: Color
Country: USA
MPAA Rating: PG
Studio: Twentieth
Century Fox

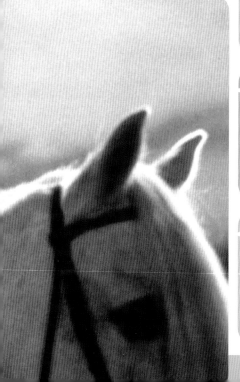

A grandfather visits his sick grandson with a special book: *The Princess Bride*. As he reads it, avoiding the "kissing parts" at his resistant grandson's request, the story comes alive. In this comedic twist on the classic fairy tale adventure, farm boy Westley, after his apparent death at sea, sets forth on a quest to rescue his childhood love, Buttercup, who has been kidnapped by a gang of villains intent on using her to start an international conflict. Unfortunately, Buttercup has agreed to marry the crafty Prince Humperdinck, who follows close behind. Westley is soon joined by a friendly giant and skilled swordsman with his own debt to settle as he continues on, motivated by the power of True Love.

Cast

Cary Elwes: Westley
Mandy Patinkin: Inigo Montoya
Chris Sarandon: Prince Humperdinck
Christopher Guest: Count Tyrone Rugen
Wallace Shawn: Vizzini
André the Giant: Fezzik
Fred Savage: The Grandson
Robin Wright Penn: Buttercup
Peter Falk: The Grandfather/Narrator

Behind the Scenes

Director: Rob Reiner
Writer: William Goldman (novel and screenplay)
Producers: Rob Reiner, Andrew Scheinman
Executive Producer: Norman Lear
Film Editor: Robert Leighton
Cinematographer: Adrian Biddle
Original Music: Mark Knopfler

Trivia

• When William Goldman originally wanted the film to be made, in the 1970's, Arnold Schwarzenegger was seriously considered for the part of Fezzik. By the time the movie was made, Schwarzenegger was too expensive to be cast and André the Giant played the part instead.

Awards

Oscar Nominations: Best Music—Original Song

1967
The Producers

Overview

Genre: Comedy
Duration: 88 min
Color: Color (Pathécolor)
Country: USA
MPAA Rating: PG
Studio: Crossbow Productions/MGM/ Springtime Productions

Max Bialystock is complete charlatan who somehow manages to finance his horrible theatrical productions by charming little old ladies out of their money. When nebbishy accountant Leo Bloom comes to take a look at Max's books, he makes the mistake of mentioning that a lot of money could be made by producing a Broadway flop. You can almost see the light bulb go on over Bialystock's head as he bullies Bloom into becoming his partner in what will hopefully be the worst show in Broadway history. While many know *The Producers* as the Tony-winning Broadway musical or its disappointing 2005 film adaptation, it's this version that is by far the funniest.

Cast

Zero Mostel: Max Bialystock
Gene Wilder: Leo Bloom
Dick Shawn: "L.S.D." (Lorenzo St. DuBois)
Kenneth Mars: Franz Liebkind
Lee Meredith: Ulla
Christopher Hewett: Roger De Bris
Andréas Voutsinas: Carmen Ghia

Behind the Scenes

Director: Mel Brooks
Writer: Mel Brooks
Producers: Sidney Glazier, Jack Grossberg
Film Editor: Ralph Rosenblum
Cinematographer: Joseph F. Coffey
Original Music: John Morris

Awards

Oscar Winners: Best Writing
Oscar Nominations: Best Supporting Actor

Trivia

• The film was banned in Germany due to the musical number "Springtime for Hitler." It finally played in that country during a festival celebrating Jewish filmmakers.

1960
Psycho

Overview

Genre: Horror/Thriller
Duration: 109 min
Color: Black and White
Country: USA
MPAA Rating: R
Studio: Paramount Pictures

Marion Crane is fed up with her job at a Phoenix real estate office and equally tired of her stagnant relationship with hardware store owner Sam Loomis. When she's asked to deposit $40,000 in cash into the bank, she instead sees a chance to change her life and takes off with the money. On her way to rendezvous with Sam, Marion gets caught in a torrential rainstorm and decides to take refuge at the Bates Motel. The proprietor of the motel is the shy and somewhat twitchy Norman Bates who generously invites her to dinner in the house that he shares with his domineering mother. What could possibly go wrong?

Cast

Anthony Perkins: Norman Bates
Janet Leigh: Marion Crane
Vera Miles: Lila Crane
John Gavin: Sam Loomis
Martin Balsam: Milton Arbogast
John McIntire: Sheriff Al Chambers
Simon Oakland: Dr. Fred Richmond

Behind the Scenes

Director: Alfred Hitchcock
Writers: Robert Bloch (novel), Joseph Stefano (screenplay)
Producer: Alfred Hitchcock (uncredited)
Film Editor: George Tomasini
Cinematographer: John L. Russell
Original Music: Bernard Herrmann

Awards

Oscar Nominations: Best Supporting Actress, Best Art Direction, Best Cinematography, Best Director

Trivia

• The Bates house was modeled on Edward Hopper's painting, *House by the Railroad*.

1994
Pulp Fiction

Overview

Genre: Drama/Crime
Duration: 154 min
Color: Color
Country: USA
MPAA Rating: R
Studio: Miramax Films

Quentin Tarantino's casserole of drugs, double-crosses, dirty deeds, and dancing mixes perfectly and bubbles over in this wildly entertaining film. Vincent and Jules are two slick hit men working for crime boss Marcellus Wiley. Mia Wallace is married to Marcellus and just looking for a fun night out. Butch Coolidge is a boxer who may be having second thoughts about taking a dive. And jittery bandits Pumpkin and Honey Bunny just want to rob a diner. Sounds simple enough, but when these various players cross paths the results are explosive. Add in an assortment of other quirky characters and a great soundtrack and you get a movie that will leave you hungry for more.

Cast

John Tavolta: Vincent Vega
Samuel L. Jackson: Jules Winnfield
Uma Thurman: Mia Wallace
Bruce Willis: Butch Coolidge
Tim Roth: Pumpkin (Ringo)
Amanda Plummer: Honey Bunny (Yolanda)
Eric Stoltz: Lance

Behind the Scenes

Director: Quentin Tarantino
Writers: Quentin Tarantino, Roger Avary
Producer: Lawrence Bender
Executive Producers: Danny DeVito, Michael Shamberg, Stacey Sher
Film Editor: Sally Menke
Cinematographer: Andrzej Sekula

Awards

Oscar Winners: Best Writing
Oscar Nominations: Best Actor, Best Supporting Actor, Best Supporting Actress, Best Director, Best Film Editing, Best Picture

Trivia

• Quentin Tarantino read the entire script to Uma Thurman over the phone to convince her to take the role of Mia Wallace, after she turned it down once.

2006
The Queen

Overview

Genre: Drama
Duration: 97 min
Color: Color
Country: UK
MPAA Rating: PG-13
Studio: Miramax Films

This film explores the Royal Family's lack of response to the death of Princess Diana in 1997. A devastated public, shocked by what it perceives as blatant disregard for the "People's Princess," demands that Queen Elizabeth II come forward to acknowledge Princess Diana's untimely death and celebrate her life of service. Stoic and inundated by years of policy, breeding, and expectation, the Queen misjudges her role in a modern society and struggles with the hostility of her people and the demands of the newly elected Tony Blair. This film offers a more personal understanding of the woman behind the monarchy.

Cast

Helen Mirren: The Queen
James Cromwell: Prince Philip
Alex Jennings: Prince Charles
Roger Allam: Robin Janvrin
Sylvia Syms: Queen Mother
Tim McMullan: Stephen Lamport
Robin Soans: Equerry

Behind the Scenes

Director: Stephen Frears
Writer: Peter Morgan
Producers: Andy Harries, Christine Langan, Tracey Seaward
Executive Producers: François Ivernel, Cameron McCracken, Scott Rudin
Cinematographer: Affonso Beato

Awards

Oscar Winners: Best Actress
Oscar Nominations: Best Costume Design, Best Director, Best Music, Best Picture, Best Writing

Trivia

• To better portray Elizabeth II, Helen Mirren studied her minutely, reviewing film and video footage and keeping photographs of the monarch in her trailer during production.

1952
The Quiet Man

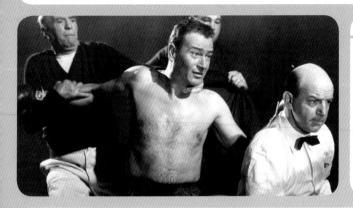

Overview

Genre: Drama/Romance
Duration: 129 min
Color: Color (Technicolor)
Country: USA
MPAA Rating: Not Rated
Studio: Argosy Pictures

John Wayne stars as Sean Thornton, a boxer who retires to Ireland after accidentally killing one of his opponents. On his way back to his birthplace of Innisfree, he spies a red-haired beauty named Mary Kate Danaher. It just so happens that Mary Kate's brutish brother Will wants to buy the same cottage that Sean eventually purchases. Sean and Mary Kate's courtship and eventual marriage only serve to further antagonize her brother. When Will Danaher refuses to give Mary Kate her wedding dowry, Sean may have to fight for it. But will his tragic past allow him to raise his hands against another man?

Cast

John Wayne: Sean Thornton
Maureen O'Hara: Mary Kate Danaher
Barry Fitzgerald: Michaleen Oge Flynn
Ward Bond: Father Peter Lonergan
Victor McLaglen: Squire "Red" Will Danaher
Charles B. Fitzsimons: Hugh Forbes
James O'Hara: Father Paul

Behind the Scenes

Director: John Ford
Writers: Maurice Walsh (story), Frank S. Nugent (screenplay)
Producers: Merian C. Cooper, G.B. Forbes, John Ford, L.T. Rosso
Film Editor: Jack Murray
Cinematographer: Winton C. Hoch

Awards

Oscar Winners: Best Cinematography, Best Director

Trivia

• John Wayne's reaction to Maureen O'Hara's whisper after the credits is genuine, just as Ford planned. O'Hara agreed to say the line only if it would remain a secret and it has.

1994
Quiz Show

Overview

Genre: Drama
Duration: 133 min
Color: Color
Country: USA
MPAA Rating: PG-13
Studio: Hollywood
Pictures/Buena Vista

R obert Redford directed this fascinating drama about the television game show scandal that rocked America in the late 1950s. An Ivy League English professor and the son of a renowned literary family, Charles Van Doren was the darling of the air waves as he dominated his competition on the popular quiz show "Twenty-One" week after week. But after disgruntled former "Twenty-One" champ Herb Stempel starts crying "foul," Congress begins investigating: were Van Doren and other contestants on the popular show given the answers to questions in advance? A terrifically entertaining look at a scandal that changed television forever, *Quiz Show* features outstanding performances by Ralph Fiennes and John Turturro as Van Doren and Stempel.

Cast

John Turturro: Herbie Stempel
Rob Morrow: Dick Goodwin
Ralph Fiennes: Charles Van Doren
Paul Scofield: Mark Van Doren
David Paymer: Dan Enright
Hank Azaria: Albert Freedman
Christopher McDonald: Jack Barry
Elizabeth Wilson: Dorothy Van Doren
Mira Sorvino: Sandra Goodwin

Behind the Scenes

Director: Robert Redford
Writers: Richard N. Goodwin (book), Paul Attanasio (screenplay)
Producers: Michael Jacobs, Julian Krainin, Michael Nozik, Robert Redford
Executive Producers: Fred Zollo, Richard Dreyfuss
Film Editor: Stu Linder

Trivia

• Because he wanted to mirror the real Charles Van Doren's accent accurately, and it was assumed that Van Doren would not want to help the film, Ralph Fiennes drove to the town where Van Doren lived and found him sitting outside his house. Fiennes pretended to be lost and asked Van Doren for directions.

Awards

Oscar Nominations: Best Supporting Actor, Best Director, Best Picture, Best Writing—Adapted Screenplay

1980
Raging Bull

Overview

Genre: Drama/Sports
Duration: 129 min
Color: Black and White
Country: USA
MPAA Rating: R
Studio: United Artists

Jake La Motta's boxing career was as brutal and tumultuous outside the ring as it was inside. Robert De Niro turns in an Oscar-winning performance as the volatile and violent middleweight champ who seems bent on destroying everything in his path as well as himself. Filmed in black and white, this 1980 biopic follows La Motta through his many clashes in the ring—including his vicious rivalry with Sugar Ray Robinson—as well as his bouts of paranoia, which prove to be equally damaging. The final result is a stark, unvarnished portrait of a single-minded fighter and seriously flawed human being. *Raging Bull* is as real a boxing movie as you are likely to see.

Cast

Robert De Niro: Jake La Motta
Cathy Moriarty: Vickie Thailer
Joe Pesci: Joey La Motta
Frank Vincent: Salvy Batts
Nicholas Colasanto: Tommy Como
Theresa Saldana: Lenore
Mario Gallo: Mario

Behind the Scenes

Director: Martin Scorsese
Writers: Jake LaMotta, Joseph Carter, and Peter Savage (book), Paul Schrader, Mardik Martin, and Martin Scorsese (screenplay)
Producers: Robert Chartoff, Irwin Winkler
Film Editor: Thelma Schoonmaker
Cinematographer: Michael Chapman

Awards

Oscar Winners: Best Actor, Best Film Editing
Oscar Nominations: Best Supporting Actor, Best Supporting Actress, Best Cinematography, Best Director, Best Pictures, Best Sound

Trivia

• Robert De Niro and Joe Pesci did not pull their punches in their infamous "hit me" exchange.
• Robert De Niro gained 60 pounds to play the older Jake La Motta.

1981
Raiders of the Lost Ark

Overview

Genre: Action/Adventure
Duration: 115 min
Color: Color
Country: USA
MPAA Rating: PG
Studio: Paramount Pictures

Hollywood heavyweights George Lucas and Steven Speilberg team up to bring you one of the best adventure films ever. Harrison Ford stars as Indiana Jones, a professor of archaeology who tracks down rare historical treasures and artifacts in his spare time, often at great personal peril. It has come to the U.S. government's attention that the Nazis are trying to locate the Ark of the Covenant, an ancient chest said to contain the Ten Commandments tablets. Legend has it that the Ark also holds a mysterious and powerful force that would make any army in its possession unbeatable. It's up to Indiana Jones to find it before the Germans do.

Cast

Harrison Ford: Indiana Jones
Karen Allen: Marion Ravenwood
Paul Freeman: Dr. Rene Belloq
Ronald Lacey: Major Arnold Toht
John Rhys-Davies: Sallah
Denholm Elliot: Dr. Marcus Brody
Alfred Molina: Satipo

Behind the Scenes

Director: Steven Spielberg
Writers: George Lucas and Philip Kaufman (story), Lawrence Kasdan (screenplay)
Producer: Frank Marshall
Executive Producers: Howard G. Kazanjian, George Lucas
Film Editor: Michael Kahn

Awards

Oscar Winners: Best Art Direction, Best Effects—Visual, Best Film Editing, Best Sound, Special Achievement Award—Sound Effects Editing

Trivia

• When Indiana finds himself face-to-face with a cobra, there is a barely detectable sheet of glass separating the two.

1988
Rain Man

Overview

Genre: Drama
Duration: 133 min
Color: Color
Country: USA
MPAA Rating: R
Studio: United Artists

After the death of his estranged father, Charlie Babbitt learns he has an autistic brother to whom his father has bequeathed the lion's share of his estate. Charlie, a materialistic wheeler-dealer, travels to see this brother—a savant living in an institution—and kidnaps him in the hopes of seeing at least some of the inheritance. His brother Raymond has difficulty traveling, agitated by the lack of routine on the road. Charlie, however, forces him onward and on the journey remembers forgotten moments from his youth. As he discovers who he really is and what he really wants, Charlie begins to understand the necessity of family, forgiveness, and unconditional love.

Cast

Dustin Hoffman: Raymond Babbitt
Tom Cruise: Charlie Babbitt
Valeria Golino: Susanna
Gerald R. Molen: Dr. Bruner
Jack Murdock: John Mooney
Michael D. Roberts: Vern
Ralph Seymour: Lenny

Behind the Scenes

Director: Barry Levinson
Writers: Barry Morrow (story and screenplay), Ronald Bass (screenplay)
Producer: Mark Johnson
Executive Producers: Peter Guber, Jon Peters
Film Editor: Stu Linder
Cinematographer: John Seale

Awards

Oscar Winners: Best Actor, Best Director, Best Picture, Best Writing
Oscar Nominations: Best Art Direction, Best Cinematography, Best Film Editing

Trivia

• Director Barry Levinson makes a cameo appearance in the film. He plays the psychiatrist at the end of the film who is determining whether Raymond should stay with Charlie or not.

1961
A Raisin in the Sun

Overview

Genre: Drama
Duration: 128 min
Color: Black and White
Country: USA
MPAA Rating: Not Rated
Studio: Columbia Pictures

The Younger family yearns to escape the conditions of their poverty, including their cramped, rundown apartment in the South Side of Chicago. Son Walter Younger wants to invest in a liquor store, which he's sure will ensure financial security for his family, matriarch Lena and Walter's wife, Ruth, want to buy a house, and sister Beneatha wants financial support in her efforts to study medicine. When the family does buy a house, they face racial intolerance as the only African American family in the neighborhood. The stars of the movie were also in the groundbreaking original Broadway production.

Cast

Sidney Poitier: Walter Lee Younger
Claudia McNeil: Lena Younger
Ruby Dee: Ruth Younger
Diana Sands: Beneatha Younger
Ivan Dixon: Asagai
John Fiedler: Mark Lindner
Louis Gossett Jr.: George Murchison

Behind the Scenes

Director: Daniel Petrie
Writer: Lorraine Hansberry (play and screenplay)
Producers: Philip Rose, David Susskind
Film Editors: William A. Lyon, Paul Weatherwax
Cinematographer: Charles Lawton Jr.
Original Music: Laurence Rosenthal

Awards

Golden Globe Nominations: Best Actor, Best Actress
Added to National Film Registry in 2005

Trivia

• This was Louis Gossett Jr.'s film debut.
• The title for this film is taken from the Langston Hughes' poem, "Harlem (What Happens to a Dream Deferred?)."

1987
Raising Arizona

Overview

Genre: Comedy
Duration: 94 min
Color: Color
Country: USA
MPAA Rating: PG-13
Studio: Twentieth
Century Fox

A repeat offender petty thief vows to go on the straight and narrow after marrying his mug shot photographer, but their wedded bliss is interrupted when they find out they can't conceive children. H.I. McDunnough and his wife Ed are in a state of depression until they hear that a man named Nathan Arizona and his wife just gave birth to quintuplets. Feeling that the Arizonas "got more than they can handle," H.I. and Ed decide to take one of the quints for themselves. This kooky kidnapping comedy from the Coen brothers boasts a host of colorful characters, the cinematography genius of Barry Sonnenfeld, and a yodel-riffic soundtrack by Carter Burwell.

Cast

Nicolas Cage: H.I. McDunnough
Holly Hunter: Edwina "Ed" McDunnough
Trey Wilson: Nathan Arizona
John Goodman: Gale Snoats
William Forsythe: Evelle Snoats
Frances McDormand: Dot
Randall "Tex" Cobb: Leonard Smalls
T.J. Kuhn: Nathan Arizona Jr.

Behind the Scenes

Director: Joel Coen, Ethan Coen (uncredited)
Writers: Ethan Coen, Joel Coen
Producers: Ethan Coen, Joel Coen (uncredited)
Executive Producer: James Jacks
Film Editor: Michael R. Miller
Cinematographer: Barry Sonnenfeld
Original Music: Carter Burwell

Trivia

• Fifteen infants were used to play the Arizona quintuplets, one of whom was fired because he learned to walk.
• The Coen brothers wrote Holly Hunter's character, Edwina McDunnough, specifically for her.
• Randall "Tex" Cobb's bounty hunter character, Leonard Smalls, shares a similar name as "Lennie" in John Steinbeck's *Of Mice and Men*.

1951
Rashômon

Overview

Genre: Drama/Crime
Duration: 88 min
Color: Black and White
Country: Japan
MPAA Rating: PG-13
Studio: Daiei Motion Picture Company/Daiei Studios

In twelfth-century Japan, a woodcutter, a priest, and a peasant shelter from a rainstorm at the decrepit gate (*rashômon*) at the entrance to Kyoto, where the woodcutter recounts the horror of what he has witnessed. This disturbing movie examines the killing of a samurai and the rape of his wife. Notorious bandit Tajomaru ties up the husband and rapes the wife, but what really happened is told from four contradictory points (the woodcutter's, the bandit's, the wife's, and the dead husband's, through a medium). The film introduced both Akira Kurosawa and Japanese cinema to the attention of Western audiences.

Cast

Toshirô Mifune: Tajômaru
Machiko Kyô: Masako Kanazawa
Masayuki Mori: Takehiro Kanazawa
Takashi Shimura: Woodcutter
Minoru Chiaki: Priest
Kichijiro Ueda: Commoner
Fumiko Honma: Medium

Behind the Scenes

Director: Akira Kurosawa
Writers: Ryunosuke Akutagawa (stories), Akira Kurosawa and Shinobu Hashimoto (screenplay)
Producer: Minoru Jingo
Executive Producer: Masaichi Nagata
Original Music: Fumio Hayasaka

Awards

Oscar Nominations: Best Art Direction, Honorary Award for the most outstanding foreign language film released in the United States during 1951

Trivia

• This film is regularly credited as the impetus behind the Academy of Motion Picture Arts and Sciences creating the Best Foreign Film category.

2004
Ray

Overview

Genre: Biography
Duration: 152 min
Color: Color
Country: USA
MPAA Rating: PG-13
Studio: Bristol Bay Productions/Universal Pictures

You know his music. You've witnessed his incredible performances. Now see the story behind the man, in Taylor Hackford's Academy Award–nominated biopic chronicling the life of Ray Charles. Jamie Foxx turns in an uncanny performance as the musical legend, all to the backdrop of Charles's most memorable compositions. The movie follows Charles's life from his youth to the end of his storied career while presenting an unvarnished look at his personal triumphs and failures. His survival and musical genius illustrate just why the man had such universal appeal. From the dizzying highs to the heartbreaking lows, *Ray* appeals to both music and movie lovers alike.

Cast

Jamie Foxx: Ray Charles
Kerry Washington: Della Bea Robinson
Regina King: Margie Hendricks
Clifton Powell: Jeff Brown
Harry J. Lennix: Joe Adams
Bokeem Woodbine: Fathead Newman
Aunjanue Ellis: Mary Ann Fisher

Behind the Scenes

Director: Taylor Hackford
Writers: Taylor Hackford (story), James L. White (screenplay)
Producers: Howard Baldwin, Karen Elise Baldwin, Stuart Benjamin, Taylor Hackford
Executive Producers: William J. Immerman, Jaime Rucker King

Awards

Oscar Winners: Best Achievement in Sound Mixing, Best Actor
Oscar Nominations: Best Costume Design, Best Director, Best Editing, Best Picture

Trivia

• The screenplay for this film was transcribed as Braille so that Ray Charles could read it.

1954
Rear Window

Overview

Genre: Thriller/Mystery

Duration: 112 min

Color: Color (Eastmancolor/Technicolor)

Country: USA

MPAA Rating: PG

Studio: Paramount Pictures

Photographer L.B. Jefferies has been stuck inside his apartment ever since breaking his leg on his last assignment. Itching to get out of his cast and back to work, Jefferies is left with nothing to do but stare out at his neighbors in New York's Greenwich Village. Meanwhile, his long-suffering girlfriend Lisa has an itch of her own involving the two of them getting married. After Jefferies is awakened by a scream late one night, all thoughts of broken bones and weddings are put on the backburner as he begins to suspect one of his neighbors of foul play. Is his imagination getting the better of him or is real danger lurking just outside his window?

Cast

James Stewart: L.B. Jefferies
Grace Kelly: Lisa Carol Fremont
Wendell Corey: Detective Lieutenant Thomas J. Doyle
Thelma Ritter: Stella
Raymond Burr: Lars Thorwald
Judith Evelyn: Miss Lonelyheart
Ross Bagdasarian: Songwriter
Georgine Darcy: Miss Torso

Behind the Scenes

Director: Alfred Hitchcock
Writers: Cornell Woolrich (story), John Michael Hayes (screenplay)
Producers: James C. Katz and Alfred Hitchcock (uncredited)
Film Editor: George Tomasini
Cinematographer: Robert Burks
Original Music: Franz Waxman

Trivia

• As usual, Alfred Hitchcock makes a cameo appearance halfway into the film when he winds the clock in the songwriter's apartment.
• Shot entirely on one set, 1,000 lights were used to produce realistic daylight.

Awards

Oscar Nominations: Best Cinematography, Best Director, Best Sound, Best Writing

1940
Rebecca

Overview

Genre: Drama/Mystery
Duration: 130 min
Color: Black and White
Country: USA
MPAA Rating: Not Rated
Studio: Selznick International Pictures/ United Artists

In Alfred Hitchcock's first American film, Laurence Olivier stars as a rich widower named Maxim de Winter who marries a young woman he meets in Monte Carlo. But, upon returning to his palatial seaside estate, the new Mrs. de Winter finds that both the house's servants and the mansion itself still seem to be under the spell of Maxim's first wife, Rebecca. Making things particularly uncomfortable for the new bride is housekeeper Mrs. Danvers who makes sure to remind her just how special the first Mrs. de Winter was. Joan Fontaine is first rate as the bewildered young woman battling her own demons as well as the haunting presence of Rebecca.

Cast

Laurence Olivier: Maxim de Winter
Joan Fontaine: The second Mrs. de Winter
George Sanders: Jack Favell
Judith Anderson: Mrs. Danvers
Nigel Bruce: Major Giles Lacy
C. Aubrey Smith: Colonel Julyan
Gladys Cooper: Beatrice Lacy
Florence Bates: Mrs. Edythe Van Hopper

Behind the Scenes

Director: Alfred Hitchcock
Writers: Daphne du Maurier (novel), Joan Harrison, Robert E. Sherwood, Philip MacDonald, and Michael Hogan (screenplay)
Producer: David O. Selznick
Film Editor: W. Donn Hayes (uncredited)
Cinematographer: George Barnes
Original Music: Franz Waxman

Trivia

• Alfred Hitchcock's first Hollywood film was also his only movie to win an Oscar for Best Picture.
• Olivier treated Fontaine poorly since his girlfriend, Vivien Leigh, had not gotten the part. Hitchcock capitalized on this, telling her she was hated to enhance her performance.

Awards

Oscar Winners: Best Cinematography, Best Picture
Oscar Nominations: Best Actor, Best Actress, Best Supporting Actress, Best Art Direction, Best Director, Best Effects—Special Effects, Best Film Editing, Best Music, Best Writing

1955
Rebel Without a Cause

Overview

Genre: Drama/ Romance
Duration: 111 min
Color: Color (Warner-color)
Country: USA
MPAA Rating: PG-13
Studio: Warner Bros. Pictures

This tale of disaffected Los Angeles teens stars James Dean as Jim Stark, a troubled young man whose parents constantly move so that he can have a fresh start. The problem with this approach is that Jim never spends enough time in one place to gain any traction. In his latest town, he once again finds himself struggling to fit in, but he's not alone. Plato is a lonely and disturbed youth who befriends Jim, and Judy, who has major issues with her father, is a potential girlfriend. Still, the same problems remain, as Jim copes with bullies and tries to act like a man, even as his own henpecked father does not.

Cast

James Dean: Jim Stark
Natalie Wood: Judy
Sal Mineo: John "Plato" Crawford
Jim Backus: Frank Stark
Ann Doran: Mrs. Carol Stark
Corey Allen: Buzz Gunderson
Dennis Hopper: Goon

Behind the Scenes

Director: Nicholas Ray
Writer: Nicholas Ray (story), Stewart Stern and Irving Shulman (screenplay)
Producer: David Weisbart
Film Editor: William H. Ziegler
Cinematographer: Ernest Haller
Original Music: Leonard Rosenman

Awards

Oscar Nominations: Best Supporting Actor, Best Supporting Actress, Best Writing

Trivia

• Director Nicholas Ray got further insight into L.A. gangs by riding around with them for several nights.

1981
Reds

Overview

Genre: Drama
Duration: 194 min
Color: Color (Technicolor)
Country: USA
MPAA Rating: PG
Studio: Paramount Pictures

This tale of larger-than-life journalist and radical sympathizer John Reed and his adventures and relationship with Louise Bryant, a Portland dentist's wife who he lured into a bohemian life caught writer/director/producer Warren Beatty's eye as early as the 1960s. The movie covers John Reed's life, from his fieldwork covering Pancho Villa's revolt to his relationships with radical Emma Goldman, playwright Eugene O'Neill, and editor Max Eastman. Despite an affair, Louise Bryant returns to her husband John, and the two together witnesses the Russian Revolution. The rosy glow of their idealized beliefs, however, begin to lose its sheen.

Cast

Warren Beatty: John Reed
Diane Keaton: Louise Bryant
Edward Herrmann: Max Eastman
Jerzy Kosinski: Grigory Zinoviev
Jack Nicholson: Eugene O'Neill
Paul Sorvino: Louis Friana
Maureen Stapleton: Emma Goldman

Behind the Scenes

Director: Warren Beatty
Writers: Warren Beatty, Trevor Griffiths
Producers: Warren Beatty, David Leigh MacLeod
Executive Producers: Dede Allen, Simon Relph
Cinematographer: Vittorio Storaro

Awards

Oscar Winners: Best Supporting Actress, Best Cinematography, Best Director

Trivia

• Gene Hackman's cameo appearance as Pete Van Wherry was uncredited. Director Warren Beatty shot 100 takes for the short scene. Hackman refused to do 101.

1984
Repo Man

Overview

Genre: Sci-Fi/Comedy
Duration: 92 min
Color: Color
Country: USA
MPAA Rating: R
Studio: Universal Pictures

Do you like your films to have endless quotable lines? Check. Strange characters? Check. Obscure jokes? Check. Filmic references to *Kiss Me Deadly* (ten years before *Pulp Fiction*)? Check. How about a soundtrack that blows the wheels off any other '80s film? Check. Maybe you just plain dig movies about consumerism, interstellar aliens, religious hypocrisy, conspiracy theory, and LA punk rock. If so, be sure to give Alex Cox's *Repo Man* a shot. Emilio Estevez plays Otto, a rudderless suburban punk indoctrinated into the world of auto repossession by a cadre of repo men, each named after a different beer. It's a nonstop thrill ride and arguably one of the best films of the decade.

Cast

Harry Dean Stanton: Bud
Emilio Estevez: Otto
Tracey Walter: Miller
Olivia Barash: Leila
Sy Richardson: Lite
Susan Barnes: Agent Rogersz
Fox Harris: J. Frank Parnell
Tom Finnegan: Oly

Behind the Scenes

Director: Alex Cox
Writer: Alex Cox
Producers: Peter McCarthy, Jonathan Wacks
Executive Producer: Michael Nesmith
Film Editor: Dennis E. Dolan
Cinematographer: Robby Muller
Original Music: Steven Hufsteter, Tito Larriva

Trivia

• The company that makes "Xmas tree" air fresheners was one of the sponsors of the movie.

Awards

Saturn Award Winner: Best Supporting Actor
Saturn Award Nomination: Best Writing

1983
Risky Business

Overview

Genre: Comedy
Duration: 98 min
Color: Color
Country: USA
MPAA Rating: R
Studio: The Geffen Company

J oel Goodsen is your stereotypical American teenager: he gets good grades in school, plays poker with his friends, and hasn't had much luck with girls. So, when his parents go out of town on a trip, Joel throws caution to the wind and decides to get a little worldly experience. After taking his dad's Porsche for a spin, he dials up an escort service for a little female companionship. But he soon finds that he got more than he bargained for in the form of a sultry prostitute named Lana and her pimp Guido. The more Joel tries to set things right, the worse things get. At this rate he'll never get into Princeton.

Cast

Tom Cruise: Joel Goodsen
Rebecca De Mornay: Lana
Joe Pantoliano: Guido
Richard Masur: Rutherford
Bronson Pinchot: Barry
Curtis Armstrong: Miles
Nicholas Pryor: Joel's father
Janet Carroll: Joel's mother

Behind the Scenes

Director: Paul Brickman
Writer: Paul Brickman
Producers: Jon Avnet, Steve Tisch
Film Editor: Richard Chew
Cinematographers: Bruce Surtees, Reynaldo Villalobos
Original Music: Tangerine Dream: Christopher Franke, Edgar Froese, Johannes Schmölling

Trivia

• The "Old Time Rock and Roll" dance sequence was not choreographed. Tom Cruise was just asked to dance to the music, and his improvisation made for one of the movie's signature scenes.

Awards

Golden Globe Nomination: Best Actor in a Motion Picture—Comedy/Musical

1976
Rocky

Overview

Genre: Drama/Sports
Duration: 119 min
Color: Color (Technicolor)
Country: USA
MPAA Rating: PG
Studio: United Artists

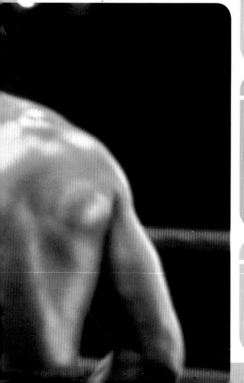

R ocky Balboa is a club fighter in Philadelphia with a one-way ticket to palookaville. Barely clinging to his boxing dreams while scratching out a hardscrabble existence, he's offered the opportunity of a lifetime when flashy heavyweight champion Apollo Creed offers him a shot at the title. Throwing everything he's got into his last big chance, Rocky hires his grizzled ex-trainer Mickey to whip him into shape. Will hard work, guts, and the love of a shy pet store clerk named Adrian be enough to carry Balboa into the ring against an undefeated champion? A true underdog story in every sense of the word, *Rocky* went on to win Best Picture of 1976.

Cast

Sylvester Stallone: Rocky Balboa
Talia Shire: Adrianna "Adrian" Pennino
Burt Young: Paulie Pennino
Carl Weathers: Apollo Creed
Burgess Meredith: Mickey Goldmill
Thayer David: Jergens
Joe Spinell: Gazzo
Jimmy Gambina: Mike
Bill Baldwin: Fight announcer

Behind the Scenes

Director: John G. Avildsen
Writer: Sylvester Stallone
Producers: Robert Chartoff, Irwin Winkler
Executive Producer: Gene Kirkwood
Cinematographer: James Crabe
Original Music: Bill Conti

Trivia

• The Rocky theme, "Gonna Fly Now," didn't have a title until Bill Conti played the song for Director John G. Avildsen, who said, "It should be almost like Rocky is flying now."
• Stallone wrote the first draft of the script in just three days after watching Chuck Wepner and Muhammad Ali's boxing match, in which Wepner almost lasted through the 15th round.

Awards

Oscar Winners: Best Director, Best Film Editing, Best Picture
Oscar Nominations: Best Actor, Best Supporting Actor, Best Actress, Best Music—Original Song, Best Sound, Best Writing

1953
Roman Holiday

Overview

Genre: Comedy/Romance
Duration: 118 min
Color: Black and White
Country: USA
MPAA Rating: Not Rated
Studio: Paramount Pictures

When Princess Ann has a tantrum about her overregimented European tour, her keepers issue her a sedative—but the princess escapes before the medication takes effect. On his way home from a poker game, American reporter Joe Bradley finds what he believes is a drunken young miss sitting on a bench. When she can't tell him where she lives, he puts her on his couch. Discovering she's a princess, Joe angles to get an exclusive from his editor, taking the girl on the town with his photographer sidekick. Love blossoms as the two have the time of their lives, but duty calls, as the princess makes her way back to the confines of her royal life, after a memorable Roman holiday.

Cast

Gregory Peck: Joe Bradley
Audrey Hepburn: Princess Ann
Eddie Albert: Irving Radovich
Hartley Power: Mr. Hennessy
Harcourt Williams: Ambassador
Margaret Rawlings: Countess Vereberg
Tullio Carminati: Gen. Provno

Behind the Scenes

Director: William Wyler
Writers: Dalton Trumbo, Ian McLellan Hunter, John Dighton
Producer: William Wyle
Film Editor: Robert Swink
Cinematographers: Henri Alekan, Franz Planer

Awards

Oscar Winners: Best Actress, Best Costume Design, Best Writing

Trivia

• Dalton Trumbo was the true writer of the film, but he was blacklisted and could not receive credit for the screenplay. He allowed his friend Ian McLellan Hunter to stand in as a front.

1968
Rosemary's Baby

Overview

Genre: Horror/Drama
Duration: 136 min
Color: Color (Technicolor)
Country: USA
MPAA Rating: R
Studio: Paramount Pictures

Roman Polanski's breakthrough hit leads the audience through a delicate maze threading the strange through the familiar, where the difference between the diabolical and unfounded paranoia is both razor thin and razor sharp. A young wife's first pregnancy drives her to such emotional extremes that she begins to distrust herself, even as her fears about the neighbors' supernatural activities and increasing alienation from her husband force her to rely on her instincts. A subtle supernatural thriller and a psychological foray into the terrors of pregnancy and motherhood, *Rosemary's Baby* inaugurated a new form of horror movie as it exposed an old form of horror.

Cast

Mia Farrow: Rosemary Woodhouse
John Cassavetes: Guy Woodhouse
Ruth Gordon: Minnie Castevet
Sidney Blackmer: Roman Castevet
Maurice Evans: Edward "Hutch" Hutchins
Ralph Bellamy: Dr. Abraham Sapirstein
Victoria Vetri: Terry Gionoffrio

Behind the Scenes

Director: Roman Polanski
Writer: Ira Levin (novel), Roman Polanski
Producer: William Castle
Film Editors: Sam O'Steen, Bob Wyman
Cinematographer: William A. Fraker
Original Music: Krzysztof Komeda

Awards

Oscar Winners: Best Supporting Actress
Oscar Nominations: Best Writing—Adapted Screenplay

Trivia

• Roman Polanski's adaptation of Ira Levin's novel was incredibly faithful to the novel. Polanski used dialogue, color schemes, and clothes directly from the text.

1990
Rosencrantz and Guildenstern Are Dead

Overview

Genre: Comedy/Drama
Duration: 117 min
Color: Color (Technicolor)
Country: USA
MPAA Rating: PG
Studio: Brandenberg International/Cinecom Pictures

William Shakespeare's *Hamlet* may be the world's most famous play, and Tom Stoppard's *Rosencrantz and Guildenstern Are Dead* its worthiest companion. Following two of *Hamlet's* minor characters as they dip in and out of their 15 minutes of fame, the audience is forced to wrestle with the grand questions of the characters' existence: just who is watching whom, and when, and why? If all the world's a stage, then *Rosencrantz and Guildenstern* is a relentlessly funny, completely modern take on the ageless questions of life—no longer "to be, or not to be," but how to be, at all?

Cast

Gary Oldman: Rosencrantz
Tim Roth: Guildenstern
Richard Dreyfuss: The Player
Iain Glen: Hamlet
Donald Sumpter: Claudius
Joanna Miles: Gertrude
Joanna Roth: Ophelia

Behind the Scenes

Director: Tom Stoppard
Writers: William Shakespeare (*The Tragedy of Hamlet*), Tom Stoppard (play and screenplay)
Producers: Emanuel Azenberg, Michael Brandman
Film Editor: Nicolas Gaster

Awards

Nominated for Independent Spirit Award for Best Male Lead

Trivia

• Throughout the film, the pieces of paper blowing around are the script of *Hamlet*.

2001
The Royal Tenenbaums

Overview

Genre: Comedy/Drama
Duration: 110 min
Color: Color (Technicolor)
Country: USA
MPAA Rating: R
Studio: Touchstone Pictures

The estranged patriarch of a gifted family, Royal Tenenbaum wants one last chance to make good with his wife and kids before he dies. Richie, a reclusive former tennis superstar, is delighted to have his dad back in his life but business tycoon Chas wants nothing to do with the father that abandoned them. Adopted daughter Margot, a playwright, is going through her own marital problems and treats her father with the same indifference he showed her. Not yet divorced from Royal, his wife Etheline is recently engaged to her accountant, Henry Sherman. A renowned archaeologist, Etheline now finds herself hosting the whole group as they collectively sift through the remains of their past and try to piece together some sort of future.

Cast

Gene Hackman: Royal Tenenbaum
Anjelica Huston: Etheline Tenenbaum
Ben Stiller: Chas Tenenbaum
Gwyneth Paltrow: Margot Tenenbaum
Luke Wilson: Richie Tenenbaum
Owen Wilson: Eli Cash
Bill Murray: Raleigh St. Clair
Danny Glover: Henry Sherman
Alec Baldwin: Narrator

Behind the Scenes

Director: Wes Anderson
Writers: Wes Anderson, Owen Wilson
Producers: Wes Anderson, Barry Mendel, Scott Rudin
Executive Producers: Rudd Simmons, Owen Wilson
Cinematographer: Robert D. Yeoman
Original Music: Mark Mothersbaugh

Trivia

• The hand with the BB between its knuckles belongs to the third Wilson brother, Andrew, not Ben Stiller. Owen Wilson is responsible for firing the BB gun that lodged the pellet in his brother's hand when they were kids.

Awards

Oscar Nominations: Best Writing

1998
Saving Private Ryan

Overview

Genre: Drama/Action
Duration: 170 min
Color: Color (Technicolor)
Country: USA
MPAA Rating: R
Studio: DreamWorks SKG/Paramount Pictures

Acclaimed actor Tom Hanks leads the way through this unusual war movie, in which an act of mercy—rescuing Private Ryan, the last of a family of brothers, from war-torn France—requires a crew of soldiers to put aside more usual battles for an unprecedented act of bravery. Before they can bring Ryan home, the band first must find him, and the wrenching trip through the lines of war requires them to ask the terrible question: how do you measure the value of one man's life? Requiring the ultimate sacrifice of its characters and total commitment of its viewers, *Saving Private Ryan* is based on a true event.

Cast

Tom Hanks: Captain John H. Miller
Adam Goldberg: Private Stanley Mellish
Tom Sizemore: Sergeant Horvath
Vin Diesel: Private Adrian Caparzo
Giovanni Ribisi: T-4 Medic Irwin Wade
Ed Burns: Private Reiben
Matt Damon: Private James Francis Ryan

Behind the Scenes

Director: Steven Spielberg
Writer: Robert Rodat
Producers: Ian Bryce, Mark Gordon, Gary Levinsohn, Steven Spielberg
Film Editor: Michael Kahn
Cinematographer: Janusz Kaminski

Awards

Oscar Winners: Best Cinematography, Best Director, Best Effects—Sound, Best Film Editing, Best Sound

Trivia

• Movie theaters were specifically instructed to turn up the volume during screenings because the sound effects play such an important role in the power of the film.

1977
Saturday Night Fever

Overview

Genre: Drama/Romance
Duration: 118 min
Color: Color
Country: USA
MPAA Rating: R
Studio: Paramount Pictures

If you were alive in the late '70s, you probably remember *Saturday Night Fever*. John Travolta stars as Tony Manero, a Brooklyn paint store employee by day and disco king by night. Still living at home with his parents, Tony cares more about his clothes and hair than his future. When he enters a dance contest with a secretary named Stephanie, her dreams and aspirations begin to rub off on him. Though the fashions, hairstyles, and lingo may all seem dated, this film is a perfect snapshot of that moment in American culture. Backing up Travolta's impressive dance moves is one of the top-selling movie soundtracks of all time, featuring the infectious beats of the Bee Gees.

Cast

John Travolta: Tony Manero
Karen Lynn Gorney: Stephanie Mangano
Barry Miller: Bobby C.
Joseph Cali: Joey
Paul Pape: Double J.
Donna Pescow: Annette
Bruce Ornstein: Gus

Behind the Scenes

Director: John Badham
Writers: Nik Cohn (article), Norman Wexler (screenplay)
Producer: Robert Stigwood
Executive Producer: Kevin McCormick
Original Music: Bee Gees: Barry Gibb, Maurice Gibb, Robin Gibb

Awards

Oscar Nominations: Best Actor

Trivia

• Travolta's response to being hit in the dinner scene, "Just watch the hair!" was not scripted. It worked well with the character of Tony, so John Badham left it in.

1989
Say Anything . . .

Overview

Genre: Drama/ Romance
Duration: 100 min
Color: Color
Country: USA
MPAA Rating: PG-13
Studio: Gracie Films/ Twentieth Century Fox

When lovable underachiever Lloyd Dobler falls for the beautiful high school valedictorian Diane`Court, the match seems anything but likely. Among those not giving them much of a chance is Diane's over-protective father, who views Lloyd as nothing more than a distraction for his daughter. As the young couple struggles with family issues, friends, and relationship challenges, their improbable romance seems just that—improbable. But it just may be their imperfections and insecurities that make them perfect for each other. A romantic coming-of-age story, *Say Anything* illustrates both the power of persistence as well as that of a good boom box.

Cast

John Cusack: Lloyd Dobler
Ione Skye: Diane Court
John Mahoney: James Court
Lili Taylor: Corey Flood
Amy Brooks: D.C.
Pamela Adlon: Rebecca
Jason Gould: Mike Cameron

Behind the Scenes

Director: Cameron Crowe
Writer: Cameron Crowe
Producer: Polly Platt
Executive Producer: James L. Brooks
Film Editors: Richard Marks, Karen I. Stern
Cinematography: Laszlo Kovacs
Original Music: Anne Dudley, Richard Gibbs

Trivia

• Lloyd's kick-boxing sparring partner is former champion Don "The Dragon" Wilson.

Trivia

• During the scene where Lloyd drives by the mall and mentions it as the site of their first date, Director Cameron Crowe and his wife Nancy Wilson briefly appear as pedestrians.

1993
Schindler's List

Overview

Genre: Drama
Duration: 195 min
Color: Black and White, Color
Country: USA
MPAA Rating: R
Studio: Universal Pictures

Steven Spielberg's gut-wrenching portrait of the Holocaust centers around the story of wartime profiteer turned humanitarian, Oskar Schindler. As the owner of a factory in Poland, Schindler first sees Jews from the Krakow ghetto as a cheap form of labor, but as they are taken away to death camps, he and his accountant come to realize that they can actually save lives by employing these people. Based on a true story, *Schindler's List* brings the horrors and sorrows of the Holocaust to the screen like no other movie. In a cast including Liam Neeson and Ben Kingsley, Ralph Fiennes delivers a chilling performance as a sadistic camp commander: a true movie villain if ever there was one.

Cast

Liam Neeson: Oskar Schindler
Ben Kingsley: Itzhak Stern
Ralph Fiennes: Amon Goeth
Caroline Goodall: Emilie Schindler
Jonathan Sagall: Poldek Pfefferberg
Embeth Davidtz: Helen Hirsch
Mark Ivanir: Marcel Goldberg
Friedrich von Thun: Rolf Czurda

Behind the Scenes

Director: Steven Spielberg
Writers: Thomas Keneally (book), Steven Zaillian (screenplay)
Producers: Branko Lustig, Gerald R. Molen, Steven Spielberg
Executive Producer: Kathleen Kennedy
Cinematographer: Janusz Kaminski
Original Music: John Williams

Trivia

• Steven Spielberg refused to be paid for the film, saying that it would be "blood money."
• The film was originally going to be in Polish and German with English subtitles, but Spielberg decided to use English to make the film more accessible.

Awards

Oscar Winners: Best Art Direction, Best Cinematography, Best Director, Best Film Editing, Best Music, Best Picture, Best Writing—Adapted Screenplay
Oscar Nominations: Best Actor, Best Supporting Actor, Best Costume Design, Best Makeup, Best Sound

1956
The Searchers

Overview

Genre: Drama/Western
Duration: 119 min
Color: Color (Technicolor)
Country: USA
MPAA Rating: Not Rated
Studio: Warner Bros. Pictures

In 1868, former Confederate soldier Ethan Edwards returns to his brother's ranch in Texas, bringing the spoils of his travels. When Edwards goes out with a team of Texas Rangers to search for stolen cattle, a Comanche raiding party kills most of Edwards's kin, and abducts his two nieces, Lucy and Debbie. After finding Lucy dead, the bitter and angry veteran spends the next five years hunting for the other, with the help of his adopted nephew who is part Native American. When he learns that Debbie has married a Comanche warrior, he is torn between rescuing and killing her. John Wayne delivers a great performance as antihero Ethan in what many consider to be John Ford's finest film.

Cast

John Wayne: Ethan Edwards
Jeffrey Hunter: Martin Pawley
Vera Miles: Laurie Jorgensen
Ward Bond: Captain Samuel Johnston Clayton
Natalie Wood: Debbie Edwards
John Qualen: Lars Jorgensen
Olive Carey: Mrs. Jorgensen
Hank Worden: Mose Harper

Behind the Scenes

Director: John Ford
Writers: Alan Le May (novel), Frank S. Nugent (screenpaly)
Producer: C.V. Whitney
Executive Producer: Merian C. Cooper
Film Editor: Jack Murray
Cinematographer: Winton C. Hoch
Original Music: Max Steiner

Trivia

• Right before the Indian raid on the Edwards homestead, the tombstone that Debbie hides near reads "Here lies Mary Jane Edwards killed by Comanches May 12, 1852. A good wife and mother in her 41st year." Though this is a small detail that many viewers do not notice, it explains Ethan's hatred for Native Americans—his own mother was killed by Comanches sixteen years earlier.
• John Wayne named one of his sons Ethan in homage to his role in this movie. Wayne's portrayal of Ethan Edwards was his all-time screen favorite.

Awards

Added to National Film Registry in 1989

1995
Se7en

Overview

Genre: Drama/Crime
Duration: 127 min
Color: Color
Country: USA
MPAA Rating: R
Studio: New Line Cinema

David Fincher's dark crime thriller centers on a serial killer acting out the seven deadly sins. Six days away from retirement, veteran detective William Somerset gets teamed up with David Mills, the young cop who will replace him. Together they investigate two separate murders, one of an obese man and the other a defense attorney, each victim with his respective sin—gluttony and greed—scrawled in blood. As Somerset and Mills fight to stop the next in a presumable series of grisly homicides, they seem to constantly be one step behind their murderer. Can Somerset and Mills catch the killer before this play reaches its denouement? And what will they lose in the process?

Cast

Brad Pitt: Detective David Mills
Morgan Freeman: Detective Lieutenant William Somerset
Kevin Spacey: John Doe
Gwyneth Paltrow: Tracy Mills
R. Lee Ermey: Police Captain
Daniel Zacapa: Detective Taylor

Behind the Scenes

Director: David Fincher
Writer: Andrew Kevin Walker
Producers: Phyllis Carlyle, Arnold Kopelson
Executive Producers: Dan Kolsrud, Anne Kopelson, Gianni Nunnari
Film Editor: Richard Francis-Bruce
Original Music: Howard Shore

Awards

Oscar Nomination: Best Film Editing

Trivia

• All of the building numbers in the opening scene begin with the number seven.

1954
The Seven Samurai

Akira Kurosawa directed this oft-imitated tale of a poor Japanese farming village that hire a group of samurai warriors to defend them against bandits. When scouts from the village witness an older samurai named Kambei rescue a young boy, they ask for his help and he assents. Kambei recruits five more warriors and heads to the village. Their number swells to seven when Kikuchiyo, a loud-mouthed straggler, is added to the group. With little reward for their services, the men band together to help train the farmers, fortify the village, and await their battle. Whatever the outcome, the samurai have already proven that they are willing to sacrifice themselves and honor their warrior legacy.

Cast

Takashi Shimura: Kambei Shimada
Toshirô Mifune: Kikuchiyo
Yoshio Inaba: Gorobei Katayama
Seiji Miyaguchi: Kyuzo
Minoru Chiaki: Heihachi Hayashida
Daisuke Katô: Shichiroji
Isao Kimura: Katsushiro Okamoto

Behind the Scenes

Director: Akira Kurosawa
Writers: Akira Kurosawa, Shinobu Hashimoto, Hideo Oguni
Producer: Sohiro Motoki
Film Editor: Akira Kurosawa
Cinematographer: Asakazu Nakai
Original Music: Fumio Hayasaka

Awards

Oscar Nominations: Best Art Direction, Best Costume Design

Trivia

• The production company, Toho, tried to kill this film several times. A huge success in both Japan and the West, it became one of the most influential films of all time.

1955
The Seven Year Itch

Overview

Genre: Comedy
Duration: 105 min
Color: Color
Country: USA
MPAA Rating: Not Rated
Studio: Twentieth Century Fox

A married book editor with an overactive imagination gets all he can handle when a beautiful blonde moves into the apartment upstairs. After seeing his wife and son off for the summer, Richard Sherman settles back into his Manhattan apartment . . . content until he meets his neighbor. Of course ideas and actions are two very different things, and Richard is anything but a smooth-talking lothario. But still, between thoughts of his wife and this new girl, that imagination of his is driving him to distraction. After the famous subway grate scene in this movie, one can only assume that Marilyn Monroe became the fodder for many a midlife crisis.

Cast

Marilyn Monroe: The Girl
Tom Ewell: Richard Sherman
Evelyn Keyes: Helen Sherman
Sonny Tufts: Tom MacKenzie
Robert Strauss: Mr. Kruhulik
Oskar Homolka: Dr. Brubaker
Marguerite Chapman: Miss Morris

Behind the Scenes

Director: Billy Wilder
Writers: Billy Wilder, George Axelrod
Producers: Charles K. Feldman, Billy Wilder
Film Editor: Hugh S. Fowler
Cinematographer: Milton R. Krasner
Original Music: Alfred Newman

Awards

Golden Globe Winner: Best Actor— Musical/Comedy

Trivia

• Even though the photograph of Marilyn Monroe with her white dress billowing up is one of America's most iconic pop images, the full-length shot never made the final cut.

1953
Shane

Overview

Genre: Drama/Western
Duration: 118 min
Color: Color (Technicolor)
Country: USA
MPAA Rating: Not Rated
Studio: Paramount Pictures

Alan Ladd stars as the iconic Shane, a lone cowboy who one day shows up on the Wyoming farm of the Starrett family. Almost immediately, the Starretts' young son Joey idolizes the mysterious stranger with the lightning fast draw. When Shane helps run off cattleman Rufe Ryker, who claims that the Starretts are living on his land, he is asked to stay by the grateful family. Nevertheless, even when the surrounding homesteaders decide to band together, they still are vulnerable to the bullying tactics of Ryker and his men. And when Ryker hires a notorious gunman to handle his dirty work, a showdown seems inevitable.

Cast

Alan Ladd: Shane
Jean Arthur: Marian Starrett
Van Heflin: Joe Starrett
Brandon De Wilde: Joe Starrett
Jack Palance: Jack Wilson
Ben Johnson: Chris Calloway
Edgar Buchanan: Fred Lewis

Behind the Scenes

Director: George Stevens
Writers: Jack Schaefer (novel), A.B. Guthrie Jr. (screenplay)
Producer: George Stevens
Film Editors: William Hornbeck, Tom McAdoo
Cinematographer: Loyal Griggs
Original Music: Victor Young

Awards

Oscar Winner: Best Cinematography
Oscar Nominations: Best Supporting Actor, Best Supporting Actor, Best Director, Best Picture, Best Writing

Trivia

• Jean Arthur came out of semi-retirement to play Marian Starrett, and she retired fully after filming was completed.

1994
The Shawshank Redemption

Overview

Genre: Drama
Duration: 142 min
Color: Color
(Technicolor)
Country: USA
MPAA Rating: R
Studio: Castle Rock
Entertainment

Andy Dusfresne is a banker who has been convicted of murdering his wife and her lover. Despite his pleas of innocence, he's shipped off to Shawshank State Prison in Maine and faced with a place populated by violent criminals, vicious guards, and a corrupt warden. Instead of cracking, Andy makes friends with a wise inmate named Red and also agrees to help the head guard and warden with their finances in exchange for small improvements in the prison. Through trials and travails, his selfless attitude and never-ending hope are two things that can't be locked up. He's even got his friends thinking that he may just be the one innocent man in Shawshank.

Cast

Tim Robbins: Andy Dufresne
Morgan Freeman: Ellis Boyd "Red" Redding
Bob Gunton: Warden Norton
William Sadler: Heywood
Clancy Brown: Captain Hadley
Gil Bellows: Tommy
Mark Rolston: Bogs Diamond
James Whitmore: Brooks Hatlen

Behind the Scenes

Director: Frank Darabont
Writers: Stephen King (story), Frank Darabont
Producer: Niki Marvin
Executive Producers: Liz Glotzer, David V. Lester
Film Editor: Richard Francis-Bruce
Cinematographer: Roger Deakins
Original Music: Thomas Newman

Trivia

• Director Frank Darabont rejected the idea of putting deleted scenes in the DVD because he was embarrassed by the cut scenes and didn't want them available to the public.
• The character, Red, was a white Irishman in the short story. Nevertheless, Darabont left in his line "Maybe it's cause I'm Irish" as a joke.

Awards

Oscar Nominations: Best Actor, Best Cinematography, Best Film Editing, Best Music, Best Picture, Best Sound, Best Writing—Adapted Screenplay

1980
The Shining

Overview

Genre: Horror
Duration: 146 min
Color: Color
Country: USA
MPAA Rating: R
Studio: Warner Bros. Pictures

The Overlook Hotel is completely isolated during the long Colorado winters—just the thing for struggling writer Jack Torrance. Bringing his wife Wendy and their young son Danny along, Jack happily accepts the job of winter caretaker, disregarding the manager's warning that the isolation can be psychologically dangerous. The hotel's spectral inhabitants, however, cannot be ignored, and Danny's psychic awareness awakens under their threatening, unseen presence. The hotel's real victim, however, is Jack. Mentally besieged by unknown horrors, Jack is driven to the depths of madness, where waiting to welcome him are the hotel's true eternal caretakers.

Cast

Jack Nicholson: Jack Torrance
Shelley Duvall: Wendy Torrance
Danny Lloyd: Danny Torrance
Scatman Crothers: Dick Hallorann
Barry Nelson: Stuart Ullman
Philip Stone: Delbert Grady
Joe Turkel: Lloyd the bartender

Behind the Scenes

Director: Stanley Kubrick
Writers: Stephen King (novel), Stanley Kubrick and Diane Johnson (screenplay)
Producer: Stanley Kubrick
Executive Producer: Jan Harlan
Cinematographer: John Alcott
Original Music: Wendy Carlos, Rachel Elkind

Awards

Saturn Award Winner: Best Supporting Actor
Saturn Award Nominations: Best Director, Best Horror Film, Best Music

Trivia

• Stanley Kubrick was protective of the young actor Danny Lloyd and did not tell Lloyd he was acting in a horror movie until after production.

2004
Sideways

Overview

Genre: Comedy/Drama
Duration: 126 min
Color: Color
Country: USA
MPAA Rating: R
Studio: Fox Searchlight Pictures

Alexander Payne's bittersweet road trip concerns two old college buddies who take off for one last fandango in California wine country before one of them gets married. Miles is a struggling writer and avid oenophile who takes his friend Jack, a former soap star, up to Northern California for a week of wine and golf before Jack's wedding. As both men fly headlong into middle age, it's clear that their individual hopes and concerns are very different. While Mile frets over his broken marriage and whether his latest novel will be published, Jack only thinks about sowing his oats one last time. Both funny and poignant, *Sideways* also succeeded in boosting the sales of Pinot Noir while simultaneously making Merlot a dirty word.

Cast

Paul Giamatti: Miles
Thomas Haden Church: Jack
Virginia Madsen: Maya
Sandra Oh: Stephanie
Marylouise Burke: Miles's mother
Jessica Hecht: Victoria
Missy Doty: Cammi

Behind the Scenes

Director: Alexander Payne
Writers: Rex Pickett (novel), Alexander Payne and Jim Taylor (screenplay)
Film Editor: Kevin Trent
Producer: Michael London
Cinematographer: Phedon Papamichael
Original Music: Rolfe Kent

Trivia

• Most of the wine used in the wine-tasting scenes was nonalcoholic. The actors drank so much of it that it occasionally made them sick.

Awards

Oscar Winner: Best Writing—Adapted Screenplay
Oscar Nominations: Best Directing, Best Picture, Best Supporting Actor, Best Supporting Actress

1991
The Silence of the Lambs

Overview

Genre: Horror/Thriller
Duration: 118 min
Color: Color
(Eastmancolor)
Country: USA
MPAA Rating: R
Studio: Orion Pictures

Clarice Starling is a rookie FBI agent who specializes in serial killers. Her particular skill set lands her on a case concerning a killer known as Buffalo Bill who murders women and removes their skin. In order to catch her man, Clarice first needs to get inside his mind. To help her do this she must visit with Dr. Hannibal Lecter, a former psychiatrist and murderous mastermind who is locked up in a maximum security facility. Lecter can indeed help Clarice catch Buffalo Bill, but in return for his insights she'll have to reveal very personal information about herself. Just how far will agent Starling go to catch the killer before he strikes again?

Cast

Jodie Foster: Clarice Starling
Anthony Hopkins: Dr. Hannibal Lecter
Scott Glenn: Jack Crawford
Anthony Heald: Dr. Frederick Chilton
Ted Levine: Jame "Buffalo Bill" Gumb
Frankie Faison: Barnie Matthews
Kasi Lemmons: Ardelia Mapp
Brooke Smith: Catherine Martin
Paul Lazar: Pilcher

Behind the Scenes

Director: Jonathan Demme
Writers: Thomas Harris (novel), Ted Tally (screenplay)
Producers: Ronald M. Bozman, Edward Saxon, Kenneth Utt
Executive Producer: Gary Goetzman
Cinematographer: Tak Fujimoto
Original Music: Howard Shore

Trivia

• Though it had already gone bankrupt, Orion Pictures still managed to raise $200,000 for the film's Oscar campaign. The film went on to become the third film in history to win the top five Academy Awards—Best Actor, Actress, Director, Picture, and Screenplay.

Awards

Oscar Winners: Best Actor, Best Actress, Best Director, Best Picture, Best Writing—Adapted Screenplay
Oscar Nominations: Best Film Editing, Best Sound

1952
Singin' in the Rain

Overview

Genre: Musical/Romance
Duration: 103 min
Color: Color (Technicolor) and Black and White
Country: USA
MPAA Rating: G
Studio: Metro-Goldwyn-Mayer (MGM)

One of the splashiest (literally) and most beloved of all of the MGM musicals, *Singin' in the Rain* features a dynamic and talented cast led by the one and only Gene Kelly. Don Lockwood is one half of a silent film romantic duo who are now faced with making the transition to "talkies." While Don has considerable song and dance chops, his partner Lina Lamont has a voice that grates on everyone. Enter talented young actress Kathy Selden, who just may be the answer to everyone's problems. Along with countless memorable musical numbers, including the famous title song, this movie has plenty of laughs, romance, and an incredible supporting cast.

Cast

Gene Kelly: Don Lockwood
Donald O'Connor: Cosmo Brown
Debbie Reynolds: Kathy Selden
Jean Hagen: Lina Lamont
Millard Mitchell: R.F. Simpson
Cyd Charisse: Dancer
Douglas Fowley: Roscoe Dexter

Behind the Scenes

Directors: Stanley Donen and Gene Kelly
Writers: Adolph Green, Betty Comden
Producer: Arthur Freed
Film Editor: Adrienne Fazan
Cinematographer: Harold Rosson
Original Music: Arthur Freed, Nacio Herb Brown

Awards

Oscar Nominations: Best Supporting Actress, Best Music

Trivia

• In the famous rain scene, the rain was made up of a mixture of water and milk. It showed up better on film, but also caused Gene Kelly's new suit to shrink.

1999
The Sixth Sense

Overview

Genre: Drama/Thriller
Duration: 107 min
Color: Color
Country: USA
MPAA Rating: PG-13
Studio: Spyglass Entertainment/Hollywood Pictures

Cole Sear is a young boy who can see dead people. Child psychologist Malcolm Crowe is a man who has his own demons to face. Together they embark on a tense journey to discover the truth. As Cole learns to trust Dr. Crowe, he begins to try and communicate with the ghosts that haunt his waking hours, offering assistance to let them continue on their journey. Dr. Crowe, on the other hand, is gaining an understanding not only of Cole's condition, but also of another patient whose distress he'd never been able to cure. With plenty of thrills, chills, and twists along the way, *The Sixth Sense* may leave you feeling as though you are not alone.

Cast

Bruce Willis: Dr. Malcolm Crowe
Haley Joel Osment: Cole Sear
Toni Collette: Lynn Sear
Olivia Williams: Anna Crowe
Donnie Wahlberg: Vincent Grey
Glenn Fitzgerald: Sean
Greg Wood: Mr. Collins

Behind the Scenes

Director: M. Night Shyamalan
Writers: M. Night Shyamalan
Producers: Kathleen Kennedy, Frank Marshall, Barry Mendel
Executive Producers: Sam Mercer
Cinematographer: Tak Fujimoto
Original Music: James Newton Howard

Awards

Oscar Nominations: Best Supporting Actor, Best Supporting Actress, Best Director, Best Editing, Best Picture, Best Writing

Trivia

• M. Night Shyamalan appears in a cameo as Dr. Hill, who examines Cole after the "accident" at the birthday party.

1977
Slap Shot

Overview

Genre: Comedy/Sports
Duration: 123 min
Color: Color (Technicolor)
Country: USA
MPAA Rating: R
Studio: Universal Pictures

The Charlestown Chiefs are a lousy minor league hockey club struggling to stay afloat in a dying town. As rumors begin to swirl that this will be their final season, player/coach Reggie Dunlop gets the bright idea that he can save the team by having them play a more violent brand of hockey. Sure enough, once the fists start flying—led by a trio of geeky goons called the Hanson Brothers—the Chiefs can't lose. The stands now packed with bloodthirsty fans, the team is not only bullying its way toward a possible league title, but there are even whispers that they could be moving to sunny Florida.

Cast

Paul Newman: Reggie "Reg" Dunlop
Strother Martin: Joe McGrath
Michael Ontkean: Ned Braden
Jennifer Warren: Francine Dunlop
Lindsay Crouse: Lily Braden
Jerry Houser: Dave "Killer" Carlson
Andrew Duncan: Jim Carr

Behind the Scenes

Director: George Roy Hill
Writer: Nancy Dowd
Producers: Robert J. Wunsch, Stephen J. Friedman
Film Editor: Dede Allen
Cinematographer: Victor J. Kemper
Original Music: Elmer Bernstein

Trivia

• Universal Pictures wanted to make a spin-off film with Steve Carlson, Jeff Carlson, and David Hanson. All three turned down the opportunity in favor of their hockey careers.

Trivia

• Ned Braden was named for real minor league hockey player Ned Dowd, brother of writer Nancy Dowd. He played for the Johnstown Jets, the basis for the Charlestown Chiefs.

1973
Sleeper

Overview

Genre: Comedy/Sci-Fi
Duration: 89 min
Color: Color
Country: USA
MPAA Rating: PG
Studio: United Artists

Woody Allen directs and stars in this zany slapstick comedy about a man who goes in for some minor surgery in the '70s and wakes up 200 years in the future. Allen is Miles Monroe, the former owner of a New York health food store who now finds himself living in a modernized dictatorship run by someone known as "The Leader." Hilarious gags abound as Miles is introduced to new technology such as "The Orgasma-tron" and a party drug known as "The Orb." Though the whole thing is played for laughs, you have to admire some of Allen's spot-on thoughts about a future where the government closely monitors everyone and human cloning is discussed. One wonders, can Jewish robot tailors be far behind?

Cast

Woody Allen: Miles Monroe
Diane Keaton: Luna Schlosser
John Beck: Erno Windt
Mary Gregory: Dr. Melik
Don Keefer: Dr. Tryon
John McLiam: Dr. Aragon
Bartlett Robinson: Dr. Orva
Chris Forbes: Rainer Krebs

Behind the Scenes

Director: Woody Allen
Writers: Woody Allen, Marshall Brickman
Producer: Jack Grossberg
Executive Producers: Charles H. Joffe, Jack Rollins
Film Editors: Ron Kalish, Ralph Rosenblum
Cinematographer: David M. Walsh
Original Music: Woody Allen

Trivia

• As Miles is brought up to speed on significant events that he missed, he is told that the world came to an end when a madman named Albert Shanker got hold of a nuclear device. Shanker was actually the president of the American Federation of Teachers.

Awards

WGA Award Nomination: Best Comedy Written Directly for the Screen

1937
Snow White and the Seven Dwarfs

Overview

Genre: Family/Musical
Duration: 83 min
Color: Color
Country: USA
MPAA Rating: G
Studio: Walt Disney Productions

Walt Disney's first full-length animated feature film is hailed as a cinematic landmark, but is also still beloved for its intristic appeal. The mistreated princess, Snow White, her villainous stepmother, the Queen, and a host of helpful woodland creatures quickly became hallmarks of a new American folklore. Perhaps the film's most memorable characters are Snow White's dwarf companions, each imbued with a comical personality of singular dimension. With elements designed to appeal to adults and children alike, *Snow White* opened the door for many more animated films—but the first may still be the fairest of them all.

Cast

Adriana Caselotti: Snow White (voice)
Lucille La Verne: Queen/Witch (voice)
Roy Atwell: Doc (voice)
Eddie Collins: Dopey (voice)
Pinto Colvig: Sleepy/Grumpy (voice)
Billy Gilbert: Sneezy (voice)
Otis Harlan: Happy (voice)

Behind the Scenes

Director: David Hand
Writers: Ted Sears, Richard Creedon, Otto Englander, Dick Rickard, Earl Hurd, Merrill De Maris, Dorothy Ann Blank, Webb Smith
Producer: Walt Disney
Original Music: Frank Churchill, Leigh Harline, Paul Smith

Awards

Oscar Nominations: Honorary Award for Best Music Score

Trivia

• The first film to have its musical score released as a soundtrack-recording album.

1984
A Soldier's Story

Overview

Genre: Drama/Mystery
Duration: 101 min
Color: Color (Metrocolor)
Country: USA
MPAA Rating: PG
Studio: Columbia Tristar

Adapted by Charles Fuller from his Pulitzer Prize–winning play, *A Soldier's Story* is a tense drama built around the murder of a black sergeant at a Louisiana military base during World War II. After Sergeant Vernon Waters is found shot to death, a black military lawyer named Captain Richard Davenport is sent down to conduct an investigation. Because of the location and nature of the case, Captain Davenport must collect his facts from uncooperative white soldiers and locals as well as the wary men of Waters' platoon. The more Davenport digs into the case and learns about his victim, the more he realizes that any number of people could be his murderer.

Cast

Howard E. Rollins Jr.: Captain Davenport
Adolph Caesar: Sergeant Waters
Art Evans: Private Wilkie
David Alan Grier: Corporal Cobb
David Harris: Private Smalls
Denzel Washington: Pfc. Peterson
Larry Riley: C.J. Memphis

Behind the Scenes

Director: Norman Jewison
Writers: Charles Fuller (play and screenplay)
Producers: Patrick Palmer, Ronald L. Schwary, Norman Jewison
Executive Producer: Chiz Schultz
Cinematographer: Russell Boyd
Original Music: Herbie Hancock

Awards

Oscar Nominations: Best Supporting Actor, Best Picture, Best Writing—Adapted Screenplay

Trivia

• David Alan Grier acted in both the film and play versions of this story, but he took on Larry Riley's role of C.J. Memphis for the play.

1959
Some Like It Hot

Overview

Genre: Comedy/Crime
Duration: 120 min
Color: Black and White
Country: USA
MPAA Rating: Not Rated
Studio: United Artists

Start with Jack Lemmon and Tony Curtis in drag, add Marilyn Monroe at her sultry best, throw in some gangsters, lies, and the lure of money and you have the makings of one of the best comedies ever. On the run from the mob, two jazz musicians dress up as women and hide out in an all-girl band. It isn't long before one of the men falls for the beautiful blonde lead singer while the other finds himself (or his female persona, more specifically) impossibly mixed up with an eccentric millionaire. All of the lunacy is pulled off to perfection and topped with perhaps the funniest final line in movie history.

Cast

Marilyn Monroe: Sugar Kane Kowalczyk
Tony Curtis: Joe/Josephine/Junior
Jack Lemmon: Jerry/Daphne
George Raft: Spats Colombo
Pat O'Brien: Det. Mulligan
Joe E. Brown: Osgood Fielding III
Nehemiah Persoff: Little Bonaparte

Behind the Scenes

Director: Billy Wilder
Writers: Robert Thoeren and Michael Logan (story), Billy Wilder and I.A.L. Diamond (screenplay)
Producer: Billy Wilder
Film Editor: Arthur P. Schmidt
Cinematographer: Charles Lang

Awards

Oscar Winners: Best Costume Design
Oscar Nominations: Best Actor, Best Art Direction, Best Cinematography, Best Director, Best Writing—Adapted Screenplay

Trivia

• Marilyn Monroe reportedly needed 47 takes to say the line "It's me, Sugar" correctly— even after take 30, when Billy Wilder had the line written on a blackboard.

1986
Something Wild

Overview

Genre: Comedy/Crime
Duration: 113 min
Color: Color
Country: USA
MPAA Rating: R
Studio: Orion Pictures

Charlie Driggs is your run-of-the-mill, clean cut New York yuppie who has a barely visible rebellious streak. It takes no time at all though for sexy, freewheeling Lulu to pick up on that streak and offer him a ride back to his office. But, before he knows what's happening, Charlie finds himself a hostage in Lulu's car as they barrel down the highway toward points unknown. Almost immediately, Lulu goes to work at tearing down Charlie's conservative façade, as well tearing off one of his shirts. Once he gives up and starts going with the flow, Charlie actually starts to enjoy himself. But there are still more surprises in store, and not all of them are pleasant.

Cast

Jeff Daniels: Charles Driggs
Melanie Griffith: Audrey Hankel
Ray Liotta: Ray Sinclair
Margaret Colin: Irene
Tracey Walter: The country squire
Jack Gilpin: Larry Dillman
Su Tissue: Peggy Dillman

Behind the Scenes

Director: Jonathan Demme
Writer: E. Max Frye
Producers: Jonathan Demme, Kenneth Utt
Executive Producer: Edward Saxon
Film Editors: Craig McKay, Camilla Toniolo
Cinematographer: Tak Fujimoto
Original Music: Laurie Anderson, John Cale

Trivia

• The two women working in the second-hand store are Dorothy Demme and Emma Byrne, the mothers of director Jonathan Demme and singer David Byrne.

Awards

Golden Globes Nominations: Best Performance by an Actor—Comedy/Musical, Best Performance by an Actress—Comedy/Musical, Best Performance by a Supporting Actor

1982
Sophie's Choice

Overview

Genre: Drama
Duration: 150 min
Color: Color (Technicolor)
Country: USA
MPAA Rating: R
Studio: Universal Pictures

Stingo is a southern writer who moves to Brooklyn after World War II. Almost immediately he meets Nathan and Sophie—a passionate and beautiful, but troubled young couple living in his building. Nathan is Jewish, enraged and disgusted by the horrors of the Holocaust, and battling a violent temper. Sophie is quiet and mysterious, and clearly covering up a difficult past. As Stingo and Sophie become closer, she reveals bits of herself to him and he realizes that he may be falling in love with her. Sophie finally opens her heart to Stingo and confesses the horrible past she has escaped and the unforgivable choices she was forced to make during the war.

Cast

Meryl Streep: Sophie Zawistowski
Kevin Kline: Nathan Landau
Peter MacNicol: Stingo
Rita Karin: Yetta
Stephen D. Newman: Larry Landau
Greta Turken: Leslie Lapidus
Josh Mostel: Morris Fink

Behind the Scenes

Director: Alan J. Pakula
Writers: William Styron (novel), Alan J. Pakula,
Producers: Keith Barish, Alan J. Pakula
Executive Producer: Martin Starger
Film Editor: Evan Lottman
Cinematographer: Néstor Almendros
Original Music: Marvin Hamlisch

Awards

Oscar Winners: Best Actress
Oscar Nominations: Best Cinematography, Best Costume Design, Best Music, Best Writing—Adapted Screenplay

Trivia

• Meryl Streep did only one take of the final "choice" scene and refused to do any others because she found the situation too painful.

1965
The Sound of Music

Overview

Genre: Musical/Family
Duration: 174 min
Color: Color
Country: USA
MPAA Rating: G
Studio: Twentieth Century Fox

This wildly popular musical stars Julie Andrews as Maria, an impetuous young nun-in-training at an Austrian convent who is sent to be governess to the children of a widowed navy captain. Upon arriving at the home of the Von Trapps, Maria finds the captain to be very cold and his seven children incorrigible. While the captain is away, Maria wins the children over by teaching them songs and loosening the restrictions that have been placed upon them. As she gets more involved in the lives of the Von Trapps, Maria starts feeling torn about her impending vows and her growing love for Captain Von Trapp.

Cast

Julie Andrews: Maria
Christopher Plummer: Captain Von Trapp
Elanor Parker: The Baroness
Richard Haydn: Max Detweiler
Peggy Wood: Mother Abbess
Charmiam Carr: Liesl
Heather Menzies: Louisa

Behind the Scenes

Director: Robert Wise
Writers: Howard Lindsay and Russel Crouse (book), Ernest Lehman (screenplay)
Producer: Robert Wise
Executive Producers: Peter Levathes (uncredited), Richard D. Zanuck (uncredited)
Cinematographer: Ted McCord

Awards

Oscar Winners: Best Picture, Best Director, Best Sound, Best Music—Adapted Score, Best Film Editing

Trivia

• The real Marla Von Trapp appears briefly— she is the older of two women in the background as Julie Andrews walks through an archway during the song "I Have Confidence."

1960
Spartacus

Overview

Genre: Drama
Duration: 184 min
Color: Color (Technicolor)
Country: USA
MPAA Rating: PG-13
Studio: Universal Pictures

Kirk Douglas stars as the title character, a proud Roman slave who has had enough. After being born into slavery, Spartacus is eventually sold to Lentulus Batiatus who trains gladiators to fight to the death for public spectacle. After weeks of training for this brutal contest, Spartacus leads a revolt against his owners and breaks free from his imprisonment. As the rebel slave ranks swell, two rival Roman senators, Gracchus and Crassus, figure out ways to exploit the uprising for their political gain. Can the merchants of power in Rome stop the growing revolution, or will Spartacus and his followers cross the sea to freedom?

Cast

Kirk Douglas: Spartacus
Laurence Olivier: Marcus Licinius Crassus
Jean Simmons: Varinia
Charles Laughton: Sempronius Gracchus
Peter Ustinov: Lentulus Batiatus
John Gavin: Julius Caesar
Nina Foch: Helena Glabrus

Behind the Scenes

Director: Stanley Kubrick
Writers: Howard Fast (novel), Dalton Trumbo (screenplay)
Producer: Edward Lewis
Executive Producer: Kirk Douglas
Cinematographer: Russell Metty
Original Music: Alex North

Awards

Oscar Winners: Best Supporting Actor, Best Art Direction, Best Cinematography, Best Costume Design

Trivia

• Kirk Douglas helped score some very famous names to play supporting roles by convincing each that his or her part would be emphasized.

2001
Spirited Away

Overview

Genre: Family/Fantasy
Duration: 125 min
Color: Color
Country: Japan
MPAA Rating: PG
Studio: Studio Ghibli/
NTV/DENTSU/Tokuma
Shoten/Buena Vista/
Tohokushinsha Film/
Mitsubishi Commercial

On the way to their new home in the countryside, Chiriro and her parents turn down a strange wooded path and discover an abandoned city with decadent food laid out at every restaurant. Her parents gorge themselves at once, but Chiriro is wary and explores instead. Along the way she meets a boy named Haku, who warns her to leave before nightfall. She returns for her parents as the sun sets and finds them transformed into pigs, while the city fills with spirits around them. Haku, promising to help, finds her a job at the bathhouse, and Chiriro embarks on a fantastical journey through the spirit-world to save her parents and find her way home.

Cast

Rumi Hîragi: Chihiro/Sen (voice)
Miyu Irino: Haku (voice)
Mari Natsuki: Yubaba/Zeniba (voice)
Takashi Naitô: Chihiro's father (voice)
Yasuko Sawaguchi: Chihiro's mother (voice)
Tatsuya Gashuin: Aogaeru, assistant manager (voice)

Behind the Scenes

Director: Hayao Miyazaki
Writers: Hayao Miyazaki (story and screenplay)
Producer: Toshio Suzuki
Executive Producer: Yasuyoshi Tokuma
Film Editor: Takeshi Seyama
Cinematographer: Atsushi Okui
Original Music: Joe Hisaishi

Awards

Oscar Winners: Best Animated Feature

Trivia

• This is the first film in history to gross $200 million worldwide prior to opening in the United States.

1939
Stagecoach

Overview

Genre: Drama/Western
Duration: 96 min
Color: Black and White
Country: USA
MPAA Rating: Not Rated
Studio: United Artists

When the Overland stage pulls out of Tonto, New Mexico, en route to the town of Lordsburg, it transports a host of colorful passengers carrying both physical and emotional baggage. Along for the trip are a woman of questionable virtue, a drunken doctor, a gambler, and the wife of a cavalry officer, among others. There is also a marshal aboard the stage who is on the lookout for an escaped outlaw named the Ringo Kid. The threat of Ringo, however, is the least of the group's problems. They are riding right into Apache territory virtually defenseless. A wild western adventure, John Ford's *Stagecoach* has it all.

Cast

Claire Trevor: Dallas
John Wayne: The Ringo Kid
Andy Devine: Buck
John Carradine: Hatfield
Thomas Mitchell: Doc Boone
Louise Platt: Lucy Mallory
George Bancroft: Marshal Curly Wilcox

Behind the Scenes

Director: John Ford
Writers: Ernest Haycox (story), Dudley Nichols
Producer: John Ford (uncredited)
Executive Producer: Walter Wanger
Original Music: Gerard Carbonara (uncredited)

Awards

Oscar Winners: Best Supporting Actor, Best Music

Trivia

• Local Navajo Indians played the Apache seen in the film. The production provided an economic shot-in-the-arm to the tribe as hundreds were employed as extras and crew.

1953
Stalag 17

Overview

Genre: Drama/War
Duration: 120 min
Color: Black and White
Country: USA
MPAA Rating: Not Rated
Studio: Paramount Pictures

Billy Wilder's excellent World War II drama stars William Holden as Sergeant J.J. Sefton, one of several U.S. soldiers held in a German prison camp. A hard-bitten cynic, Sefton is not exactly loved by his fellow detainees as he has no qualms about making bets on, and winning money off of, failed escape attempts. Before long, many in the barracks start suspecting him of being an informer. In-between the serious business of escape plans and possible moles, there is comic relief as the men find interesting ways to pass the time. But it's Holden who steals the show here. Whether he's really the one tipping off the Germans or just too wise for his own good, he's a first-class S.O.B.

Cast

William Holden: Sergeant J.J. Sefton
Don Taylor: Lieutenant James Dunbar
Otto Preminger: Colonel von Scherbach
Robert Strauss: Stanislas Kasava
Harvey Lembeck: Harry Shapiro
Richard Erdman: Sergeant "Hoffy" Hoffman
Peter Graves: Price

Behind the Scenes

Director: Billy Wilder
Writer: Donald Bevan and Edmund Trzcinski (play), Billy Wilder and Edwin Blum (screenplay)
Producer: Billy Wilder
Cinematographer: Ernest Laszlo
Original Music: Leonid Raab

Awards

Oscar Winners: Best Actor in a Leading Role
Oscar Nominations: Best Actor in a Supporting Role, Best Director

Trivia

• William Holden, winner of the Best Actor Oscar for his performance in *Stalag 17*, gave the shortest acceptance speech in Academy history, saying only, "Thank you."

1986
Stand by Me

Overview

Genre: Drama/Adventure
Duration: 89 min
Color: Color (Technicolor)
Country: USA
MPAA Rating: R
Studio: Columbia TriStar

Based on a short story by Stephen King, *Stand by Me* is the tale of four close friends who set out on a trek to uncover the body of a missing boy. One of the four boys, Gordie Lachance, is coping with the recent death of his brother Denny and trying to move on with his life. Narrated by the now grown-up Gordie, he recounts the unforgettable trip with his friends Chris, Teddy, and Vern. With little money, food, or supplies, the boys aim to get to the body before a group of ne'er-do-well teenagers from their town get there first. On the road, their bond grows stronger and they realize that the power of friendship is the real reward of their journey.

Cast

Wil Wheaton: Gordie Lachance
River Phoenix: Chris Chambers
Corey Feldman: Teddy Duchamp
Jerry O'Connell: Vern Tession
Kiefer Sutherland: Ace Merrill
Casey Siemaszko: Billy Tessio
Richard Dreyfuss: The writer
John Cusack: Denny Lachance

Behind the Scenes

Director: Rob Reiner
Writers: Stephen King (story), Bruce A. Evans and Raynold Gideon (screenplay)
Producers: Bruce A. Evans, Raynold Gideon, Andrew Scheinman
Film Editing: Robert Leighton
Cinematographer: Thomas Del Ruth
Original Music: Jack Nitzsche

Trivia

• To get a better sense of his character, Kiefer Sutherland often picked on Wil Wheaton, River Phoenix, Corey Feldman, and Jerry O'Connell even while the camera wasn't rolling.

Awards

Oscar Nominations: Best Writing—Adapted Screenplay

1977
Star Wars

Overview

Genre: Sci-Fi/ Adventure
Duration: 121 min
Color: Color (Technicolor)
Country: USA
MPAA Rating: PG
Studio: Twentieth Century Fox

This high-octane 1977 space fantasy is like nothing that came before it and influenced sci-fi movies for years to come. In a far-off galaxy Luke Skywalker is living on a farm with his aunt and uncle when he stumbles upon a distress message from a captured princess, held by the evil Empire on something called the Death Star. Before you can say "hyperspace," Luke joins up with the sage Ben Kenobi, mercenary pilot Han Solo, Chewbacca the Wookie, and a pair of curious droids in an effort to free Princess Leia from the Empire and their ominous enforcer, Darth Vader. This special effects laden clash between good and evil is pure popcorn-chomping fun.

Cast

Mark Hamill: Luke Skywalker
Harrison Ford: Han Solo
Carrie Fisher: Princess Leia Organa
Peter Cushing: Grand Moff Tarkin
Alec Guinness: Ben Obi-Wan Kenobi
Anthony Daniels: C-3PO (voice)
Kenny Baker: R2-D2 (voice)
Peter Mayhew: Chewbacca
James Earl Jones: Darth Vader (voice)

Behind the Scenes

Director: George Lucas
Writer: George Lucas
Producer: Gary Kurtz
Executive Producer: George Lucas
Film Editors: Richard Chew, Paul Hirsch, Marcia Lucas
Cinematographer: Gilbert Taylor
Original Music: John Williams

Trivia

• Harrison Ford did not memorize his lines for the intercom conversation in the cell block in order to make the dialogue sound spontaneous and realistic.
• Famed Warner Bros. voice man Mel Blanc auditioned for the voice of C-3PO.

Awards

Oscar Winners: Best Art Direction, Best Costume Design, Best Effects—Visual, Best Film Editing, Best Music, Best Sound, Special Achievement Award: Ben Burtt for Sound Effects
Oscar Nominations: Best Supporting Actor, Best Director, Best Picture, Best Writing

1973
The Sting

Overview

Genre: Comedy/Crime
Duration: 129 min
Color: Color
(Technicolor)
Country: USA
MPAA Rating: PG
Studio: Universal
Pictures

When a smalltime con man and his partner unwittingly rip off a mob courier, one of them pays with his life while the other looks to avenge his friend. Having nowhere else to go, Johnny Hooker seeks out Henry Gondorff in hopes that the seasoned confidence man will teach him the "long con" and help him take down mob boss Doyle Lonnegan—the man responsible for his partner's death. It may take some doing, but Gondorff is willing to show the kid the ropes. The only problem is, Gondorff has the feds looking for him and Lonnegan still has a contract out on Hooker. They're going to need a little help from their friends and a whole lot of luck.

Cast

Paul Newman: Henry Gondorff
Robert Redford: Johnny Hooker
Robert Shaw: Doyle Lonnegan
Charles Durning: Lieutenant William Snyder
Ray Walston: J.J. Singleton
Eileen Brennan: Billie
Harold Gould: Kid Twist
Dana Elcar: FBI Agent Polk

Behind the Scenes

Director: George Roy Hill
Writer: David S. Ward
Producers: Tony Bill, Julia Phillips, Michael Phillips
Film Editior: William Reynolds
Cinematographer: Robert Surtees

Trivia

• Robert Shaw was nursing a bad ankle and used a limp as part of Doyle Lonnegan's character.
• This was the first Universal Pictures film to win the Best Picture Academy Award in more than 40 years—when *All Quiet on the Western Front* won in 1930.

Awards

Oscar Winners: Best Art Decoration, Best Costume Design, Best Director, Best Film Editing, Best Music—Original Song, Best Picture, Best Writing
Oscar Nominations: Best Actor, Best Cinematography, Best Sound

1951
A Streetcar Named Desire

Overview

Genre: Drama
Duration: 122 min
Color: Black and White
Country: USA
MPAA Rating: PG
Studio: Warner Bros. Pictures

An aging Southern belle comes to New Orleans to live with her sister and her brutish husband in this screen adaptation of the Tennessee Williams play. When Blanche Dubois shows up on her sister Stella's doorstep, she does so as a broken woman who has lost the family home. Nevertheless, she's not too keen on Stella's cramped apartment and even less fond of her husband, Stanley Kowalski. Blanche and Stanley get along like cats and dogs, with Stella caught in the middle. Into this dysfunctional mix comes Mitch, one of Stanley's poker buddies who is a possible suitor for Blanche. But Stanley may have to do something about this.

Cast

Vivien Leigh: Blanche DuBois
Marlon Brando: Stanley Kowalski
Kim Hunter: Stella Kowalski
Karl Malden: Harold "Mitch" Mitchell
Rudy Bond: Steve
Nick Dennis: Pablo Gonzales
Peg Hillias: Eunice

Behind the Scenes

Director: Elia Kazan
Writers: Tennessee Williams (play and screenplay), Oscar Saul (screenplay)
Producer: Charles K. Feldman
Film Editor: David Weisbart
Cinematographer: Harry Stradling Sr.
Original Music: Alex North

Awards

Oscar Winners: Best Supporting Actor, Best Actress, Best Supporting Actress, Best Art Direction

Trivia

• During production, the crew built the set of the Kowalski apartment progressively smaller in order to hint at Blanche's growing claustrophobia.

1981
Stripes

Overview

Genre: Comedy
Duration: 106 min
Color: Color (Metrocolor)
Country: USA
MPAA Rating: R
Studio: Columbia Pictures

After quitting his job and losing his girlfriend, John Winger decides to join the army . . . but does the army want him? Thinking that the military would be a great way to get in shape and pick up chicks, Winger convinces his friend Russell Ziskey to enlist with him. But, after reporting for duty, they find themselves in a platoon of morons and screw-ups led by no-nonsense drill instructor Sergeant Hulka. As wisecracking Winger and gruff Hulka continually butt heads, it looks like this could have been a huge mistake. And, even if this platoon manages to bumble its through basic training, are these really the guys we want protecting our country?

Cast

Bill Murray: John Winger
Harold Ramis: Russell Ziskey
Warren Oates: Sergeant Hulka
P.J. Soles: MP Stella Hansen
Sean Young: MP Louise Cooper
John Candy: Private Dewey "Ox" Oxberger
John Larroquette: Captain Stillman

Behind the Scenes

Director: Ivan Reitman
Writers: Len Blum, Daniel Goldberg, Harold Ramis
Producers: Daniel Goldberg, Ivan Reitman
Cinematographers: Bill Butler, James Connell
Original Music: Elmer Bernstein

Trivia

• Nearly all of the dialogue when the cast sits around telling their back stories was improvised.

Trivia

• This film was originally meant for Cheech and Chong, but the deal fell through. Most of the "stoner" humor stayed in the film but was transferred to the character Elmo.

1942
Sullivan's Travels

Overview

Genre: Comedy
Duration: 90 min
Color: Black and White
Country: USA
MPAA Rating: Not Rated
Studio: Paramount Pictures

Conscientious Hollywood film director John L. Sullivan is tired of making comedies and instead would like his next picture to focus on the plight of the poor. With this in mind, Sullivan dresses up as a hobo and earnestly takes to the road to research his subject. His incognito efforts are undermined, however, when the studio sends along a support staff to look after his needs. Along the way he meets up with a struggling actress. When he shares his true identity and mission with her, the two ditch his staff and really experience the life of poverty. *Sullivan's Travels* is not your typical screwball comedy; like Sullivan himself, this movie has a heart that beats for the downtrodden.

Cast

Joel McCrea: John L. Lloyd "Sully" Sullivan
Veronica Lake: The Girl
Robert Warwick: Mr. Lebrand
William Demarest: Mr. Jones
Franklin Pangborn: Mr. Casalsis
Porter Hall: Mr. Hadrian
Byron Foulger: Mr. Johnny Valdelle
Margaret Hayes: Secretary

Behind the Scenes

Director: Preston Sturges
Writer: Preston Sturges
Producer: Preston Sturges (uncredited)
Executive Producer: Buddy G. DeSylva (uncredited)
Film Editor: Stuart Gilmore
Cinematographer: John F. Seitz
Original Music: Charles Bradshaw, Leo Shuken

Trivia

• In the film, John Sullivan plans to make a movie called *O Brother, Where Art Thou?* Fifty-eight years later, Joel Coen and Ethan Coen used this title for their own movie.

Awards

Added to National Film Registry in 1990

1950
Sunset Boulevard

Overview

Genre: Drama/ Romance
Duration: 110 min
Color: Black and White
Country: USA
MPAA Rating: Not Rated
Studio: Paramount Pictures

William Holden plays struggling screenwriter Joe Gillis who unwittingly gets entangled in the odd world of former silent star Norma Desmond, eerily portrayed by Gloria Swanson. Having very little money and precious few resources, Gillis agrees to work on a disastrous screenplay with Desmond and soon becomes a kept man within her creepy mansion. A movie featuring some hysterically dark comedic moments, *Sunset Boulevard* is also a drama of the highest order with great performances all the way around. Billy Wilder perfectly captures all of the pitfalls of Hollywood; from fleeting stardom to uncaring studios to sycophantic relationships, not a trick is missed.

Cast

William Holden: Joe Gillis
Gloria Swanson: Norma Desmond
Erich von Stroheim: Max von Mayerling
Nancy Olson: Betty Schaefer
Fred Clark: Sheldrake
Jack Webb: Artie Green
Buster Keaton: Himself

Behind the Scenes

Director: Billy Wilder
Writers: Charles Brackett, Billy Wilder, and D.M. Marshman Jr.
Producer: Charles Brackett
Film Editor: Arthur P. Schmidt
Cinematographer: John F. Seitz
Original Music: Franz Waxman

Trivia

• Fearful that Hollywood would react harshly to an unflattering portrarit of the film industry, writers code-named the film "A Can of Beans."
• The young Norma Desmond photos that decorate the house are all authentic publicity photos from Gloria Swanson's early career.

Awards

Oscar Winners: Best Art Direction, Best Music, Best Writing
Oscar Nominations: Best Actor, Best Actress, Best Supporting Actress, Best Supporting Actor, Best Cinematography, Best Director, Best Film Editing, Best Picture

1978
Superman: The Movie

Overview

Genre: Action/ Adventure
Duration: 143 min
Color: Color (Technicolor)
Country: UK/USA
MPAA Rating: PG
Studio: Warner Bros. Pictures

Christopher Reeve stars as the man of steel in this 1978 big screen adaptation of the popular DC comic. Following Superman's beginnings on his home planet of Krypton through his formative years living with his adoptive parents in Kansas, we flash forward to present day as Clark Kent (aka Superman) works as a reporter for the *Daily Planet* in Metropolis. Cleverly disguising his awesome powers behind a pair of glasses and a suit, it's not long before Clark has to don his cape and come to the rescue of his coworker Lois Lane, facing off against master criminal Lex Luthor. Along for the high-flying action are two acting supermen: Marlon Brando and Gene Hackman.

Cast

Christopher Reeve: Superman (Clark Kent)
Margot Kidder: Lois Lane
Marlon Brando: Jor-El
Gene Hackman: Lex Luthor
Ned Beatty: Otis
Jackie Cooper: Perry White
Glenn Ford: Jonathan Kent

Behind the Scenes

Director: Richard Donner
Writers: Jerry Siegel and Joe Shuster (character), Mario Puzo (story and screenplay), David Newman, Leslie Newman, and Robert Benton (screenplay)
Producers: Alexander Salkind, Pierre Spengler, Michael Thau, Richard Lester

Awards

Oscar Winners: Special Achievement Award—Visual Effects
Oscar Nominations: Best Film Editing, Best Music, Best Sound

Trivia

• Aside from the glasses, another noticeable difference between Clark Kent and Superman is that they part their hair on opposite sides.

1957
Sweet Smell of Success

Overview

Genre: Drama
Duration: 96 min
Color: Black and White
Country: USA
MPAA Rating: Not Rated
Studio: United Artists

Parasitic press agent Sidney Falco will do anything to get an item in J.J. Hunsecker's popular newspaper column. So when J.J. asks for assistance in breaking up his sister Susie's relationship with jazz musician Steve Dallas, Sidney jumps at the chance. Since disappointing a powerful man like J.J. is career suicide, Sidney will stop at nothing to ruin Dallas's reputation. Sidney double-talks his way in and out of various situations, all the while using people like chess pieces in his attempts to slander the young musician. Meanwhile J.J. has a capable backup plan in the person of Harry Kello, a corrupt cop in Hunsecker's pocket. The dialogue crackles, and New York never seemed so dirty, in this biting drama.

Cast

Burt Lancaster: J.J. Hunsecker
Tony Curtis: Sidney Falco
Susan Harrison: Susan Hunsecker
Martin Milner: Steve Dallas
Sam Levene: Frank D'Angelo
Barbara Nichols: Rita
Jeff Donnell: Sally
Joe Frisco: Herbie Temple

Behind the Scenes

Director: Alexander Mackendrick
Writers: Ernest Lehman (story and screenplay), Clifford Odets (screenplay)
Producer: James Hill
Executive Producers: Tony Curtis, Harold Hecht, Burt Lancaster (uncredited)
Cinematographer: James Wong Howe
Original Music: Elmer Bernstein

Trivia

• The character J.J. Hunsecker is loosely based on famous New York entertainment columnist Walter Winchell.
• Tony Curtis's role of Sidney Falco was a career-changing role. It allowed Curtis to finally break out of his typecast of a juvenile delinquent or a swashbuckling hero and take on more serious dramatic roles.

Awards

BAFTA Nominations: Best Foreign Actor

1974
The Taking of Pelham One Two Three

Overview

Genre: Drama/Thriller
Duration: 104 min
Color: Color
Country: USA
MPAA Rating: R
Studio: United Artists

When four armed men take over a New York City subway train, it's up to transit Police Lieutenant Zachary Garber to meet their demands before time runs out. Using code names, Mr. Blue, Mr. Green, Mr. Grey, and Mr. Brown methodically hijack the lead car of an eastside local and pull it into a tunnel between stations. Their demands are one million dollars within the hour or they will start killing hostages. Working against the clock, as well as the mayor's office, subway dispatch, and the general chaos of the city, Garber hustles to meet their deadline. As he ponders who could pull off such a heist, he also wonders how they plan to escape.

Cast

Walter Matthau: Lieutenant Zachary "Z" Garber
Robert Shaw: Blue (Bernard Ryder)
Martin Balsam: Green (Harold Longman)
Hector Elizondo: Grey (Joe Welcome)
Earl Hindman: Brown (George Steever)
James Broderick: Denny Doyle
Dick O'Neill: Frank Correll
Jerry Stiller: Lieutenant Rico Patrone

Behind the Scenes

Director: Joseph Sargent
Writers: John Godey (novel), Peter Stone (screenplay)
Producers: Gabriel Katzka, Edgar J. Scherick
Film Editors: Gerald B. Greenberg, Robert Q. Lovett
Cinematographers: Enrique Bravo, Owen Roizman

Trivia

• Since the release of the film, no #6 train has ever been scheduled to leave the Pelham Bay Park station at 1:23 (a.m. or p.m.)
• Producers noted that this film was a box office success in New York, Toronto, London, and Paris—all cities with major subway systems—but less successful elsewhere.

Awards

BAFTA Nominations: Anthony Asquith Award for Film Music, Best Supporting Actor

1976
Taxi Driver

Overview

Genre: Drama
Duration: 113 min
Color: Color (Metro-color)
Country: USA
MPAA Rating: R
Studio: Columbia Pictures

The gritty streets of 1970s' New York are home to all sorts of miscreants, and cabbie Travis Bickle has seen them all. Cruising around picking up fares, Travis is a loner who finds few redeeming qualities in those he encounters. When he works up the courage to ask a beautiful blonde political volunteer for a date, the results are disastrous. Becoming increasingly isolated and influenced by the malevolence all around him, Travis decides to arm himself and strike back against what he perceives to be the ills of society. After Robert DeNiro's portrayal of paranoid Travis, New Yorkers never looked at cabbies the same way again.

Cast

Robert De Niro: Travis Bickle
Cybill Shepherd: Betsy
Peter Boyle: Wizard
Jodie Foster: Iris Steensma
Harvey Keitel: "Sport" Matthew
Leonard Harris: Senator Charles Palantine
Albert Brooks: Tom

Behind the Scenes

Director: Martin Scorsese
Writer: Paul Schrader
Producers: Julia Phillips, Michael Phillips
Film Editors: Marcia Lucas, Tom Rolf, Melvin Shapiro
Cinematographer: Michael Chapman
Original Music: Bernard Herrmann

Awards

Oscar Nominations: Best Actor, Best Supporting Actress, Best Music—Original Song, Best Picture

Trivia

• Robert De Niro ad-libbed Travis Bickle's "you talkin' to me?" scene.
• Since Jodie Foster was only 14, her older sister played her double for explicit scenes.

1956
The Ten Commandments

Overview

Genre: Drama/Adventure
Duration: : 220 min
Color: Color (Technicolor)
Country: USA
MPAA Rating: G
Studio: Paramount Pictures

Cecil B. DeMille's sweeping religious epic follows the life and times of Moses. As a baby, Moses is set in a basket on the Nile to escape the Pharaoh's death sentence for first-born Hebrew males. There he is discovered by the Pharaoh's daughter and raised among the Egyptians. After his true roots are revealed and he's cast out of Egypt, Moses returns years later armed with a message from God and a demand that the Hebrews be released. You know the rest: there are plagues, a Red Sea crossing, and wrath aplenty. Most of all there's Charlton Heston, with a screen presence as commanding as Moses himself. This entertaining film is also biblically long, but what did you expect?

Cast

Charlton Heston: Moses
Yul Brynner: Rameses
Anne Baxter: Nefretiri
Edward G. Robinson: Dathan
Yvonne De Carlo: Sephora
Debra Paget: Lilia
John Derek: Joshua

Behind the Scenes

Director: Cecil B. DeMille
Writers: Dorothy Clarke Wilson, A.E. Southon, and J.H. Ingraham (novel), Æneas MacKenzie, Jesse Lasky Jr., Jack Gariss, and Fredric M. Frank (screenplay)
Producer: Cecil B. DeMille
Film Editor: Anne Bauchens

Awards

Oscar Winners: Best Effects—Special
Oscar Nominations: Best Art Direction, Best Cinematography, Best Costume Design, Best Film Editing, Best Picture, Best Sound

Trivia

• While Charlton Heston is known as the actor who plays Moses in this film, his son Fraser Clarke Heston played Moses as a baby.

1984
The Terminator

Overview

Genre: Sci-Fi/Action
Duration: 108 min
Color: Color
Country: USA/UK
MPAA Rating: R
Studio: Orion Pictures

Before he became the "king of the world" with *Titanic*, James Cameron was directing this sci-fi thriller about a futuristic cyborg that is sent back in time to kill a woman of some significance. That woman's name is Sarah Connor, and in the year 1984 she is living the fairly inconsequential life of a waitress. But when she starts noticing that women sharing her name are turning up dead, she's not worrying about tips, she's running for her life. Lucky for Sarah, a human soldier has also been sent back to protect her; but is he any match for the terminator? Arnold Schwarzenegger isn't kidding when he utters the line "I'll be back," as he reprised his role in two sequels.

Cast

Arnold Schwarzenegger: The Terminator
Linda Hamilton: Sarah Connor
Michael Biehn: Kyle Reese
Paul Winfield: Lieutenant Ed Traxler
Lance Henriksen: Detective Hal Vukovich
Bess Motta: Ginger Ventura
Earl Boen: Dr. Peter Silberman

Behind the Scenes

Director: James Cameron
Writers: James Cameron, Gale Anne Hurd
Producer: Gale Anne Hurd
Executive Producers: John Daly, Derek Gibson
Cinematographer: Adam Greenberg
Original Music: Brad Fiedel

Trivia

• Gale Anne Hurd, wife of writer/director James Cameron, acquired the initial draft of this film for only one dollar.

Trivia

• Producers passed on O.J. Simpson for the role of the Terminator, believing that nobody would take "a nice guy like O.J." seriously as a heartless killer.

1983
Terms of Endearment

Overview

Genre: Drama/ Romance
Duration: 132 min
Color: Color (Metrocolor)
Country: USA
MPAA Rating: PG
Studio: Paramount Pictures

Aurora and Emma Greenway are a mother and daughter who rarely see eye to eye. So, of course, when Emma decides to marry college professor Flap Horton, Aurora is not fond of her choice. But is it her future son-in-law or the thought of becoming a grandma that has her in such a state? While Emma copes with the ups and downs of marriage and parenthood, Aurora lives the somewhat quiet life of a widow. Her salvation, however, may lay right next door in the form of Garret Breedlove, a hard-partying former astronaut. Featuring outstanding acting and a storyline filled with laughter and tears, *Terms of Endearment* won Best Picture for 1983.

Cast

Shirley MacLaine: Aurora Greenway
Debra Winger: Emma Greenway Horton
Jack Nicholson: Garrett Breedlove
Danny DeVito: Vernon Dahlart
Jeff Daniels: Flap Horton
John Lithgow: Sam Burns
Lisa Hart Carroll: Patsy Clark
Betty King: Rosie Dunlop

Behind the Scenes

Director: James L. Brooks
Writers: Larry McMurtry (novel), James L. Brooks (screenplay)
Producer: James L. Brooks
Film Editor: Richard Marks
Cinematographer: Andrzej Bartkowiak
Original Music: Michael Gore

Trivia

• John Lithgow signed on as a last-minute replacement. On a brief break from *Footloose*, he filmed all of his scenes in only three days.
• The character of Garrett Breedlove wasn't in the novel and was written specifically for Burt Reynolds. Reynolds loved the script, but had already signed on for another film.

Awards

Oscar Winners: Best Actor, Best Actress, Best Director, Best Picture, Best Writing—Adapted Screenplay
Oscar Nominations: Best Supporting Actor, Best Actress, Best Art Direction, Best Film Editing, Best Music, Best Sound

1949
The Third Man

Overview

Genre: Drama/Mystery
Duration: 104 min
Color: Black and White
Country: UK
MPAA Rating: Not Rated
Studio: London Film Productions

Struggling American novelist Holly Martins travels to post-war Vienna at the behest of his friend Harry Lime who has promised him a job. However, when Martins arrives he finds that Lime has died in a traffic accident. At the funeral Martins notices a beautiful young woman who was Lime's girlfriend and also makes the acquaintance of Major Calloway, a British officer who tells him that his old friend was a criminal of the lowest order. Martins vows to clear his friend's name and contacts Lime's girlfriend to help him. As they dig for the truth, they find that Harry was indeed involved in some unsavory business and that there was a mysterious third man present at his fatal accident.

Cast

Joseph Cotten: Holly Martins
Alida Valli: Anna Schmidt
Orson Welles: Harry Lime
Trevor Howard: Major Calloway
Bernard Lee: Sergeant Paine
Paul Hoerbinger: Harry's Porter
Ernst Deutsch: "Baron" Kurtz

Behind the Scenes

Director: Carol Reed
Writer: Graham Greene (story and screenplay)
Producer: Carol Reed
Film Editor: Oswald Hafenrichter
Cinematographer: Robert Krasker
Original Music: Anton Karas

Awards

Oscar Winners: Best Cinematography
Oscar Nominations: Best Director, Best Film Editing

Trivia

• Orson Welles refused to film several scenes in the sewers. As a result, sets replicating the sewers had to be constructed on a sound stage.

1984
This Is Spinal Tap

Overview

Genre: Comedy
Duration: 82 min
Color: Color
Country: USA
MPAA Rating: R
Studio: Embassy Pictures

This sidesplitting "rockumentary" follows the doomed North American tour of aging British metal band Spinal Tap. Fronted by the delightfully clueless trio of David St. Hubbins, Nigel Tufnel, and Derek Smalls, Spinal Tap looks back on their colorful past—which includes multiple ill-fated drummers—as they gear up to take American by storm. But, even with a new album titled *Smell the Glove* and amps that go to 11, their best-laid plans hit a few snags. Plagued by awful record reviews, increasingly apathetic fans, malfunctioning stage props, and the intrusion of a band member's girlfriend into the group, Spinal Tap is on a hilarious road to irrelevance.

Cast

Michael McKean: David St. Hubbins
Christopher Guest: Nigel Tufnel
Harry Shearer: Derek Smalls
Rob Reiner: Marty DiBergi
R.J. Parnell: Mick Shrimpton
David Kaff: Viv Savage
Tony Hendra: Ian Faith

Behind the Scenes

Director: Rob Reiner
Writers: Christopher Guest, Michael McKean, Harry Shearer, Rob Reiner
Producer: Karen Murphy
Cinematographer: Peter Smokler
Original Music: Christopher Guest, Michael McKean, Rob Reiner, Harry Shearer

Awards

Added to National Film Registry in 2002

Trivia

• The actors really perform all of the numbers.
• In the first dinner interview scene, Christopher Guest wears a t-shirt from the company that supplied many of the guitars for the movie.

1997
Titanic

Overview

Genre: Drama/Romance
Duration: 194 min
Color: Color
Country: USA
MPAA Rating: PG-13
Studio: Twentieth
Century Fox/Paramount
Pictures

The story of the "unsinkable" ship that hit the ocean's floor on April 15, 1912, comes to life through the eyes of Jack Dawson and Rose DeWitt Bukater, an unlikely pair who fall in love on the *Titanic's* ill-fated inaugural trip. Challenged by class affairs, jealousy, and destiny, Jack and Rose's romance is as fraught with peril as the ship itself. When Rose's fiancé Caledon Hockley becomes suspicious of Jack, he does everything in his power to take him out of the picture. But after the *Titanic* encounters an iceberg, survival becomes the only priority among the terrified passengers. Only a lucky few will live to tell the tale of the nightmare voyage aboard the "ship of dreams."

Cast

Leonardo DiCaprio: Jack Dawson
Kate Winslet: Rose DeWitt Bukater
Billy Zane: Caledon "Cal" Hockley
Kathy Bates: Molly Brown
Frances Fisher: Ruth Dewitt Bukater
Gloria Stuart: Old Rose
Bill Paxton: Brock Lovett

Behind the Scenes

Director: James Cameron
Writer: James Cameron
Producers: James Cameron, Jon Landau
Executive Producer: Rae Sanchini
Film Editors: Conrad Buff, Richard A. Harris
Cinematographer: Russell Carpenter
Original Music: James Horner

Awards

Oscar Winners: Best Art Direction, Best Cinematography, Best Costume Design, Best Director, Best Film Editing, Best Music, Best Music—Original Song, Best Picture

Trivia

• *Titanic* is the highest grossing film in North American and global box office history, with a total of $1.2 billion worldwide. It also had the longest cinematic release in history.

1962
To Kill a Mockingbird

Overview

Genre: Drama
Duration: 129 min
Color: Black and White
Country: USA
MPAA Rating: Not Rated
Studio: Universal International Pictures

Harper Lee's Pulitzer Prize–winning novel about racial inequality in the South translates beautifully to the screen with Gregory Peck playing Atticus Finch, a widowed father of two and lawyer defending a black man accused of rape. So much more than a trial film, the action is seen through the eyes of Finch's young daughter Scout who, along with her older brother Jem, reveres her father. The Finch children also have a bright and quirky friend in Dill Harris and together the three of them train their imaginations on mysterious town resident Boo Radley. Along the way, the children learn important lessons that some adults will never grasp.

Cast

Gregory Peck: Atticus Finch
Mary Badham: Scout Finch
Philip Alford: Jem Finch
John Megna: Dill Harris
Frank Overton: Sheriff Heck Tate
Rosemary Murphy: Miss Maudie Atkinson
Brock Peters: Tom Robinson

Behind the Scenes

Director: Robert Mulligan
Writers: Harper Lee (novel), Horton Foote (screenplay)
Producer: Alan J. Pakula
Film Editor: Aaron Stell
Cinematographer: Russell Harlan
Original Music: Elmer Bernstein

Awards

Oscar Winners: Best Actor, Best Art Direction, Best Writing—Adapted Screenplay

Trivia

• Dill was modeled after author Harper Lee's childhood friend, Truman Capote.
• Finch was the maiden name of author Harper Lee's mother.

1982
Tootsie

Overview

Genre: Comedy
Duration: 116 min
Color: Color (Technicolor)
Country: USA
MPAA Rating: PG
Studio: Columbia Pictures

Michael Dorsey is a terrific actor but no one will work with him. He desperately wants to raise money to help produce his roommate's play. After his good friend Sandy unsuccessfully auditions for a daytime soap opera, Michael decides to dress up as a woman and audition for the role himself. Not only does he land the part, but his newfound fame soon makes him the toast of New York. There are a few problems though. How can he tell his co-star Julie that he's falling for her when she thinks he's a woman? What will Sandy say if she finds out he got her part? And how long can he keep up this charade?

Cast

Dustin Hoffman: Michael Dorsey/Dorothy Michaels
Jessica Lange: Julie Nichols
Teri Garr: Sandy Lester
Dabney Coleman: Ron Carlisle
Bill Murray: Jeff Slater
Geena Davis: April Page
Charles Durning: Leslie "Les" Nichols
George Gaynes: John Van Horn

Behind the Scenes

Director: Sydney Pollack
Writers: Don McGuire (story), Larry Gelbart (story and screenplay), Murray Schisgal (screenplay)
Producers: Sydney Pollack, Dick Richards
Executive Producer: Charles Evans
Cinematographer: Owen Roizman
Original Music: Dave Grusin

Trivia

• Director Sydney Pollack appears in the film as Michael/Dorothy's agent George Fields.
• Almost all of Bill Murray's dialogue in the movie is improvised.

Awards

Oscar Winners: Best Supporting Actress
Oscar Nominations: Best Actor, Best Supporting Actress, Best Cinematography, Best Director, Best Film Editing, Best Music — Original Song, Best Picture, Best Sound, Best Writing

1995
Toy Story

Overview

Genre: Family/Comedy
Duration: 81 min
Color: Color (Technicolor)
Country: USA
MPAA Rating: G
Studio: Walt Disney Pictures/Pixar

This film, the first animated entirely with computer-generated graphics, centers on Andy and his roomful of toys, who unbeknownst to him, come alive when he leaves the room. But these toys' paradise is threatened when Woody's position as Andy's favorite toy is filled by the arrogant Buzz Lightyear, who thinks he is a real space ranger. When Buzz and Woody's fight leaves them separated from Andy and the other toys, including Mr. Potato Head, Rex the plastic T-Rex, Slinky Dog, and Hamm the piggy bank, they have to band together to reach home before they are left behind as Andy moves to a new house.

Cast

Tom Hanks: Woody (voice)
Tim Allen: Buzz Lightyear (voice)
Don Rickles: Mr. Potato Head (voice)
Jim Varney: Slinky Dog (voice)
Wallace Shawn: Rex (voice)
John Ratzenberger: Hamm (voice)
Annie Potts: Bo Peep (voice)

Behind the Scenes

Director: John Lasseter
Writers: John Lasseter, Pete Docter, Andrew Stanton, Joe Ranft, Joss Wheldon, Joel Cohen, Alec Sokolow
Producers: Bonnie Arnold, Ralph Guggenheim
Original Music: Randy Newman

Awards

Oscar Nominations: Best Music, Best Music—Original Song, Best Writing

Trivia

• The Pizza Planet truck makes its debut appearance in *Toy Story*, but can be glimpsed in many Pixar films since, including *Monsters Inc.*, *Finding Nemo*, and *Cars*.

1983
Trading Places

Overview

Genre: Comedy
Duration: 118 min
Color: Color (Technicolor)
Country: USA
MPAA Rating: R
Studio: Paramount Pictures

Are good genes or your environment more responsible for social standing? This nature versus nurture argument becomes the impetus for a bet between commodity broker giants Randolph and Mortimer Duke. The Duke brothers decide to ruin stuffy, Harvard-educated financial executive Louis Winthorpe III while elevating two-bit con man Billy Ray Valentine to his former position. This experiment produces some incredibly funny moments as Winthorpe descends from prince to pauper and Valentine becomes a natural in the commodities racket. But when the guinea pigs catch wind of this wager, you can bet your bottom dollar that they aren't going to take it lying down.

Cast

Eddie Murphy: Billy Ray Valentine
Dan Aykroyd: Louis Winthorpe III
Jamie Lee Curtis: Ophelia
Ralph Bellamy: Randolph Duke
Don Ameche: Mortimer Duke
Denholm Elliott: Coleman
Kristin Holby: Penelope

Behind the Scenes

Director: John Landis
Writers: Timothy Harris, Herschel Weingrod
Producer: Aaron Russo
Executive Producer: George Folsey Jr.
Film Editor: Malcom Campbell
Cinematographer: Robert Paynter
Original Music: Elmer Bernstein

Awards

Oscar Nominations: Best Music—Original Song

Trivia

• Actor Don Ameche's juggling act when Valentine returns Mortimer's money clip was unintentional, but left in because neither Ameche nor Ralph Bellamy broke character.

1948
The Treasure of the Sierra Madre

Overview

Genre: Drama/ Adventure
Duration: 126 min
Color: Black and White
Country: USA
MPAA Rating: Not Rated
Studio: Warner Bros. Pictures

There's gold in them thar hills, and two down-on-their-luck Americans and a crusty old prospector aim to find it. Fred C. Dobbs and Bob Curtin meet while working in the oil fields of Mexico. One night they're told tales of gold in the mountains by an old man named Howard, and before you can say "eureka!" the trio decide to team up and seek their fortune. But, as Howard has warned, prospecting has its pitfalls. The hills are full of Mexican bandits, and men in the throes of gold fever are likely to do anything to protect their claim.

Cast

Humphrey Bogart: Fred C. Dobbs
Walter Huston: Howard
Tim Holt: Bob Curtin
Bruce Bennett: James Cody
Barton MacLane: Pat McCormick
Alfonso Bedoya: Gold Fat
Arturo Soto Rangel: Presidente

Behind the Scenes

Director: John Huston
Writers: B. Traven (novel), John Huston (screenplay)
Producer: Henry Blanke
Executive Producer: Jack L. Warner
Film Editor: Owen Marks
Cinematographer: Ted McCord
Original Music: Max Steiner

Trivia

• When the film began shooting in Tampico, Mexico, the production was temporarily halted by the Mexican government because a newspaper had printed a false story that the film put the country in a bad light.

Awards

Oscar Winners: Best Supporting Actor, Best Director, Best Writing
Oscar Nominations: Best Picture

1957
12 Angry Men

Overview

Genre: Drama
Duration: 96 min
Color: Black and White
Country: USA
MPAA Rating: Not Rated
Studio: United Artists

This classic courtroom drama begins with a jury being given instructions on a murder case and adjourning to deliberate. Henry Fonda stars as Juror #8, the one man on the jury that wants to take a closer look at the evidence against a young man accused of stabbing his father to death. As a sultry New York day approaches evening, the tempers in the jury room get as hot as the weather outside. A fantastic ensemble cast led by Lee J. Cobb, the angriest of the 12 men, lends a combustible chemistry to the heated deliberations. The proceedings aren't only about innocence and guilt, but also how they are perceived and colored by individual experience.

Cast

Martin Balsam: Juror #1
John Fiedler: Juror #2
Lee J. Cobb: Juror #3
E.G. Marshall: Juror #4
Jack Klugman: Juror #5
Ed Binns: Juror #6
Jack Warden: Juror #7
Henry Fonda: Juror #8
Joseph Sweeney: Juror #9

Behind the Scenes

Director: Sidney Lumet
Writer: Reginald Rose (story and screenplay)
Producers: Henry Fonda, Reginald Rose
Film Editor: Carl Lerner
Cinematographer: Boris Kaufman
Original Music: Kenyon Hopkins

Trivia

• The cameras all begin the film above eye level and with wide-angle lenses. As the film continues, the camera slides to eye level and finally to below eye level. By the end, all shots are close-ups and all cameras equipped with telephoto lenses to induce a sense of claustrophobia.

Awards

Oscar Nominations: Best Director, Best Picture, Best Writing—Adapted Screenplay

1968
2001: A Space Odyssey

Overview

Genre: Sci-Fi/ Adventure
Duration: 141 min
Color: Color (Technicolor)
Country: UK/US
MPAA Rating: G
Studio: Metro- Goldwyn-Mayer (MGM)

S tanley Kubrick's mind-blowing space adventure is as thought-provoking today as it was in 1968. At the dawn of civilization a pack of apes come in contact with a mysterious black monolith which seems to impart to them the wisdom to use tools and evolve. Flash forward to the 21st century where a similar monolith has been discovered on the moon and appears to be sending signals to Jupiter. The resulting space mission to find the source of these signals and their significance imperils the human crew and provides the movie with a villain in the form of the HAL 9000 computer. *2001: A Space Odyssey* remains a brilliant look at the mysteries of the universe and the soul of man.

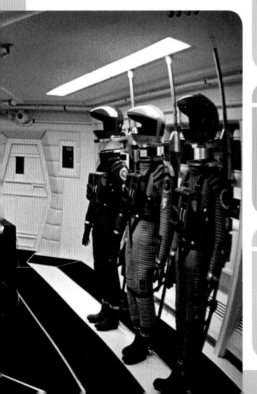

Cast

Keir Dullea: Dr. Dave Bowman
Gary Lockwood: Dr. Frank Poole
William Sylvester: Dr. Heywood R. Floyd
Daniel Richter: Moon-Watcher
Leonard Rossiter: Dr. Andrei Smyslov
Margaret Tyzack: Elena
Robert Beatty: Dr. Ralph Halvorsen
Sean Sullivan: Dr. Bill Michaels
Douglas Rain: HAL 9000 (voice)

Behind the Scenes

Director: Stanley Kubrick
Writers: Arthur C. Clarke (story and screenplay), Stanley Kubrick (screenplay)
Producer: Stanley Kubrick
Film Editor: Ray Lovejoy
Cinematographer: Geoffrey Unsworth

Trivia

• Even though incrementing each letter of "HAL" gives you "IBM," Arthur C. Clarke said it was purely a coincidence. The acronym HAL actually stands for Heuristic Algorithmic Computer.

Awards

Oscar Winners: Best Effects—Special Effects
Oscar Nominations: Best Art Direction, Best Director, Best Writing

1995
The Usual Suspects

Overview

Genre: Drama/Thriller
Duration: 106 min
Color: Color (Technicolor)
Country: USA
MPAA Rating: R
Studio: PolyGram

After an explosion on a ship docked near Los Angeles kills 27 and leaves the police searching for a suspect and a motive, a witness named Verbal is brought in for questioning. Tracked by agent Kujan during the weeks preceding the mysterious explosion, Verbal is questioned about low-level criminals based in New York. Verbal lays out his story for Kujan, implicating a mysterious lawyer named Kobayashi and the terrifying and inescapable Keyser Söze. An unstoppable chain of events brought about by the workings of an intricate web of criminals and motives leads to the baffling explosion, and in the final, unforgettable plot twist, the truth behind it all is masterfully revealed.

Cast

Stephen Baldwin: Michael McManus
Gabriel Byrne: Dean Keaton
Benicio Del Toro: Fred Fenster
Kevin Pollak: Todd Hockney
Kevin Spacey: Roger "Verbal" Kint
Chazz Palminteri: Dave Kujan, US Customs
Pete Postlethwaite: Kobayashi

Behind the Scenes

Director: Bryan Singer
Writer: Christopher McQuarrie
Producers: Michael McDonnell, Bryan Singer
Executive Producers: Hans Brockmann, François Duplat, Art Horan, Robert Jones
Cinematographer: Newton Thomas Sigel

Awards

Oscar Winners: Best Supporting Actor, Best Writing

Trivia

• A cigarette flicked at Stephen Baldwin's McManus was meant to hit him in the chest rather than his face. Director Bryan Singer liked his reaction and left it in.

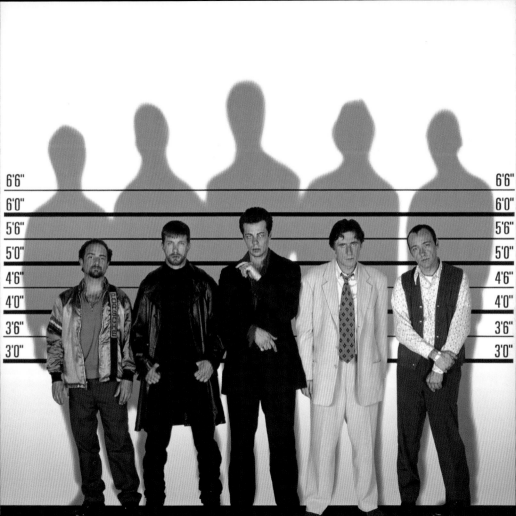

1982
The Verdict

Overview

Genre: Drama
Duration: 129 min
Color: Color (Technicolor)
Country: USA
MPAA Rating: R
Studio: Twentieth Century Fox

Paul Newman gives a riveting performance as Frank Galvin, a hard-drinking, ambulance-chasing lawyer who's got one last chance to revive both his flagging career and his dignity. When Galvin agrees to take on a medical malpractice suit on behalf of the family of a woman who was left in a coma by a botched operation, he sees a settlement and an easy payday. But after visiting the victim's bedside, he has a change of heart and decides to take on the powerful Catholic hospital. The odds stacked against him, Galvin will have to beat a team of lawyers from a prestigious law firm, as well as his own demons, to see justice done.

Cast

Paul Newman: Frank Galvin
Charlotte Rampling: Laura Fischer
Jack Warden: Mickey Morrissey
Jame Mason: Ed Concannon
Ed Binns: Bishop Brophy
Roxanne Hart: Sally Doneghy
James Handy: Kevin Doneghy

Behind the Scenes

Director: Sidney Lumet
Writers: Barry Reed (novel), David Mamet (screenplay)
Producers: David Brown, Richard D. Zanuck
Executive Producer: Burtt Harris
Cinematographer: Andrzej Bartkowiak
Original Music: Johnny Mandel

Awards

Oscar Nominations: Best Actor, Best Supporting Actor, Best Director, Best Picture, Best Writing—Adapted Screenplay

Trivia

• Both Bruce Willis and Jerry Seinfeld, as uncredited extras, are among the crowd in the courtroom during the climactic closing speech.

1958
Vertigo

Overview

Genre: Drama/Thriller
Duration: 128 min
Color: Color (Technicolor)
Country: USA
MPAA Rating: PG
Studio: Paramount Pictures

John "Scottie" Ferguson is a San Francisco police detective who retires from the force after a rooftop tragedy reveals that he suffers from an acute fear of heights. While coping with his vertigo, Scottie is contacted by an old friend who wants to hire him to tail his wife Madeleine, who has been acting very strangely. Scottie half-heartedly agrees to look into it, but he soon finds himself attracted to the woman, even though she seems strangely possessed by a spirit from the past. After Madeleine throws herself into the Frisco Bay, Scottie is, literally and figuratively, in deep. Featuring a haunting score by Bernard Herrmann, *Vertigo* has more twists and turns than the Pacific Coast Highway.

Cast

James Stewart: Detective John "Scottie" Ferguson
Kim Novak: Madeleine Elster/Judy Barton
Barbara Bel Geddes: Marjorie "Midge" Wood
Tom Helmore: Gavin Elster
Ellen Corby: Manager of McKittrick Hotel
Henry Jones: Coroner
Raymond Bailey: Scottie's doctor
Konstantin Shayne: Pop Leibel

Behind the Scenes

Director: Alfred Hitchcock
Writers: Pierre Boileau and Thomas Narcejac (novel), Alec Coppel and Samuel Taylor (screenplay)
Producer: Alfred Hitchcock (uncredited)
Film Editor: George Tomasini
Cinematographer: Robert Burks
Original Music: Bernard Herrmann

Trivia

• The famous "vertigo" effect was invented for this film by tracking in the camera while zooming out. It is now referred to as "contra-zoom" or a "trombone shot."
• As he does in all of his films, Alfred Hitchcock makes a brief cameo. About 11 minutes in, he walks past Gavin Elster's shipyard in a gray suit.

Awards

Oscar Nominations: Best Art Direction, Best Sound

1985
Vision Quest

Overview

Genre: Drama/Sports
Duration: 105 min
Color: Color
Country: USA
MPAA Rating: R
Studio: The Guber-Peters Company/ Warner Bros. Pictures

Louden Swain just turned 18 and decided that this is the year he's going to make his mark on the world. He plans on doing this by dropping two weight classes and getting on the mat with the best wrestler in Washington state, Brian Shute. Louden's coach, teachers, and teammates all think he's crazy but taking on the undefeated and dangerous Shute is all he wants. Well, that is until a beautiful young artist named Carla moves in with Louden and his dad on her way to San Francisco. With Carla around, Louden's training focus is seriously tested. But this schoolboy crush just may get him crushed by Shute if he doesn't watch out.

Cast

Matthew Modine: Louden Swain
Linda Fiorentino: Carla
Michael Schoeffling: Kuch
Ronny Cox: Larry Swain
Harold Sylvester: Gene Tanneran
Daphne Zuniga: Margie Epstein
Charles Hallahan: The Coach

Behind the Scenes

Director: Harold Becker
Writers: Terry Davis (novel), Darryl Ponicsan
Producers: Peter Guber, Jon Peters
Cinematographer: Owen Roizman
Original Music: Tangerine Dream: Christopher Frankie, Edgar Froese, Johannes Schmölling

Trivia

• Linda Fiorentino landed this part in her first audition ever, straight out of drama school. This was her onscreen debut.

Trivia

• Matthew Modine, who plays Louden Swain, once said that he thought the film's title was inappropriate because it sounded like a science fiction film.

1953
The Wages of Fear

Overview

Genre: Action/Thriller
Duration: 131 min
Color: Color
Country: France/Italy
MPAA Rating: Not Rated
Studio: Compagnie Industrielle et Commerciale Cinematographique

Oh how France's Henri-Georges Clouzot could craft a suspense film. Hitchcock himself is said to have heard competitive footsteps from Clouzot. Coincidentally, Hitch attempted to secure the rights to the novel from which the film was based, but novelist Georges Arnaud announced that only Clouzot could do his story justice. The film is set in a hellish Central American town where the American manager of an oilfield offers a bunch of desperate characters big money to drive trucks carrying nitro-glycerin through a not-exactly-smooth jungle, in order to extinguish an oil well fire. Suffice to say, it's white knuckles and clenched teeth from there on in.

Cast

Yves Montand: Mario
Charles Vanel: Jo
Folco Lulli: Luigi
Peter van Eyck: Bimba
Vera Clouzot: Linda
William Tubbs: Bill O'Brien
Dario Moreno: Hernandez

Behind the Scenes

Director: Henri-Georges Clouzot
Writers: Georges Arnaud (novel), Henri-Georges Clouzot and Jerome Geronimi (screenplay)
Producers: Raymond Borderie, Henri-Georges Clouzot
Cinematographer: Armand Thirard

Awards

BAFTA Winners: Best Film
Cannes Film Festival Winners: Grand Prize of the Festival, Special Mention for the Acting Performance of Charles Vanel

Trivia

• Accused of being anti-American, the film had several important scenes cut for the U.S. release of the film.

1996
Waiting for Guffman

Overview

Genre: Comedy
Duration: 84 min
Color: Color
Country: USA
MPAA Rating: R
Studio: Castle Rock Entertainment/Sony Pictures

Community theater was never so entertaining as it is under the steady directorial hand of flamboyant transplanted New Yorker Corky St. Clair. *Waiting for Guffman* is a hilarious "mockumentary," following Corky and his inept cast of local yokels as they attempt to stage a musical theater production for their small community of Blaine, Missouri. But even the most modest productions have high aspirations, and when word arrives that a Broadway theater representative will be watching, Corky and company can barely contain themselves. Ridiculous song lyrics, ludicrous costumes, and an audience of eccentrics make this one performance you won't soon forget.

Cast

Christopher Guest: Corky St. Clair
Eugene Levy: Allan Pearl
Fred Willard: Ron Albertson
Catherine O'Hara: Sheila Albertson
Parker Posey: Libby Mae Brown
Bob Balaban: Lloyd Miller

Behind the Scenes

Director: Christopher Guest
Writers: Christopher Guest, Eugene Levy
Producer: Karen Murphy
Film Editor: Andrew Blumenthal
Cinematographer: Roberto Schaefer
Original Music: Christopher Guest, Michael McKean, Harry Shearer

Awards

Independent Spirit Award Nominations: Best Feature, Best Male Lead, Best Screenplay

Trivia

• Guest and Blumenthal spent over a year editing 60 hours of footage.
• The only scripted part of this film are the lines in the musical "Red, White, and Blaine."

1961
West Side Story

Overview

Genre: Musical/Romance
Duration: 152 min
Color: Color (Technicolor)
Country: USA
MPAA Rating: Not Rated
Studio: United Artists

The story of Romeo and Juliet is brought to New York City and set to music in this 1961 "Best Picture" winner. Tony is a former member of a white street gang known as the Jets and Maria is the sister of the leader of their Puerto Rican rivals, the Sharks. The moment the two star-crossed teens lock eyes, they fall for each other and their love only stokes the fires of hatred between the two gangs. Filled with the songs of Broadway heavyweights Leonard Bernstein and Stephen Sondheim and choreographed by Jerome Robbins, *West Side Story* keeps the action lively even as the dramatic storyline unfolds.

Cast

Natalie Wood: Maria
Richard Beymer: Tony
Russ Tamblyn: Riff
Rita Moreno: Anita
George Chakiris: Bernardo
Simon Oakland: Lieutenant Schrank
Tucker Smith: Ice

Behind the Scenes

Directors: Jerome Robbins, Robert Wise
Writers: Jerome Robbins and Arthur Laurents (play), Ernest Lehman (screenplay)
Producer: Robert Wise
Executive Producer: Walter Mirisch (uncredited)
Cinematographer: Daniel L. Fapp
Original Music: Leonard Bernstein

Trivia

• The original story centered on a romance between a Catholic boy and Jewish girl and was originally titled *East Side Story*. It was later changed after an influx of Puerto Rican immigrants in the 1940s–'50s.

Awards

Oscar Winners: Best Supporting Actor, Best Supporting Actress, Best Art Direction, Best Cinematography, Best Costume Design, Best Director, Best Film Editing, Best Music, Best Picture, Best Sound
Oscar Nominations: Best Writing—Adapted Screenplay

1989
When Harry Met Sally . . .

Overview

Genre: Comedy/
Romance
Duration: 96 min
Color: Color
Country: USA
MPAA Rating: R
Studio: Castle Rock
Entertainment

haring a car ride home from college, Harry Burns tells Sally Albright that men and women can't be friends because sex always gets in the way. Years later the two run into each other in New York and put that maxim to the test. Harry is in the midst of a divorce and Sally is also coming out of a long-term relationship and neither is looking for romance. As they spend time together, they become friends and share thoughts on the male/female dynamic. But can this friendship last without sex getting in the way? *When Harry Met Sally . . .* may not have all the answers, but the questions sure are a lot of fun.

Cast

Billy Crystal: Harry Burns
Meg Ryan: Sally Albright
Carrie Fisher: Marie
Bruno Kirby: Jess
Steven Ford: Joe
Lisa Jane Persky: Alice
Michelle Nicastro: Amanda Reese

Behind the Scenes

Director: Rob Reiner
Writer: Nora Ephron
Producers: Rob Reiner, Andrew Scheinman
Film Editor: Robert Leighton
Cinematographer: Barry Sonnenfeld

Trivia

• Sally's precise and picky eating habits were added to the film when Rob Reiner saw writer Nora Ephron ordering her food in exactly that manner. Sally's line "I just like it the way I like it" was what Ephron said when Reiner asked her about her habits.

Awards

Oscar Nominations: Best Writing

1949
White Heat

Overview

Genre: Drama/Crime
Duration: 114 min
Color: Black and White
Country: USA
MPAA Rating: Not Rated
Studio: Warner Bros. Pictures

James Cagney stars as Cody Jarrett, a psychotic gangster only a mother could love. After Jarrett and his gang knock over a train, they hide out with his beloved mother and none-too-saintly wife Verna. Like most criminals, Cody's got plenty to worry about, including Big Ed Somers who has his eye on taking over the gang and Verna. When the feds link Cody to the train robbery, he concocts an alibi copping to a lesser crime. While he serves a short sentence, the government sends in an undercover agent to be his cellmate. On the outside, Big Ed doesn't want to see Cody leave prison alive. But as long as Ma is looking out for him, Cody will be just fine.

Cast

James Cagney: Arthur "Cody" Jarrett
Virginia Mayo: Verna Jarrett
Edmond O'Brien: Vic Pardo
Margaret Wycherly: Mia Jarrett
Steve Cochran: Big Ed Somers
John Archer: Philip Evans
Wally Cassell: "Cotton" Valletti

Behind the Scenes

Director: Raoul Walsh
Writers: Virginia Kellogg (story), Ivan Goff and Ben Roberts (screenplay)
Producer: Louis F. Edelman
Film Editor: Owen Marks
Cinematographer: Sidney Hickox
Original Music: Max Steiner

Awards

Oscar Nominations: Best Writing

Trivia

• The surprise seen on the faces of Cody's fellow inmates during the prison mess hall scene is real. Only Cagney and the director were aware of his planned outburst.

1966
Who's Afraid of Virginia Woolf?

Overview

Genre: Drama
Duration: 131 min
Color: Black and White
Country: USA
MPAA Rating: Not Rated
Studio: Warner Bros. Pictures

Based on Edward Albee's Tony Award–winning play, *Who's Afraid of Virginia Woolf?* is a searing portrait of marital domesticity and a commentary on 1950s' society. George, an aging professor, and Martha, his wife, are an abusive couple who invite Nick, George's youthful colleague, and his wife Honey over for a drink. Almost immediately, George and Martha begin to air their dirty laundry for the benefit of their unsuspecting guests. Using a series of mind games, George and Martha uncover hurtful information about Nick and Honey and force the naive young couple to play along. Elizabeth Taylor, Richard Burton, George Segal, and Sandy Dennis all received Oscar nominations for their emotionally complex performances.

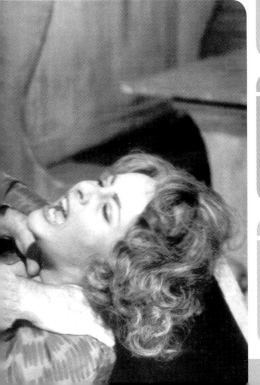

Cast

Elizabeth Taylor: Martha
Richard Burton: George
George Segal: Nick
Sandy Dennis: Honey
Agnes Flanagan: Roadhouse waitress (uncredited)
Frank Flanagan: Roadhouse manager (uncredited)

Behind the Scenes

Director: Mike Nichols
Writers: Edward Albee (play), Ernest Lehman
Producer: Ernest Lehman
Film Editor: Sam O'Steen
Cinematographer: Haskell Wexler
Original Music: Alex North

Trivia

• Elizabeth Taylor gained almost 30 pounds just to play the character of Martha. Cinematographer Harry Stradling Sr. was fired just after filming began, supposedly because he was attempting to "beautify" Taylor.

Awards

Oscar Winners: : Best Actress, Best Supporting Actress, Best Art Direction, Best Cinematography, Best Costume Design
Oscar Nominations: Best Actor, Best Supporting Actor, Best Director, Best Film Editing, Best Music, Best Picture, Best Sound, Best Writing—Adapted Screenplay

1969
The Wild Bunch

Overview

Genre: Drama/Action
Duration: 134 min
Color: Color (Technicolor)
Country: USA
MPAA Rating: R
Studio: Warner Bros.–Seven Arts

Pike Bishop is the leader of an aging gang of gun-slinging bank robbers who are nearing the end of their times. After a botched robbery at a railroad office yields only a violent shootout and sacks of iron washers, Pike and his men head towards Mexico. In pursuit is a posse led by Pike's former friend Deke Thornton. But, no matter where the gang goes, they are faced with consequences of their outlaw ways. Running from their pursuers and straight into more trouble in a Mexican border town, their destiny awaits. Before there was *No Country for Old Men* there was *The Wild Bunch*, and a more appropriately titled film you'd be hard pressed to find.

Cast

William Holden: Pike Bishop
Ernest Borgnine: Dutch Engstrom
Robert Ryan: Deke Thornton
Edmond O'Brien: Freddie Sykes
Warren Oates: Lyle Gorch
Jaime Sanchez: Angel
Ben Johnson: Tector Gorch

Behind the Scenes

Director: Sam Peckinpah
Writers: Roy N. Sickner (story), Walon Green (story and screenplay), Sam Peckinpah (screenplay)
Producer: Phil Feldman
Film Editor: Lou Lombardo

Awards

Oscar Nominations: Best Music, Best Writing

Trivia

• More blank rounds (totaling 90,000) were supposedly discharged during the production of this film than live rounds were fired in the Mexican Revolution of 1914.

1959
Wild Strawberries

Overview

Genre: Drama
Duration: 91 min
Color: Black and White
Country: Sweden
MPAA Rating: Not Rated
Studio: Svensk Filmindustri (SF)

Elderly professor Dr. Isak Borg gets driven to Stockholm by his daughter-in-law, Sara, to receive an honorary degree. On the road, the characters the two pick up and drop off—young students, a bickering married couple—prompt Borg to remember significant incidents in his own life. He dozes off, experiencing disturbing dreams, and considers his problematic relationships with his mother, son, and late wife, lamenting his neglect of them. At the moment of his greatest triumph, the esteemed doctor must come to terms with the toll his professional success has taken on his personal life, even as he confronts his own impending mortality.

Cast

Victor Sjöström: Dr. Isak Borg
Bibi Andersson: Sara
Ingrid Thulin: Marianne Borg
Gunnar Björnstrand: Dr. Evald Borg
Jullan Kindahl: Agda
Folke Sundquist: Anders
Björn Bjelfvenstam: Viktor

Behind the Scenes

Director: Ingmar Bergman
Writer: Ingmar Bergman
Producer: Allan Ekelund (uncredited)
Film Editor: Oscar Rosander
Cinematographer: Gunnar Fischer
Original Music: Erik Nordgren

Awards

Oscar Nominations: Best Writing

Trivia

- Ingmar Bergman wrote the script for this film while he was in a hospital.
- This was the final on-screen appearance of Victor Sjöström.

1971
Willy Wonka & the Chocolate Factory

Overview

Genre: Family/Musical
Duration: 100 min
Color: Color
(Technicolor)
Country: USA
MPAA Rating: G
Studio: Warner Bros.
Pictures

More Brothers Grimm than *Benji, Willy Wonka & the Chocolate Factory* is a terrifically edgy children's movie. Gene Wilder stars as the ultra-eccentric candy maker who promises a factory tour and lifetime supply of candy for the finders of five golden tickets hidden in his Wonka Bars. Of course, five children find those tickets; four of them are spoiled brats and one is a humble newspaper boy named Charlie Bucket. The factory itself is a colorful confectionary fantasy. But there are harsh lessons to be learned along the way as Wonka, the wild-eyed pied piper, leads the dwindling tour group to their fates. Parents, and especially kids, have to appreciate a movie that challenges its young audience to let their imaginations run wild.

Cast

Gene Wilder: Willy Wonka
Jack Albertson: Grandpa Joe
Peter Ostrum: Charlie Bucket
Roy Kinnear: Henry Salt
Julie Dawn Cole: Veruca Salt
Leonard Stone: Sam Beauregarde
Denise Nickerson: Violet Beauregarde
Nora Denney: Mrs. Teevee

Behind the Scenes

Director: Mel Stuart
Writer: Roald Dahl (play and screenplay)
Producers: Stan Marguiles, David L. Wolper
Film Editor: David Saxon
Cinematographer: Arthur Ibbetson
Original Music: Leslie Bricusse, Anthony Newley, Walter Scharf

Trivia

• The scene for the opening credits was filmed at a real Swiss chocolate factory.
• Most of the chocolate bars pictured in the film were actually cardboard props in wrappers.

Awards

Oscar Nominations: Best Music

1939
The Wizard of Oz

Overview

Genre: Musical/Fantasy
Duration: 101 min
Color: Black and White (Sepiatone), Color (Technicolor)
Country: USA
MPAA Rating: G
Studio: Metro-Goldwyn-Mayer (MGM)

An eye-popping fantasy movie, with musical numbers too! Judy Garland stars as Dorothy Gale, a girl who longs to leave her drab Kansas home for greener pastures. A sudden tornado grants her wish, as she, her dog Toto, and their house are blown into the sky and transported to the magical land of Oz. In this strange and beautiful place Dorothy encounters munchkins, witches, flying monkeys and even manages to make three friends along the way in the forms of a scarecrow, a tin man, and a cowardly lion. As she and her friends seek out the elusive Wizard, Dorothy comes to realize that home wasn't such a bad place after all. A great film for kids and adults alike.

Cast

Judy Garland: Dorothy Gale
Ray Bolger: Hunk/Scarecrow
Bert Lahr: Zeke/Cowardly Lion
Jack Haley: Hickory/Tin Man
Billie Burke: Glinda
Margaret Hamilton: Elmira Gulch/Wicked Witch of the West

Behind the Scenes

Director: Victor Fleming
Writers: L. Frank Baum (novel), Noel Langley, Florence Ryerson, and Edgar Allan Woolf (screenplay)
Producer: Mervyn LeRoy
Film Editor: Blanche Sewell
Cinematographer: Harold Rosson

Awards

Oscar Winners: Best Music—Original Song
Oscar Nominations: Best Art Direction, Best Cinematography, Best Effects—Special Effects, Best Picture

Trivia

• The horses of the Emerald City were coated with Jell-O crystals. Their scenes were filmed quickly, before the horses started licking their sugary coating.

2000
Wonder Boys

Overview

Genre: Comedy/Drama
Duration: 111 min
Color: Color
Country: USA
MPAA Rating: R
Studio: Mutual Film Company/Paramount Pictures

nglish Professor Grady Tripp has got a few problems. On top of his wife just leaving him, he can't seem to finish writing his latest book, and he just found out that his girlfriend—his department head's wife—is pregnant with his child. Adding to his woes, Grady finds himself looking after his talented yet troubled student, James Leer. With the college hosting an annual literary symposium called Wordfest, Grady must do his best to keep his anxious editor at bay, make sure James Leer stays out of trouble, and still try to figure out his romantic issues. If that sounds like more than one man can possibly handle . . . it is.

Cast

Michael Douglas: Professor Grady Tripp
Tobey Maguire: James Leer
Frances McDormand: Dean Sara Gaskell
Robert Downey Jr.: Terry Crabtree
Katie Holmes: Hannah Green
Rip Torn: Quentin "Q" Morewood
Richard Knox: Vernon Hardapple
Jane Adams: Oola

Behind the Scenes

Director: Curtis Hanson
Writers: Michael Chabon (novel), Steve Kloves (screenplay)
Producers: Curtis Hanson, Scott Rudin
Executive Producers: Ned Dowd, Adam Schroeder
Cinematographer: Dante Spinotti
Original Music: Christopher Young

Trivia

• Author James Ellroy appears as an extra at the party thrown by the Gaskells.
• James tells Grady that his parents live in Carvel, which is the same town name from an Andy Hardy movie he had watched.

Awards

Oscar Winners: Best Music—Original Song
Oscar Nominations: Best Editing, Best Writing—Adapted Screenplay

1988
Working Girl

Overview

Genre: Comedy/Romance
Duration: 113 min
Color: Color
Country: USA
MPAA Rating: R
Studio: Twentieth Century Fox

Melanie Griffith received an Oscar nomination for her portrayal of Tess McGill, a bright, hard-working secretary from Staten Island hell bent on clawing her way to the top of New York's cutthroat corporate ladder. She has fire and determination to spare but just can't seem to get any of her bosses to take her seriously. However, when she takes a job working for top female executive Katharine Parker, her luck may be about to change. Featuring a top-notch supporting cast including Harrison Ford and Sigourney Weaver, *Working Girl* is a heart-warming and hilarious comedy that will resonate with anyone who ever strove for something bigger, brighter, and better.

Cast

Melanie Griffith: Tess McGill
Harrison Ford: Jack Trainer
Sigourney Weaver: Katharine Parker
Alec Baldwin: Mick Dugan
Joan Cusack: Cyn
Philip Bosco: Oren Trask
Kevin Spacey: Bob Speck

Behind the Scenes

Director: Mike Nichols
Writer: Kevin Wade
Producer: Douglas Wick
Executive Producers: Robert Greenhut, Laurence Mark
Film Editor: Sam O'Steen
Cinematographer: Michael Ballhaus

Awards

Oscar Winners: Best Music—Original Song
Oscar Nominations: Best Actress, Best Supporting Actress, Best Director, Best Picture

Trivia

• The stuffed gorilla Katharine is toting as she exits the helicopter may be a knowing wink to Sigourney Weaver's role in *Gorillas in the Mist*, which came out the same year.

1939
Wuthering Heights

Overview

Genre: Drama/Romance
Duration: 103 min
Color: Black and White
Country: USA
MPAA Rating: Not Rated
Studio: The Samuel Goldwyn Company

A traveler seeking refuge from a storm stops at the estate of Wuthering Heights and, after a horrid night within its walls, asks the history of its reproachable host—and so begins the story of *Wuthering Heights*. Heathcliff was a beggar's child, whom Catherine's father took pity on and brought home. Growing up free and in love, things change for Catherine and Heathcliff when a young man from a wealthy family proposes to her. Bowed but not broken, Heathcliff goes off to seek his fortune knowing that he will one day return for her. Laurence Olivier turns in another spectacular performance as Heathcliff in this adaptation of Emily Brontë's classic novel.

Cast

Merle Oberon: Cathy
Laurence Olivier: Heathcliff
David Niven: Edgar Linton
Flora Robson: Ellen Dean
Donald Crisp: Dr. Kenneth
Geraldine Fitzgerald: Isabella Linton
Hugh Williams: Hindley Earnshaw

Behind the Scenes

Director: William Wyler
Writers: Emily Brontë (novel), Charles MacArthur and Ben Hecht (screenplay)
Producer: Samuel Goldwyn
Film Editor: Daniel Mandell
Cinematographer: Gregg Toland
Original Music: Alfred Newman

Awards

Oscar Winners: Best Cinematography
Oscar Nominations: Best Actor, Best Supporting Actress, Best Art Direction, Best Director, Best Music, Best Picture, Best Writing

Trivia

• The film covers only 16 of the novel's 34 chapters.

1942
Yankee Doodle Dandy

Overview

Genre: Comedy/ Musical
Duration: 126 min
Color: Black and White
Country: USA
MPAA Rating: Not Rated
Studio: Warner Bros. Pictures

The life and times of show business legend George M. Cohan are brought to life in this inspirational biopic. The great James Cagney takes on the daunting role of the entertainer with such gusto that you sometimes forget that it's not Cohan himself. Asked to appear before President Franklin D. Roosevelt, Cohan tells the chief executive his life story. From his days as a young vaudeville star to his work as an actor, singer, dancer and songwriter, Cohan's rich history plays out like the history of entertainment itself. For those who only know Cagney for his snarling gangster roles, *Yankee Doodle Dandy* will open your eyes as to just how seriously talented he was.

Cast

James Cagney: George M. Cohan
Joan Leslie: Mary
Walter Huston: Jerry Cohan
Richard Whorf: Sam Harris
Irene Manning: Fay Templeton
George Tobias: Dietz
Douglas Croft: George M. Cohan (at age 13)

Behind the Scenes

Director: Michael Curtiz
Writer: Robert Bruckner (story and screenplay), Edmund Joseph (screenplay)
Executive Producers: Hal B. Wallis, Jack L. Warner
Original Music: Ray Heindorf (uncredited), Heinz Roemheld (uncredited)

Awards

Oscar Winners: Best Actor, Best Music, Best Sound

Trivia

• So many facts were changed about his life to spice up the story that the real George M. Cohan, after seeing the film, commented, "It was a good movie. Who was it about?"

1974
Young Frankenstein

Overview

Genre: Comedy
Duration: 106 min
Color: Black and White
Country: USA
MPAA Rating: PG
Studio: Twentieth Century Fox

Gene Wilder and Mel Brooks cooked up one howlingly funny script about the infamous mad scientist's grandson. Wilder plays the title role to perfection. At first he wants nothing to do with his family's legacy, even insisting his name be pronounced Fronk-un-shteen, but once he gets to his Grandfather's castle the switch gets flipped—time to dig up a corpse! But bringing the dead back to life is no easy task, and good help is so hard to find. Full of quotable lines and memorable scenes, *Young Frankenstein* also features a monster supporting cast including Madeline Kahn, Peter Boyle, Marty Feldman, and Teri Garr. Whoever doesn't find this one funny is downright "abby normal."

Cast

Gene Wilder: Dr. Frankenstein
Peter Boyle: The Monster
Marty Feldman: Igor
Cloris Leachman: Frau Blücher
Teri Garr: Inga
Kenneth Mars: Inspector Kemp
Madeline Kahn: Elizabeth

Behind the Scenes

Director: Mel Brooks
Writers: Mary Shelley (novel), Gene Wilder and Mel Brooks (screenplay)
Producer: Michael Gruskoff
Film Editor: John C. Howard
Cinematographer: Gerald Hirschfeld
Original Music: John Morris

Awards

Oscar Nominations: Best Sound, Best Writing—Adapted Screenplay

Trivia

• Marty Feldman had been moving Igor's hump back and forth secretly for days, and once cast members finally noticed, it was added to the script.

1964
Zorba the Greek

Overview

Genre: Drama/ Adventure
Duration: 142 min
Color: Black and White
Country: USA/UK/ Greece
MPAA Rating: Not Rated
Studio: Twentieth Century Fox

Based on the novel by Nikos Kazantza-kis, *Zorba the Greek* is the story of the friendship between the rather naïve middle class English writer Basil, and salt-of-the-earth Greek peasant—and sometimes confidence man—Alexis Zorba. Basil travels to the Greek island of Crete, after inheriting his father's dis-used mine, where he meets and employs Zorba to help him get the mine up and running again. Two more different characters you could not find: Basil the staid, reserved Englishman and Zorba, the gruff, philosophical product of the earth. Zorba's exuberance and zest lead the young writer to reach out and "grab" life rather than watch it go by. Punctuated by a terrific score by Mikis Theodorakis, *Zorba the Greek* is at turns, dark, funny, and touching.

Cast

Anthony Quinn: Alexis Zorba
Alan Bates: Basil
Irene Papas: Widow
Lila Kedrova: Madame Hortense
Sotiris Moustakas: Mimithos
Anna Kyriakou: Soul
Eleni Anousaki: Lola
Yorgo Voyagis: Pavlo
Takis Emmanuel: Manolakas

Behind the Scenes

Director: Mihalis Kakogiannis
Writer: Nikos Kazantzakis (novel), Mihalis Kakogiannis (screenplay)
Producer: Mihalis Kakogiannis
Film Editor: Mihalis Kakogiannis (uncredited)
Cinematographer: Walter Lassally
Original Music: Mikio Theodorakis

Trivia

• Lila Kedrova became Mihalis Kakogiannis's choice for Madame Hortense after filming began. In an uncharacteristic leap of faith, Darryl F. Zanuck agreed to Kakogiannis's request to hire her even though he had no idea who Kedrova was or what she looked like, because he trusted Kakogiannis so much.

Awards

Oscar Winners: Best Supporting Actress, Best Art Direction, Best Cinematography
Oscar Nominations: Best Actor, Best Director, Best Picture, Best Writing—Adapted Screenplay

More Must-See Movies

The Accidental Tourist 1988
Genre: Drama/Romance **Duration:** 121 min **Color:**
Color **Country:** USA **MPAA Rating:** R **Studio:** Warner
Bros. Pictures **Director:** Lawrence Kasdan **William
Hurt:** Macon Leary **Kathleen Turner:** Sarah Leary
Geena Davis: Muriel Pritchett **Amy Wright:** Rose Leary

Ace in the Hole 1951
Genre: Drama/Romance **Duration:** 111 min
Color: Black and White **Country:** USA **MPAA Rating:**
Not Rated **Studio:** Paramount Pictures **Director:** Billy
Wilder **Kirk Douglas:** Charles "Chuck" Tatum **Jan
Sterling:** Lorraine Minosa **Robert Arthur:** Herbie Cook
Porter Hall: Jacob Q. Boot

Adam's Rib 1949
Genre: Comedy/Romance **Duration:** 101 min
Color: Black and White **Country:** USA **MPAA Rating:**
Not Rated **Studio:** Metro-Goldwyn-Mayer (MGM)
Director: George Cukor **Spencer Tracy:** Adam Bonner
Katharine Hepburn: Amanda Bonner **Judy Holliday:**
Doris Attinger **Tom Ewell:** Warren Attinger

The Adventures of Robin Hood 1938
Genre: Action/Adventure **Duration:** 102 min
Color: Color **Country:** USA **MPAA Rating:** PG
Studio: Warner Bros. Pictures **Director:** Michael Curtiz,
William Keighley **Errol Flynn:** Robin Hood **Olivia de
Havilland:** Maid Marian **Basil Rathbone:** Sir Guy of
Gisbourne **Claude Rains:** Prince John

Alfie 1966
Genre: Comedy/Drama **Duration:** 114 min
Color: Color (Technicolor) **Country:** UK **MPAA Rating:**
PG **Studio:** Lewis Gilbert/Sheldrake Films **Director:**
Lewis Gilbert **Michael Caine:** Alfie Elkins **Shelley
Winters:** Ruby **Millicent Martin:** Siddie **Julia Foster:**
Gilda

Amarcord 1973
Genre: Comedy/Drama **Duration:** 123 min **Color:** Color

Country: Italy **MPAA Rating:** R **Studio:** F.C. Produzioni/
PECF **Director:** Federico Fellini **Bruno Zanin:** Titta
Magali Noel: Gradisca **Pupella Maggio:** Miranda
Biondi **Armando Brancia:** Aurelio Biondi

American Movie 1999
Genre: Documentary **Duration:** 107 min **Color:** Color
Country: USA **MPAA Rating:** R **Studio:** Bluemark
Prod./C-Hundred Film Corp. **Director:** Chris
Smith **Mark Borchardt:** Filmmaker **Tom Schimmels:**
Actor in *Coven* **Monica Borchardt:** Herself (Mark's
mother) **Alex Borchardt:** Himself (Mark's brother)

Anatomy of a Murder 1959
Genre: Drama/Thriller **Duration:** 160 min
Color: Black and White **Country:** USA **MPAA Rating:**
Not Rated **Studio:** Columbia Pictures **Director:** Otto
Preminger **James Stewart:** Paul Biegler **Lee Remick:**
Laura Manion **Ben Gazzara:** Lt. Frederick Manion
Arthur O'Connell: Parnell Emmett McCarthy

Around the World in 80 Days 1956
Genre: Comedy/Adventure **Duration:** 175 min
Color: Color (Technicolor) **Country:** Azerbaijan/USA
MPAA Rating: G **Studio:** Michael Todd Company
Directors: Michael Anderson **David Niven:** Phileas
Fogg **Cantinflas:** Passepartout **John Gielgud:** Mr.
Foster **Shirley MacLaine:** Princess Aouda

Arsenic and Old Lace 1944
Genre: Comedy/Thriller **Duration:** 118 min **Color:** Black
and White **Country:** USA **MPAA Rating:** Not Rated
Studio: Warner Bros. Pictures **Director:** Frank Capra
Cary Grant: Mortimer Brewster **Priscilla Lane:** Elaine
Harper **Jack Carson:** O'Hara **Peter Lorre:** Dr. Einstein

Atlantic City 1980
Genre: Drama/Crime **Duration:** 104 min
Color: Color **Country:** USA/Canada/France **MPAA
Rating:** R **Studio:** International Cinema Corp./Selta Films
Director: Louis Malle **Burt Lancaster:** Lou Pascal
Susan Sarandon: Sally Matthews **Michel Piccoli:**
Joseph **Hollis McLaren:** Chrissie

Babe 1995
Genre: Family/Comedy **Duration:** 89 min **Color:**
Color **Country:** Australia, USA **MPAA Rating:** PG
Studio: Universal Pictures **Director:** Chris Noonan
James Cromwell: Farmer Arthur Hoggett **Christine
Cavanaugh:** Babe (voice) **Magda Szubanski:** Esme
Hoggett **Miriam Margolyes:** Fly the Sheepdog (voice)

Back to the Future 1985
Genre: Comedy/Adventure **Duration:** 117 min
Color: Color **Country:** USA **MPAA Rating:** PG
Studio: Amblin Entertainment/Universal Pict.
Director: Robert Zemeckis **Michael J. Fox:** Marty
McFly **Christopher Lloyd:** Dr. Emmett Brown **Lea
Thompson:** Lorraine Baines McFly **Crispin Glover:**
George McFly

Barry Lyndon 1975
Genre: Drama/Romance **Duration:** 184 min
Color: Color (Eastmancolor) **Country:** USA **MPAA
Rating:** PG **Studio:** Warner Bros. **Director:** Stanley
Kubrick **Ryan O'Neal:** Barry Lyndon **Marisa Berenson:**

Lady Lyndon **Patrick Magee:** The Chevalier **Hardy
Kruger:** Captain Potzdorf

Beauty and the Beast 1946
Genre: Drama/Family/Romance **Duration:** 93 min
Color: Black and White **Country:** France **MPAA Rating:**
G **Studio:** DisCina **Director:** Jean Cocteau
Jean Marais: the beast/the prince **Josette Day:** Belle
Marcel André: Belle's father **Mila Parély:** Félicie

Belle de Jour 1967
Genre: Drama **Duration:** 101 min **Color:** Color
Country: France **MPAA Rating:** R **Studio:** Paris Film
Director: Luis Bruñuel **Catherine Deneuve:** Séverine
Serizy **Jean Sorel:** Pierre Serizy **Michel Piccoli:** Henri
Husson **Geneviève Page:** Madame Anais

Ben-Hur 1959
Genre: Action/Adventure **Duration:** 212 min **Color:**
Color (Technicolor) **Country:** USA **MPAA Rating:**
G **Studio:** Metro-Goldwyn-Mayer (MGM) **Director:**
William Wyler **Charlton Heston:** Judah Ben-Hur **Jack
Hawkins:** Quintus Arrius **Haya Harareet:** Esther
Stephen Boyd: Messala

The Bicycle Thief 1948
Genre: Drama **Duration:** 93 min **Color:** Black and
White **Country:** Italy **MPAA Rating:** Not Rated
Studio: Produzioni De Sica **Director:** Vittorio De Sica
Lamberto Maggiorani: Antonio Ricci **Enzo Staiola:**
Bruno Ricci **Lianella Carell:** Maria Ricci **Vittorio
Antonucci:** The thief

The Big Sleep 1946
Genre: Drama/Crime **Duration:** 114 min **Color:** Black
and White **Country:** USA **MPAA Rating:** Not Rated
Studio: Warner Bros. Pictures **Director:** Howard Hawks
Humphrey Bogart: Philip Marlowe **Lauren Bacall:**
Vivian Sternwood Rutledge **John Ridgely:** Eddie Mars
Martha Vickers: Carmen Sternwood

Blade Runner 1982
Genre: Action/Adventure **Duration:** 117 min **Color:**
Color (Technicolor) **Country:** USA **MPAA Rating:** R
Studio: Warner Bros. **Director:** Ridley Scott **Harrison**

Ford: Rick Deckard **Rutger Hauer:** Roy Batty **Sean Young:** Rachael **Edward J. Olmos:** Gaff

Blow-Up 1966
Genre: Drama/Romance **Duration:** 111 min
Color: Color **Country:** UK/Italy/USA **MPAA Rating:** Not Rated **Studio:** Bridge Films **Director:** Michelangelo Antonioni **Vanessa Redgrave:** Jane **Sarah Miles:** Patricia **David Hemmings:** Thomas **John Castle:** Bill

The Blues Brothers 1980
Genre: Comedy/Action **Duration:** 133 min
Color: Color **Country:** USA **MPAA Rating:** R
Studio: Universal Pictures **Director:** John Landis
John Belushi: "Joliet" Jake Blues **Dan Aykroyd:** Elwood Blues **James Brown:** Reverend Cleophus **Kathleen Freeman:** Sister Mary Stigmata

Born Yesterday 1950
Genre: Comedy/Romance **Duration:** 103 min
Color: Black and White **Country:** USA **MPAA Rating:** Not Rated **Studio:** Columbia Pictures Corporation
Director: George Cukor **Judy Holliday:** Emma "Billie" Dawn **Broderick Crawford:** Harry Brock **William Holden:** Paul Verrall **Howard St. John:** Jum Devery

Boyz n the Hood 1991
Genre: Comedy **Duration:** 107 min **Color:** Color
Country: USA MPAA **Rating:** R **Studio:** Columbia Pictures Corporation **Director:** John Singleton
Laurence Fishburne: Jason "Furious" Styles **Cuba Gooding Jr.:** Tré Styles **Ice Cube:** Darin "Doughboy" Baker **Morris Chestnut:** Ricky Baker

Braveheart 1995
Genre: Drama/Action **Duration:** 177 min
Color: Color **Country:** USA **MPAA Rating:** R
Studio: Paramount Pictures **Director:** Mel Gibson
Mel Gibson: William Wallace **Sophie Marceau:** Princess Isabelle **Patrick McGoohan:** Longshanks—King Edward I **Catherine McCormack:** Murron

Breakfast at Tiffany's 1961
Genre: Comedy/Romance **Duration:** 115 min **Color:**

Color (Technicolor) **Country:** USA **MPAA Rating:** Not Rated **Studio:** Paramount Pictures **Director:** Blake Edwards **Audrey Hepburn:** Holly Golightly **George Peppard:** Paul "Fred" Varjak **Patricia Neal:** 2-E **Buddy Ebsen:** Doc Golightly

A Bridge Too Far 1977
Genre: Drama/Action **Duration:** 175 min **Color:** Color
Country: USA **MPAA Rating:** PG **Studio:** United Artists
Director: Richard Attenborough **Dirk Bogarde:** Lt. Gen. Frederick A.M. Browning **James Caan:** SSgt. Eddie Dohun **Michael Caine:** Lt. Col. John Vandeleur **Sean Connery:** Maj. Gen. Robert E. Urquhart

Brief Encounter 1945
Genre: Drama/Romance **Duration:** 86 min
Color: Black and White **Country:** UK **MPAA Rating:** Not Rated **Studio:** Cineguild **Director:** David Lean
Celia Johnson: Laura JessonTrevor **Howard:** Dr. Alec Harvey **Stanley Holloway:** Albert Godby **Joyce Carey:** Myrtle Bagot

Broadcast News 1987
Genre: Comedy/Drama **Duration:** 133 min **Color:** Color
Country: USA **MPAA Rating:** R **Studio:** Twentieth Century-Fox Film Corp. **Director:** James L. Brooks
William Hurt: Tom Grunick **Albert Brooks:** Aaron Altman **Holly Hunter:** Jane Craig **Robert Prosky:** Ernie Merriman

Bugsy 1991
Genre: Drama/Crime **Duration:** 134 min **Color:** Color
Country: USA **MPAA Rating:** R **Studio:** TriStar Pictures
Director: Barry Levinson **Warren Beatty:** Ben "Bugsy" Siegel **Annette Bening:** Virginia Hill **Harvey Keitel:** Mickey Cohen **Ben Kingsley:** Meyer Lansky

The Caine Mutiny 1954
Genre: Drama **Duration:** 124 min **Color:** Color (Technicolor) **Country:** USA **MPAA Rating:** Not Rated **Studio:** Columbia Pictures **Director:** Edward Dmytryk
Humphrey Bogart: Lt. Cmdr. Philip Francis Queeg **José Ferrer:** Lt. Barney Greenwald **Van Johnson:** Lt. Steve Maryk **Fred MacMurray:** Lt. Thomas Keefer

Cape Fear 1962
Genre: Thriller **Duration:** 105 min **Color:** Black and White **Country:** USA **MPAA Rating:** Not Rated **Studio:** Universal Pictures **Director:** J. Lee Thompon **Gregory Peck:** Sam Bowden **Robert Mitchom:** Max Cordy **Polly Bergen:** Peggy Bowden **Martin Balsam:** Mark Dutton

Cat on a Hot Tin Roof 1958
Genre: Drama **Duration:** 108 min **Color:** Color (Metrocolor) **Country:** USA **MPAA Rating:** Not Rated **Studio:** Metro-Goldwyn-Mayer (MGM) **Director:** Richard Brooks **Elizabeth Taylor:** Margaret "Maggie the Cat" Pollitt **Paul Newman:** Brick Pollitt **Burl Ives:** Harvey "Big Daddy" Pollitt **Jack Carson:** Cooper "Gooper" Pollitt

Celine and Julie Go Boating 1974
Genre: Drama/Mystery **Duration:** 193 min **Color:** Color **Country:** France **MPAA Rating:** Not Rated **Studio:** Action Films **Director:** Jacques Rivette **Juliet Berto:** Celine **Dominique Labourier:** Julie **Bulle Ogier:** Camille **Marie-France Pisier:** Sophie

Chariots of Fire 1981
Genre: Drama/Sports **Duration:** 123 min **Color:** Color **Country:** UK **MPAA Rating:** PG **Studio:** Warner Bros. Pictures **Director:** Hugh Hudson **Nicholas Farrell:** Aubrey Montague **Nigel Havers:** Lord Andrew Lindsay

Ian Charleston: Eric Liddell **Ben Cross:** Harold Abrahams

Chocolat 2000
Genre: Comedy/Drama **Duration:** 121 min **Color:** Color **Country:** UK/USA **MPAA Rating:** PG-13 **Studio:** Miramax Films **Director:** Lasse Hallström **Juliette Binoche:** Vianne Rocher **Alfred Molina:** Comte Paul de Reynaud **Carrie-Anne Moss:** Caroline Clairmont **Judi Dench:** Armande Voizin

Christmas Vacation 1989
Genre: Comedy **Duration:** 97 min **Color:** Color **Country:** USA **MPAA Rating:** PG-13 **Studio:** Warner Bros. Pictures **Director:** Jeremiah S. Chechik **Chevy Chase:** Clark Griswold **Beverly D'Angelo:** Ellen Griswold **Juliette Lewis:** Audrey Griswold **Johnny Galecki:** Russell "Rusty" Griswold

City Lights 1931
Genre: Comedy **Duration:** 87 min **Color:** Black and White **Country:** USA **MPAA Rating:** G **Studio:** United Artists **Director:** Charles Chaplin **Charles Chaplin:** A Tramp **Virginia Cherrill:** A Blind Girl **Florence Lee:** The Blind Girl's Grandmother **Harry Myers:** An Eccentric Millionaire

City of God 2002
Genre: Drama/Crime **Duration:** 130 min **Color:** Color **Country:** Brazil/France **MPAA Rating:** R **Studio:** O2 Filmes **Director:** Fernando Meirelles, Katia Lund **Alexandre Rodrigues:** Buscape/Rocket **Leandro Firmino:** Ze Pequeno/Li'l Ze **Phellipe Haagensen:** Bene/Benny **Douglas Silva:** Dadinho/Li'l Dice

Coal Miner's Daughter 1980
Genre: Drama/Biography **Duration:** 125 min **Color:** Color (Technicolor) **Country:** USA **MPAA Rating:** PG **Studio:** Universal Pictures **Director:** Michael Apted **Sissy Spacek:** Loretta Lynn **Tommy Lee Jones:** "Mooney" Lynn **Levon Helm:** Ted Webb **Phyllis Boyens:** "Clary" Webb

Coming Home 1978
Genre: Drama/War **Duration:** 127 min **Color:** Color
Country: USA **MPAA Rating:** R **Studio:** United Artists
Director: Hal Ashby **Jane Fonda:** Sally Hyde **Jon
Voight:** Luke Martin **Bruce Dern:** Capt. Bob Hyde
Penelope Milford: Vi Munson

The Conversation 1974
Genre: Drama/Crime **Duration:** 113 min **Color:** Color
(Technicolor) **Country:** USA **MPAA Rating:** PG
Studio: Paramount Pictures **Director:** Francis Ford
Coppola **Gene Hackman:** Harry Caul **John Cazale:**
Stan **Allen Garfield:** William P. "Bernie" Moran **Frederic
Forrest:** Mark

Crouching Tiger, Hidden Dragon 2000
Genre: Action/Adventure **Duration:** 120 min **Color:**
Color (Technicolor) **Country:** Taiwan/USA/China **MPAA
Rating:** PG-13 **Studio:** Columbia Pictures Film Prod.
Asia **Director:** Ang Lee **Chow Yun Fat:** Master Li Mu
Bai **Michelle Yeoh:** Yu Shu Lien **Zhang Ziyi:** Jen Yu
Chen Chang: Lo "Dark Cloud"/Luo Xiao Hu

Darling 1965
Genre: Drama/Romance **Duration:** 128 min **Color:**
Black and White **Country:** UK **MPAA Rating:** Not Rated
Studio: Joseph Janni Prod./Vic Films/Appia Films Ltd.
Director: John Schlesinger **Laurence Harvey:** Miles
Brand **Dirk Bogarde:** Robert Gold **Julie Christie:**
Diana Scott José **Luis de Villalonga:** Cesare

Day for Night 1973
Genre: Comedy/Drama **Duration:** 115 min **Color:**
Black and White, Color **Country:** France **MPAA Rating:**
PG **Studio:** Les Films du Carrosse **Director:** François
Truffaut **Jacqueline Bisset:** Julie **Valentina Cortese:**
Severine **Dani:** Liliane **Alexandra Stewart:** Stacey

The Defiant Ones 1958
Genre: Drama/Crime **Duration:** 97 min **Color:** Black
and White **Country:** USA **MPAA Rating:** Not Rated
Studio: United Artists **Director:** Stanley Kramer **Tony
Curtis:** John "Joker" Jackson **Sidney Poitier:** Noah
Cullen **Theodore Bikel:** Sheriff Max Muller **Charles
McGraw:** Capt. Frank Gibbons

Deliverance 1972
Genre: Drama/Adventure **Duration:** 109 min **Color:**
Color (Technicolor) **Country:** USA **MPAA Rating:** R
Studio: Warner Bros. Pictures **Director:** John Boorman
Jon Voight: Ed **Burt Reynolds:** Lewis **Ned Beatty:**
Bobby **Ronny Cox:** Drew

Dial M for Murder 1954
Genre: Drama/Mystery **Duration:** 105 min **Color:**
Color **Country:** USA **MPAA Rating:** PG **Studio:** Warner
Bros. Pictures **Director:** Alfred Hitchcock **Ray Milland:**
Tony Wendice **Grace Kelly:** Margot Mary Wendice
Robert Cummings: Mark Halliday **John Williams:**
Chief Insp. Hubbard

The Dirty Dozen 1967
Genre: Action/Adventure **Duration:** 149 min **Color:**
Color (Metrocolor) **Country:** UK/USA **MPAA Rating:** Not
Rated **Studio:** Metro-Goldwyn-Mayer (MGM) **Director:**
Robert Aldrich **Lee Marvin:** Major Reisman **Ernest
Borgnine:** General Worden **Charles Bronson:** Joseph
Wladislaw **Jim Brown:** Robert Jefferson

Dodsworth 1936
Genre: Drama/Romance **Duration:** 101 min **Color:**
Black and White **Country:** USA **MPAA Rating:** Not
Rated **Studio:** The Samuel Goldwyn Company **Director:**
William Wyler **Walter Huston:** Sam Dodsworth **Ruth
Chatterton:** Fran Dodsworth **Paul Lukas:** Arnold Iselin
Mary Astor: Mrs. Edith Cortright

Driving Miss Daisy 1989
Genre: Comedy/Drama **Duration:** 99 min **Color:** Color
Country: USA **MPAA Rating:** PG **Studio:** Warner Bros.
Director: Bruce Beresford **Morgan Freeman:** Hoke
Colburn **Jessica Tandy:** Daisy Werthan **Dan Aykroyd:**
Boolie Werthan **Patti LuPone:** Florine Werthan

Ed Wood 1994
Genre: Comedy/Drama **Duration:** 127 min **Color:** Black
and White **Country:** USA **MPAA Rating:** R **Studio:**
Touchstone Pictures **Director:** Tim Burton **Johnny
Depp:** Ed Wood **Martin Landau:** Bela Lugosi
Sarah Jessica Parker: Dolores Fuller **Patricia
Arquette:** Kathy O'Hara

Eight Men Out 1988
Genre: Drama/Sports **Duration:** 119 min **Color:**
Color **Country:** USA **MPAA Rating:** PG **Studio:** Orion
Pictures Corporation **Director:** John Sayles **John
Cusack:** George "Buck" Weaver **Clifton James:** Charles
Comiskey **Michael Lerner:** Arnold Rothstein **David
Strathairn:** Eddie Cicotte

Elmer Gantry 1960
Genre: Drama **Duration:** 146 min **Color:** Color
(Eastmancolor) **Country:** USA **MPAA Rating:** Not Rated
Studio: United Artists **Director:** Richard Brooks **Burt
Lancaster:** Elmer Gantry **Jean Simmons:** Sister
Sharon Falconer **Arthur Kennedy:** Jim Lefferts **Dean
Jagger:** William L. Morgan

The English Patient 1996
Genre: Drama/Romance **Duration:** 162 min **Color:**
Color **Country:** USA **MPAA Rating:** R **Studio:** Miramax
Films **Director:** Anthony Minghella **Ralph Fiennes:**
Count Laszlo de Almásy **Juliette Binoche:** Hana
Willem Dafoe: David Caravaggio **Kristin Scott
Thomas:** Katharine Clifton

Eternal Sunshine of the Spotless Mind 2004
Genre: Drama/Romance **Duration:** 108 min **Color:**
Color **Country:** USA **MPAA Rating:** R **Studio:** Focus
Features **Director:** Michael Gondry **Jim Carrey:** Joel
Barish **Kate Winslet:** Clementine Kruczynski **Kirsten
Dunst:** Mary **Mark Ruffalo:** Stan **Elijah Wood:** Patrick

F for Fake 1974
Genre: Documentary **Duration:** 85 min
Color: Color **Country:** France/Iran/W. Germany **MPAA
Rating:** Not Rated **Studio:** Janus Film **Director:** Orson
Welles **Orson Welles:** Himself **Oja Kodar:** Girl
**Joseph Cotten, Francois Reichenbach, Richard
Wilson, Paul Stewart, Alexander Welles, Gary
Graver:** Special Participants

Fail-Safe 1964
Genre: Sci-Fi/Thriller **Duration:** 112 min **Color:** Black
and White **Country:** USA **MPAA Rating:** Not Rated
Studio: Columbia Pictures Corp. **Director:** Sidney Lumet
Henry Fonda: President **Walter Matthau:** Prof.

Groeteschele **Frank Overton:** Gen. Bogan **Ed Binns:**
Col. Jack Grady

Fandango 1985
Genre: Comedy **Duration:** 91 min **Color:** Color
Country: USA **MPAA Rating:** PG **Studio:** Amblin
Entertainment/Warner Bros. Pict. **Director:** Kevin
Reynolds **Kevin Costner:** Gardner Barnes **Judd
Nelson:** Phil Hicks **Sam Robards:** Kenneth Waggener
Chuck Bush: Dorman

Fantasia 1940
Genre: Family/Fantasy **Duration:** 120 min **Color:** Color
(Technicolor) **Country:** USA **MPAA Rating:** G **Studio:**
Walt Disney Pictures **Directors:** James Algar ("The
Sorcerer's Apprentice"), Samuel Armstrong ("Toccata and
Fugue in D Minor" and "The Nutcracker Suite") **Leopold
Stokowski:** Himself **Deems Taylor:** Narrator **Walt
Disney:** Mickey Mouse (uncredited)

Fiddler on the Roof 1971
Genre: Musical/Drama **Duration:** 181 min **Color:** Color
Country: USA **MPAA Rating:** G **Studio:** United Artists
Director: Norman Jewison **Topol:** Tevye **Norma Crane:**
Golde **Leonard Frey:** Motel Kamzoil **Molly Picon:** Yente

Five Easy Pieces 1970
Genre: Drama **Duration:** 98 min **Color:** Color
(Technicolor) **Country:** USA **MPAA Rating:** R
Studio: Columbia Pictures Corporation **Director:** Bob
Rafelson **Jack Nicholson:** Robert Eroica Dupea **Karen
Black:** Rayette Dipesto **Billy Green Bush:** Elton **Fannie
Flagg:** Stoney

Force of Evil 1948
Genre: Drama/Crime **Duration:** 78 min **Color:**
Black and White **Country:** USA **MPAA Rating:** PG
Studio: Enterprise Productions **Director:** Abraham
Polonsky **John Garfield:** Joe Morse **Thomas Gomez:**
Leo Morse **Marie Windsor:** Edna Tucker **Howland
Chamberlain:** Freddie Bauer

48 Hours 1982
Genre: Comedy/Action **Duration:** 96 min
Color: Color **Country:** USA **MPAA Rating:** R **Studio:**
Paramount Pictures **Director:** Walter Hill **Nick Nolte:**
Jack Cates **Eddie Murphy:** Reggie
Hammond **Annette O'Toole:** Elaine **Frank
McRae:** Captain Haden

The 400 Blows 1959
Genre: Drama/Crime **Duration:** 99 min
Color: Black and White **Country:** France
MPAA Rating: Not Rated
Studio: Les Films du Carrosse/Sédif Prod.
Director: François Truffaut **Jean-Pierre
Léaud:** Antoine Doinel **Claire Maurier:**
Gilberte Doinel (the mother) **Albert Rémy:**
Julien Doinel **Guy Decomble:** "Petite Feuille"
(the French teacher)

From Russia with Love 1964
Genre: Action/Adventure **Duration:** 110 min
Color: Color **Country:** UK **MPAA Rating:**
PG **Studio:** United Artists **Director:** Terence

Young **Sean Connery:** James Bond **Daniela Bianchi:**
Tatiana Romanova **Pedro Armendáriz:** Ali Kerim Bey
Lotte Lenya: Rosa Klebb

Gentleman's Agreement 1947
Genre: Drama/Romance **Duration:** 118 min
Color: Black and White **Country:** USA **MPAA Rating:**
Not Rated **Studio:** Twentieth Century-Fox Film Corp.
Director: Elia Kazan **Gregory Peck:** Philip Schuyler
Green **Dorothy McGuire:** Kathy Lacy **John Garfield:**
Dave Goldman **Celeste Holm:** Anne Dettrey

Get Shorty 1995
Genre: Comedy/Crime **Duration:** 105 min **Color:**
Color **Country:** USA **MPAA Rating:** R **Studio:** Metro-
Goldwyn-Mayer (MGM) **Director:** Barry Sonnenfeld
John Travolta: Chili Palmer **Gene Hackman:** Harry
Zimm **Rene Russo:** Karen Flores **Danny DeVito:**
Martin Weir

Giant 1956
Genre: Drama/Romance **Duration:** 201 min
Color: Color (Warnercolor) **Country:** USA **MPAA
Rating:** Not Rated **Studio:** Warner Bros. Pictures
Director: George Stevens **Elizabeth Taylor:** Leslie
Benedict **Rock Hudson:** Jordan "Bick" Benedict Jr.

James Dean: Jett Rink **Caroll Baker:** Luz Benedict II

Gigi 1958
Genre: Musical/Comedy **Duration:** 116 min **Color:** Color (Metrocolor) **Country:** USA **MPAA Rating:** G **Studio:** Metro-Goldwyn-Mayer (MGM) **Director:** Vincente Minnelli **Leslie Caron:** Gilberte/Gigi **Maurice Chevalier:** Honoré Lachaille **Louis Jourdan:** Gason Lachaille **Hermione Gingold:** Madam Alvarez

Glory 1989
Genre: Drama/War **Duration:** 122 min **Color:** Color **Country:** USA **MPAA Rating:** R **Studio:** TriStar Pictures **Director:** Edward Zwick **Matthew Broderick:** Col. Robert Gould Shaw **Denzel Washington:** Pvt. Trip **Cary Elwes:** Maj. Cabot Forbes **Morgan Freeman:** Sgt. Maj. John Rawlins

Going My Way 1944
Genre: Musical/Comedy **Duration:** 130 min **Color:** Black and White **Country:** USA **MPAA Rating:** Not Rated **Studio:** Paramount Pictures **Director:** Leo McCarey **Bing Crosby:** Father Chuck O'Malley **Barry Fitzgerald:** Father Fitzgibbon **Frank McHugh:** Father Timothy O'Dowd **James Brown:** Ted Haines Jr.

Good Night, and Good Luck 2005
Genre: Drama/History **Duration:** 93 min **Color:** Black and White **Country:** USA **MPAA Rating:** PG **Studio:** Warner Independent Pictures (WIP) **Director:** George Clooney **Jeff Daniels:** Sig Mickelson **David Strathairn:** Edward R. Murrow **Alex Borstein:** Natalie **Reed Diamond:** John Aaron

The Great Dictator 1940
Genre: Comedy/Drama **Duration:** 124 min **Color:** Black and White **Country:** USA **MPAA Rating:** G **Studio:** United Artists **Director:** Charles Chaplin **Charles Chaplin:** Adenoid Hynkel/a Jewish barber **Paulette Goddard:** Hannah **Jack Oakie:** Benzini Napaloni **Reginald Gardiner:** Commander Schultz

Great Expectations 1946
Genre: Drama/Romance **Duration:** 118 min **Color:** Black and White **Country:** UK **MPAA Rating:** Not Rated

Studio: Cineguild **Director:** David Lean **John Mills:** Pip (as an adult) **Valerie Hobson:** Estella (as an adult) **Anthony Wager:** Young Pip **Jean Simmons:** Young Estella

Guess Who's Coming to Dinner 1967
Genre: Drama/Romance **Duration:** 108 min **Color:** Color (Technicolor) **Country:** USA **MPAA Rating:** Not Rated **Studio:** Columbia Pictures Corporation **Director:** Stanley Kramer **Spencer Tracy:** Matt Drayton **Sidney Poitier:** Dr. John Wade Prentice **Katharine Hepburn:** Christina Drayton **Katharine Houghton:** Joey Drayton

Hamlet 1948
Genre: Drama **Duration:** 155 min **Color:** Black and White **Country:** UK **MPAA Rating:** Not Rated **Studio:** Two Cities Films **Director:** Laurence Olivier **Basil Sydney:** Claudius Eileen **Herlie:** Gertrude **Laurence Olivier:** Hamlet **Norman Wooland:** Horatio

Hannah and Her Sisters 1986
Genre: Comedy/Drama **Duration:** 103 min **Color:** Color (Technicolor) **Country:** USA **MPAA Rating:** PG-13 **Studio:** Orion Pictures Corporation **Director:** Woody Allen **Barbara Hershey:** Lee **Dianne Wiest:** Holly **Michael Caine:** Elliot **Mia Farrow:** Hannah

The Haunting 1963
Genre: Horror/Thriller **Duration:** 112 min **Color:** Black and White **Country:** USA MPAA **Rating:** G **Studio:** Metro-Goldwyn-Mayer (MGM) **Director:** Robert Wise **Julie Harris:** Eleanor "Nell" Vance **Richard Johnson:** Dr. John Markway **Claire Bloom:** Theo **Russ Tamblin:** Luke Sanderson

The Heartbreak Kid 1972
Genre: Comedy/Romance **Duration:** 106 min **Color:** Color (TVC) **Country:** USA **MPAA Rating:** PG **Studio:** Twentieth Century Fox **Director:** Elaine May **Charles Grodin:** Lenny Cantrow **Cybill Shepard:** Kelly Corcoran **Jeannie Berlin:** Lila Kolodny **Audra Lindley:** Mrs. Corcoran

Heat 1995
Genre: Action/Crime **Duration:** 171 min

Color: Color **Country:** USA **MPAA Rating:** R
Studio: Warner Bros. Pictures **Director:** Michael Mann
Al Pacino: Lt. Vincent Hanna **Robert De Niro:** Neil
McCauley **Val Kilmer:** Chris Shiherlis **Jon Voight:** Nate

His Girl Friday 1940
Genre: Comedy/Romance **Duration:** 92 min **Color:**
Black and White **Country:** USA **MPAA Rating:** PG
Studio: Columbia Pictures Corporation **Director:** Howard
Hawks **Cary Grant:** Walter Burns **Rosalind Russell:**
Hildegaard "Hildy" Johnson **Ralph Bellamy:** Bruce
Baldwin **Gene Lockhart:** Sheriff Peter B."Pinky" Hartwell

Hollywood Shuffle 1987
Genre: Comedy **Duration:** 78 min **Color:** Color
Country: USA **MPAA Rating:** R **Studio:** Samuel
Goldwyn Company **Director:** Robert Townsend **Robert
Townsend:** Bobby Taylor/Jasper/Speed/Sam Ace/
Rambro **Keenan Ivory Wayans:** Stevie Donald/Jheri
Curl **Anne-Marie Johnson:** Lydia/Willie Mae

Home Alone 1990
Genre: Family/Comedy **Duration:** 103 min **Color:** Color
Country: USA **MPAA Rating:** PG **Studio:** Twentieth
Century Fox **Director:** Chris Columbus **Macaulay
Culkin:** Kevin McCallister **Joe Pesci:** Harry **Daniel
Stern:** Marv **John Heard:** Peter
McCallister

Hud 1963
Genre: Drama/Western **Duration:** 112
min **Color:** Black and White **Country:**
USA **MPAA Rating:** Not Rated **Studio:**
Paramount Pictures **Director:** Martin Ritt
Paul Newman: Hud Bannon **Melvyn
Douglas:** Homer Bannon **Patricia Neal:**
Alma Brown **Brandon De Wilde:** Lonnie
Bannon

The Hustler 1961
Genre: Drama/Sports **Duration:** 134
min **Color:** Black and White **Country:**
USA **MPAA Rating:** Not Rated
Studio: Twentieth Century-Fox Film
Corp. **Director:** Robert Rossen **Paul

Newman: Eddie Felson **Jackie Gleason:** Minnesota
Fats **Piper Laurie:** Sarah Packard **George C. Scott:**
Bert Gordon

Il Postino 1994
Genre: Drama/Romance **Duration:** 108 min **Color:**
Color **Country:** Italy **MPAA Rating:** PG **Studio:**
Blue Dahlia/Cecchi Gori Group Tiger Cine./Esterno
Mediterraneo Film/Penta Films **Director:** Michael Radford
Philippe Noiret: Pablo Neruda **Massimo Troisi:** Mario
Ruoppolo **Maria Grazia Cucinotta:** Beatrice Russo
Renato Scarpa: Telegrapher

Invasion of the Body Snatchers 1956
Genre: Sci-Fi/Horror **Duration:** 80 min **Color:** Black and
White **Country:** USA **MPAA Rating:** Not Rated **Studio:**
Allied Artists **Director:** Don Siegel **Kevin McCarthy:**
Dr. Miles J. Bennell **Dana Wynter:** Becky Driscoll **Larry
Gates:** Dr. Dan Kauffman **King Donovan:** Jac Belicec

Jackie Brown 1997
Genre: Drama/Thriller **Duration:** 154 min **Color:** Color
Country: USA **MPAA Rating:** R **Studio:** Miramax Films
Director: Quentin Tarantino **Pam Grier:** Jackie Brown
Samuel L. Jackson: Ordell Robbie **Robert Forster:**
Max Cherry **Bridget Fonda:** Melanie Ralston

The Jazz Singer 1927
Genre: Drama/Romance **Duration:** 88 min
Color: Black and White **Country:** USA **MPAA Rating:**
Not Rated **Studio:** Warner Bros. Pictures **Director:** Alan
Crosland **Al Jolson:** Jackie Rabinowitz **May McAvoy:**
Mary Dale **Warner Oland:** Cantor Rabinowitz **Eugenie
Besserer:** Sara Rabinowitz

Johnny Belinda 1948
Genre: Drama **Duration:** 102 min **Color:** Black and
White **Country:** USA **MPAA Rating:** Not Rated **Studio:**
Warner Bros. Pictures **Director:** Jean Negulesco
Jane Wyman: Belinda McDonald **Lew Ayres:** Dr.
Robert Richardson **Charles Bickford:** Black McDonald
Agnes Moorehead: Aggie McDonald

Judgment at Nuremberg 1961
Genre: Drama **Duration:** 186 min **Color:** Black and
White **Country:** USA **MPAA Rating:** Not Rated **Studio:**
United Artists **Director:** Stanley Kramer **Spencer Tracy:**
Chief Judge Dan Haywood **Burt Lancaster:** Dr. Ernst
Janning **Richard Widmark:** Col. Tad Lawson **Marlene
Dietrich:** Mrs. Bertholt

The Killing 1956
Genre: Drama/Thriller **Duration:** 85 min **Color:**
Black and White **Country:** USA **MPAA Rating:** Not
Rated **Studio:** United Artists **Director:** Stanley Kubrick
Sterling Hayden: Johnny Clay **Coleen Gray:** Fay
Vince Edwards: Val Cannon **Jay C. Flippen:** Marvin
Unger

The Killing of a Chinese Bookie 1976
Genre: Drama/Crime **Duration:** 109 min **Color:**
Color **Country:** USA **MPAA Rating:** R **Studio:** Faces
Distribution **Director:** John Cassavetes **Ben Gazzara:**
Cosmo Vitelli **Timothy Carey:** Flo **Seymour Cassel:**
Mort Weil **Robert Phillips:** Phil

Kiss of the Spider Woman 1985
Genre: Drama **Duration:** 120 min **Color:** Color
(Metrocolor) **Country:** Brazil/USA **MPAA Rating:** R
Studio: FilmDallas Pictures/HB Filmes/Sugarloaf Films
Inc. **Director:** Hector Babenco **William Hurt:** Luis
Molina **Raul Julia:** Valentin Arregui **Sonia Braga:** Leni

Lamaison/Marta/Spider Woman **José Lewgoy:** Warden

L.A. Confidential 1997
Genre: Drama/Thriller **Duration:** 139 min **Color:**
Color **Country:** USA **MPAA Rating:** R **Studio:** TriStar
Pictures/Gracie Films **Director:** Curtis Hanson **Kevin
Spacey:** Det. Sgt. Jack Vincennes **Russell Crowe:**
Officer Wendell "Bud" White **Guy Pearce:** Det. Lt.
Edmund "Ed" Exley **Kim Basinger:** Lynn Margaret
Bracken

La Dolce Vita 1960
Genre: Drama **Duration:** 174 min **Color:** Black and
White **Country:** Italy **MPAA Rating:** Not Rated **Studio:**
Riama Film **Director:** Frederico Fellini **Marcello
Mastroianni:** Marcello Rubini **Anita Ekberg:** Sylvia
Anouk Aimée: Maddalena **Yvonne Furneaux:** Emma

The Lady Eve 1941
Genre: Drama/Romance **Duration:** 101 min **Color:**
Black and White **Country:** USA **MPAA Rating:** Not
Rated **Studio:** The Samuel Goldwyn Company **Director:**
Preston Sturges **Barbara Stanwyck:** Jean Harrington
Henry Fonda: Charles Pike **Charles Coburn:** Colonel
Harrington **Eugene Pallette:** Horace Pike

The Lady Vanishes 1938
Genre: Drama/Mystery **Duration:** 97 min **Color:**
Black and White **Country:** UK **MPAA Rating:** Not
Rated **Studio:** Gainsborough Pictures **Director:** Alfred
Hitchcock **Margaret Lockwood:** Iris Henderson
Michael Redgrave: Gilbert **Paul Lukas:** Dr. Hartz
Dame May Whitty: Miss Froy

The Last Detail 1973
Genre: Comedy/Drama **Duration:** 103 min **Color:** Color
(Metrocolor) **Country:** USA **MPAA Rating:** R **Studio:**
Columbia Pictures Corporation **Director:** Hal Ashby **Jack
Nicholson:** SM1 Billy "Bad Ass" Buddusky **Otis Young:**
GM1 "Mule" Mulhall **Randy Quaid:** Seaman Larry
Meadows **Clifton James:** M.A.A.

The Last Emperor 1987
Genre: Drama/Biography **Duration:** 160 min
Color: Color (Technicolor) **Country:** China/Italy/UK/

France **MPAA Rating:** PG-13 **Studio:** Yanco Films Ltd./
TAO Film/RPC/Screenframe Ltd./AAA Prod./Soprofilms
Director: Bernardo Bertolucci **John Lone:** Emperor Pu
Yi/Henry **Joan Chen:** Empress Wan Jung/Elizabeth
Peter O'Toole: Reginald F. "R.J." Johnston **Ruocheng
Ying:** Governor of detention center

Le Cercle Rouge 1970
Genre: Drama/Thriller **Duration:** 140 min **Color:** Color
Country: France **MPAA Rating:** Not Rated **Studio:**
Euro Intl. Film (EIA)/Les Films Corona/Selenia Cine.
Director: Jean-Pierre Melville **Alain Delon:** Corey
André Bourvil: Le Commissaire Mattei **Gian Maria
Volontè:** Vogel **Yves Montand:** Jansen

The Leopard 1963
Genre: Drama/History **Duration:** 187 min **Color:** Color
Country: Italy/France **MPAA Rating:** Not Rated **Studio:**
Titanus **Director:** Luchino Visconti **Burt Lancaster:**
Prince Don Fabrizio **Salina Claudia Cardinale:** Angelica
Sedara/Bertiana **Alain Delon:** Tancredi **Falconeri
Paolo Stoppa:** Don Calogero Sedara

Let It Ride 1989
Genre: Comedy/Action **Duration:** 90 min **Color:**
Color **Country:** USA **MPAA Rating:** PG-13 **Studio:**
Paramount Pictures **Director:** Joe Pytka **Richard
Dreyfuss:** Jay Trotter **David Johansen:** Looney **Teri
Garr:** Pam **Jennifer Tilly:** Vicki

Lethal Weapon 1987
Genre: Action/Crime **Duration:** 110 min
Color: Color (Techinicolor) **Country:** USA **MPAA
Rating:** R **Studio:** Warner Bros. Pictures **Director:**
Richard Donner **Mel Gibson:** Sergeant Martin Riggs
Danny Glover: Sergeant Roger Murtaugh **Gary Busey:**
Mr. Joshua **Mitch Ryan:** General Peter McAllister

The Lion in Winter 1968
Genre: Drama/History **Duration:** 134 min **Color:** Color
(Eastmancolor) **Country:** UK **MPAA Rating:** PG
Studio: AVCO Embassy/Haworth Production **Director:**
Anthony Harvey **Peter O'Toole:** Henry II **Katharine
Hepburn:** Eleanor of Aquitaine **Anthony Hopkins:**
Richard **John Castle:** Geoffrey

Little Big Man 1970
Genre: Comedy/Drama **Duration:** 139 min **Color:** Color
(Technicolor) **Country:** USA **MPAA Rating:** PG-13
Studio: Cinema Center Films/Stockbridge-Hiller Prod.
Director: Arthur Penn **Dustin Hoffman:** Jack Crabb
Faye Dunaway: Mrs. Louise Pendrake **Chief Dan
George:** Old Lodge Skins **Martin Balsam:**
Mr. Merriweather

Little Caesar 1931
Genre: Drama/Crime **Duration:** 79 min **Color:** Black
and White **Country:** USA **MPAA Rating:** R **Studio:** First
National Pictures **Director:** Mervyn LeRoy **Edward G.
Robinson:** Little Caesar aka "Rico" **Douglas Fairbanks
Jr.:** Joe Massara **Glenda Farrell:** Olga Stassoff **William
Collier Jr.:** Tony Passa

The Longest Day 1962
Genre: Drama/Action **Duration:** 178 min **Color:** Black
and White **Country:** USA **MPAA Rating:** G **Studio:**
Twentieth Century-Fox Film Corporation **Directors:**
Ken Annakin (British/French episodes), Andrew Marton
(American episodes), Bernhard Wicki (German episodes)
John Wayne: Lt. Col Vandervoort **Richard Burton:**
Flight Officer David Campbell **Robert Mitchum:** Brig.
Gen Norman Cota **Henry Fonda:** Brig. Gen Theodore
Roosevelt

The Longest Yard 1974
Genre: Comedy/Sports **Duration:** 121 min **Color:** Color
(Technicolor) **Country:** USA **MPAA Rating:** R **Studio:**
Paramount Pictures **Director:** Robert Aldrich **Burt
Reynolds:** Paul Crewe **Eddie Albert:** Warden Hazen
Ed Lauter: Captain Knauer **Michael Conrad:** Nate
Scarboro

Love Story 1970
Genre: Drama/Romance **Duration:** 99 min **Color:** Color
Country: France **MPAA Rating:** PG **Studio:** Paramount
Pictures **Director:** Arthur Hiller **Ali MacGraw:** Jennifer
Cavalleri **Ryan O'Neal:** Oliver Barrett IV **John Marley:**
Phil Cavalleri **Ray Milland:** Oliver Barrett III

A Man and a Woman 1966
Genre: Drama/Romance **Duration:** 102 min **Color:**
Black and White/Color (Eastmancolor) **Country:** France
MPAA Rating: Not Rated **Studio:** Les Films 13
Director: Claude Lelouch **Anouk Aimée:** Anne Gauthir
Jean-Louis Trintignant: Jean-Louis Duroc **Pierre
Barouh:** Pierre Gauthier **Valérie Lagrange:** Valerie
Duroc

A Man for All Seasons 1966
Genre: Drama/Biography **Duration:** 120 min **Color:**
Color (Technicolor) **Country:** USA **MPAA Rating:** G
Studio: Columbia Pictures **Director:** Fred Zinnemann
Paul Scofield: Sir Thomas More **Wendy Hiller:** Alice
More **Leo McKern:** Thomas Cromwell **Robert Shaw:**
King Henry VIII

Marathon Man 1976
Genre: Drama/Crime **Duration:** 125 min **Color:** Color
(Metrocolor) **Country:** USA **MPAA Rating:** R **Studio:**
Paramount Pictures **Director:** John Schlesinger **Dustin
Hoffman:** Thomas "Babe" Levy **Laurence Olivier:** Dr.
Christian Szell **Roy Scheider:** Henry "Doc" Levy **William
Devane:** Peter Janeway

Marty 1955
Genre: Drama/Romance **Duration:** 91 min **Color:** Black
and White **Country:** USA **MPAA Rating:** Not Rated
Studio: United Artists **Director:** Delbert Mann **Ernest
Brognine:** Marty Piletti **Betsey Blair:** Clara Snyder

Esther Miniciotti: Mrs. Theresa Piletti **Augusta Ciolli:**
Aunt Catherine

Meet John Doe 1941
Genre: Comedy/Drama **Duration:** 122 min **Color:** Black
and White **Country:** USA **MPAA Rating:** Not Rated
Studio: Warner Bros. **Director:** Frank Capra **Gary
Cooper:** John Doe/Long John Willoughby **Barbara
Stanwyck:** Ann Mitchell **Edward Arnold:** D.B. Norton
Walter Brennan: The colonel

Metropolis 1927
Genre: Sci-Fi/Drama **Duration:** 153 min **Color:** Black
and White (Tinted) **Country:** Germany **MPAA Rating:**
Not Rated **Studio:** Universum Film (UFA) **Director:** Fritz
Lang **Alfred Abel:** Joh Fredersen **Gustav Fröhlich:**
Freder **Rudolf Klein-Rogge:** C. A. Rotwang **Fritz Rasp:**
The thin man

Midnight Express 1978
Genre: Drama/Crime **Duration:** 121 min **Color:** Color
(Eastmancolor) **Country:** UK/USA **MPAA Rating:** R
Studio: Columbia Pictures **Director:** Alan Parker
Brad Davis: Billy Hayes **Irene Miracle:** Susan **Bo
Hopkins:** Tex **Paolo Bonacelli:** Rifki

Million Dollar Baby 2005
Genre: Drama/Sports **Duration:** 132 min **Color:** Color
Country: USA **MPAA Rating:** PG-13 **Studio:** Warner
Bros. Pictures **Director:** Clint Eastwood **Clint Eastwood:**
Frankie Dunn **Hilary Swank:** Maggie Fitzgerald **Morgan
Freeman:** Eddie "Scrap-Iron" Dupris

The Miracle of Morgan's Creek 1944
Genre: Comedy **Duration:** 98 min **Color:** Black
and White **Country:** USA **MPAA Rating:** Not Rated
Studio: Paramount Pictures **Director:** Preston Sturges
Eddie Bracken: Norval Jones **Betty Hutton:** Trudy
Kockenlocker **Diana Lynn:** Emmy Kockenlocker **William
Demarest:** Constable Edmund Kockenlocker

Missing 1982
Genre: Drama/Crime **Duration:** 122 min **Color:** Color
(Technicolor) **Country:** USA **MPAA Rating:** PG
Studio: Universal Pictures **Director:** Costa-Gavras

Jack Lemmon: Ed Horman **Sissy Spacek:** Beth Horman **Melanie Mayron:** Terry Simon **John Shea:** Charles Horman

Modern Times 1936
Genre: Comedy **Duration:** 87 min **Color:** Black and White **Country:** USA **MPAA Rating:** Not Rated **Studio:** United Artists **Director:** Charles Chaplin **Charles Chaplin:** A factory worker **Paulette Goddard:** A gamin **Henry Bergman:** Café proprietor **Tiny Sandford:** Big Bill

Mr. Blandings Builds His Dream House 1948
Genre: Comedy/Romance **Duration:** 94 min **Color:** Black and White **Country:** USA **MPAA Rating:** Not Rated **Studio:** RKO Radio Pictures **Director:** H.C. Potter **Cary Grant:** Jim Blandings **Myrna Loy:** Muriel Blandings **Melvyn Douglas:** Bill Cole **Reginald Denny:** Simms

Mrs. Miniver 1942
Genre: Drama/Romance **Duration:** 134 min **Color:** Black and White **Country:** USA **MPAA Rating:** Not Rated **Studio:** Loew's/Metro-Goldwyn-Mayer (MGM) **Director:** William Wyler **Greer Carson:** Mrs. Miniver **Walter Pidgeon:** Clem Miniver **Teresa Wright:** Carol Beldon **Dame May Whitty:** Lady Beldon

Murder by Death 1976
Genre: Comedy/Mystery **Duration:** 94 min **Color:** Color **Country:** English **MPAA Rating:** Not Rated **Studio:** Columbia Pictures Corporation **Director:** Robert Moore **Eileen Brennan:** Tess Skeffington **Truman Capote:** Lionel Twain **James Coco:** Milo Perrier **Peter Falk:** Sam Diamond **Peter Sellers:** Sidney Wang

My Fair Lady 1964
Genre: Musical/Romance **Duration:** 170 min **Color:** Color (Technicolor) **Country:** USA **MPAA Rating:** G **Studio:** Warner Bros. Pictures **Director:** Gorge Cukor **Audrey Hepburn:** Eliza Doolittle **Rex Harrison:** Professor Henry Higgins **Stanley Holloway:** Alfred P. Doolittle **Wilfrid Hyde-White:** Colonel Hugh Pickering

My Favorite Wife 1940
Genre: Comedy/Romance **Duration:** 88 min **Color:** Black and White **Country:** USA **MPAA Rating:** Not Rated **Studio:** RKO Radio Pictures **Director:** Garson Kanin **Irene Dunne:** Ellen **Cary Grant:** Nick **Randolph Scott:** Burkett **Gail Patrick:** Bianca

My Left Foot 1989
Genre: Drama/Biography **Duration:** 103 min **Color:** Color **Country:** Ireland/UK **MPAA Rating:** R **Studio:** Ferndale Films/Granada Tel./Radio Telefis Eireann **Director:** Jim Sheridan **Daniel Day-Lewis:** Christy Brown **Brenda Fricker:** Mrs. Brown **Alison Whelan:** Sheila **Kirsten Sheridan:** Sharon

Nashville 1975
Genre: Drama **Duration:** 159 min **Color:** Color (Metrocolor) **Country:** USA **MPAA Rating:** R **Studio:** Paramount Pictures **Director:** Robert Altman **David Arkin:** Norman **Barbara Baxley:** Lady Pearl **Ned Beatty:** Delbert Reese **Karen Black:** Connie White

Ninotchka 1939
Genre: Comedy/Romance **Duration:** 110 min **Color:** Black and White **Country:** USA **MPAA Rating:** Not Rated **Studio:** Metro-Goldwyn-Mayer (MGM) **Director:** Ernst Lubitsch **Greta Garbo:** Nina Yakushova "Ninotchka" Ivanoff **Melvyn Douglas:** Léon Compte d'Agoult **Ina Claire:** Grand Duchess Swana **Bela Lugosi:** Kommissar Razinin

No Way Out 1950
Genre: Drama/Thriller **Duration:** 106 min **Color:** Black and White **Country:** USA **MPAA Rating:** Not Rated **Studio:** Twentieth Century-Fox Film Corporation **Director:** Joseph L. Mankiewicz **Richard Widmark:** Ray Biddle **Linda Darnell:** Edie Johnson **Stephen McNally:** Dr. Dan Wharton **Sidney Poitier:** Dr. Luther Brooks

Nobody's Fool 1994
Genre: Drama **Duration:** 110 min **Color:** Color **Country:** USA **MPAA Rating:** R **Studio:** Paramount Pictures **Director:** Robert Benton **Paul Newman:** Sully Sullivan **Jessica Tandy:** Beryl Peoples **Bruce Willis:**

Carl Roebuck **Melanie Griffith:** Toby Roebuck

Notorious 1946
Genre: Drama/Thriller **Duration:** 101 min **Color:** Black and White **Country:** USA **MPAA Rating:** Not Rated **Studio:** Vanguard Films **Director:** Alfred Hitchcock **Cary Grant:** T.R. Devlin **Ingrid Bergman:** Alicia Huberman **Claude Rains:** Alexander Sebastian **Louis Calhern:** Captain Paul Prescott

Notting Hill 1999
Genre: Comedy/Romance **Duration:** 124 min **Color:** Color **Country:** UK/USA **MPAA Rating:** PG-13 **Studio:** Polygram Filmed Ent./Working Title Films **Director:** Roger Michell **Julia Roberts:** Anna Scott **Hugh Grant:** William Thacker **Emma Chambers:** Honey Thacker **Rhys Ifans:** Spike

Now Voyager 1942
Genre: Drama/Romance **Duration:** 117 min **Color:** Black and White **Country:** USA **MPAA Rating:** Not Rated **Studio:** Warner Bros. Pictures **Director:** Irving Rapper **Bette Davis:** Charlotte Vale **Paul Henreid:** Jerry Durrance **Claude Rains:** Dr. Jaquith **Gladys Cooper:** Mrs. Henry Windle Vale

On Golden Pond 1981
Genre: Drama **Duration:** 109 min **Color:** Color **Country:** USA **MPAA Rating:** PG **Studio:** Universal Pictures **Director:** Mark Rydell **Katharine Hepburn:** Ethel Thayer **Henry Fonda:** Norman Thayer Jr. **Jane Fonda:** Chelsea Thayer Wayne **Doug McKeon:** Billy Ray

On the Town 1949
Genre: Musical/Comedy **Duration:** 98 min **Color:** Color (Technicolor) **Country:** USA **MPAA Rating:** Not Rated **Studio:** Metro-Goldwyn-Mayer (MGM) **Directors:** Stanley Donen, Gene Kelly **Gene Kelly:** Gabey **Frank Sinatra:** Chip **Betty Garrett:** Brunhilde Esterhazy **Ann Miller:** Claire Huddesen

Out of Africa 1985
Genre: Drama/Biography **Duration:** 150 min **Color:** Color **Country:** USA **MPAA Rating:** PG **Studio:** Universal Pictures **Director:** Sydney Pollack **Meryl Streep:** Karen Blixen **Robert Redford:** Denys Finch Hatton **Klaus Maria Brandauer:** Bror Blixen/Hans Blixen **Michael Kitchen:** Berkeley

Out of the Past 1947
Genre: Drama/Thriller **Duration:** 97 min **Color:** Black and White **Country:** USA **MPAA Rating:** PG **Studio:** RKO Radio Pictures **Director:** Daniel Mainwaring **Robert Mitchum:** Jeff Bailey **Jane Greer:** Kathie Moffat **Kirk Douglas:** Whit Sterling **Rhonda Fleming:** Meta Carson

The Ox-Bow Incident 1943
Genre: Drama/Western **Duration:** 75 min **Color:** Black and White **Country:** USA **MPAA Rating:** Not Rated **Studio:** Twentieth Century-Fox Film Corporation **Director:** William A. Wellman **Henry Fonda:** Gil Carter **Dana Andrews:** Donald Martin **Mary Beth Hughes:** Rose Mapen/Rose Swanson **Anthony Quinn:** Juan Martinez/Francisco Morez

A Passage to India 1984
Genre: Drama/Adventure **Duration:** 163 min **Color:** Color (Technicolor) **Country:** UK/USA **MPAA Rating:** PG **Studio:** EMI Films/HBO/Thorn EMI Screen Ent. **Director:** David Lean **Judy Davis:** Adela Quested **Victor**

Banerjee: Dr. Aziz H. Ahmed **Peggy Ashcroft:** Mrs. Moore **James Fox:** Richard Fielding

Paths of Glory 1957
Genre: Drama/War **Duration:** 87 min **Color:** Black and White **Country:** USA **MPAA Rating:** Not Rated **Studio:** United Artists **Director:** Stanley Kubrick **Kirk Douglas:** Col. Dax **Ralph Meeker:** Cpl. Phillipe Paris **Adolphe Menjou:** Gen. George Broulard **George Macready:** Gen. Paul Mireau

Peyton Place 1957
Genre: Drama/Romance **Duration:** 157 min **Color:** Color **Country:** USA **MPAA Rating:** Not Rated **Studio:** Twentieth Century Fox **Director:** Mark Robson **Lana Turner:** Constance MacKenzie **Lee Philips:** Michael Rossi **Lloyd Nolan:** Dr. Swain **Arthur Kennedy:** Lucas Cross

Philadelphia 1993
Genre: Drama **Duration:** 125 min **Color:** Color (Technicolor) **Country:** USA **MPAA Rating:** PG-13 **Studio:** TriStar Pictures **Director:** Jonathan Demme **Tom Hanks:** Andrew Beckett **Denzel Washington:** Joe Miller **Jason Robards:** Charles Wheeler **Antonio Banderas:** Miguel Alvarez

The Piano 1993
Genre: Drama/Romance **Duration:** 121 min **Color:** Color **Country:** Australia **MPAA Rating:** R **Studio:** Australian Film Com./CiBy 2000/Jan Chapman Prod./New S. Wales Film & Television Office **Director:** Jane Campion **Holly Hunter:** Ada McGrath **Harvey Keitel:** George Baines **Sam Neill:** Alisdair Stewart **Anna Paquin:** Flora McGrath

A Place in the Sun 1951
Genre: Drama/Romance **Duration:** 122 min **Color:** Black and White **Country:** USA **MPAA Rating:** Not Rated **Studio:** Paramount Pictures **Director:** George Stevens **Montgomery Clift:** George Eastman **Elizabeth Taylor:** Angela Vickers **Shelley Winters:** Alice Tripp **Anne Revere:** Hannah Eastman

Places in the Heart 1984
Genre: Drama **Duration:** 112 min **Color:** Color (Technicolor) **Country:** USA **MPAA Rating:** PG **Studio:** TriStar Pictures **Director:** Robert Benton **Sally Field:** Edna Spalding **Lindsay Crouse:** Margaret Lomax **Ed Harris:** Wayne Lomax **Amy Madigan:** Viola Kelsey

The Player 1992
Genre: Comedy/Thriller **Duration:** 124 min **Color:** Color **Country:** USA **MPAA Rating:** R **Studio:** Avenue Pictures Prod./Guild/Spelling Entertainment **Director:** Robert Altman **Tim Robbins:** Griffin Mill **Greta Scacchi:** June Gudmundsdottir **Fred Ward:** Walter Stuckel **Whoopi Goldberg:** Detective Susan Avery

Prizzi's Honor 1985
Genre: Drama/Crime **Duration:** 130 min **Color:** Color **Country:** USA **MPAA Rating:** R **Studio:** ABC Motion Pictures **Director:** John Hudson **Jack Nicholson:** Charley Partanna **Kathleen Turner:** Irene Walker **Robert Loggia:** Eduardo Prizzi **John Randolph:** Angelo "Pop" Partanna

Putney Swope 1969
Genre: Comedy **Duration:** 84 min **Color:** Black and White, Color **Country:** USA **MPAA Rating:** R **Studio:** Herald **Director:** Robert Downey Sr. **Stanley Gottlieb:** Nathan **Allen Garfield:** Elias, Jr. **Archie Russell:** Joker **Ramon Gordon:** Bissinger **Arnold Johnson:** Putney Swope

Quick Change 1990
Genre: Comedy/Crime **Duration:** 89 min **Color:** Color
Country: USA **MPAA Rating:** R **Studio:** Warner Bros.
Directors: Howard Franklin & Bill Murray **Bill Murray:**
Grimm **Randy Quaid:** Loomis **Jason Robards:** Chief
Rotzinger **Geena Davis:** Phyllis Potter

Ran 1985
Genre: Drama/Action **Duration:** 160 min **Color:** Color
Country: Japan **MPAA Rating:** R **Studio:** Greenwich
Film Productions **Director:** Akira Kurosawa **Tatsuya
Nakadai:** Lord Hidetora Ichimonji **Akira Terao:** Taro
Takatora Ichimonji **Jinpachi Nezu:** Jiro Masatora
Ichimonji **Daisuke Ryu:** Saburo Naotora Ichimonji

Red River 1948
Genre: Action/Adventure **Duration:** 133 min
Color: Black and White **Country:** USA **MPAA Rating:**
Not Rated **Studio:** United Artists **Director:** Howard
Hawks and Arthur Rosson **John Wayne:** Thomas Dunson
Montgomery Clift: Matthew Garth **Joanne Dru:** Tess
Millay **Walter Brennan:** "Groot" Nadine

The Red Shoes 1948
Genre: Drama/Romance **Duration:** 133 min **Color:**
Color **Country:** UK **MPAA Rating:** Not Rated **Studio:**
The Archers/Independent Producers **Director:** Jan de
Bont **Marius Goring:** Julian Craster **Jean Short:** Terry
Gordon Littmann: Ike **Julia Lang:** A balletomane

Remains of the Day 1993
Genre: Drama/Romance **Duration:** 134 min **Color:**
Color **Country:** UK and USA **MPAA Rating:** PG **Studio:**
Columbia Pictures Corporation **Director:** James Ivory
Christopher Reeve: Jack Lewis **Anthony Hopkins:**
James Stevens **Emma Thompson:** Mary Kenton
James Fox: Lord Darlington

The Right Stuff 1983
Genre: Drama/Adventure **Duration:** 193 min **Color:**
Color (Technicolor) **Country:** USA **MPAA Rating:** PG
Studio: Warner Bros. **Director:** Philip Kaufman **Sam
Shepard:** Chuck Yeager **Scott Glenn:** Alan Shepard
Ed Harris: John Glenn **Dennis Quaid:** Gordon Cooper

The Road Warrior 1981
Genre: Action/Adventure **Duration:** 91 min **Color:** Black
and White/Color **Country:** Australia **MPAA Rating:** R
Studio: Kennedy Miller Productions **Director:** George
Miller **Mel Gibson:** "Mad" Max Rockatansky/The Road
Warrior **Bruce Sence:** The gyro captain **Michael
Prestion:** Pappagallo **Max Phipps:** the toadie

Room at the Top 1959
Genre: Drama **Duration:** 115 min **Color:** Black and
White **Country:** UK **MPAA Rating:** Not Rated **Studio:**
Remus **Director:** Jack Clayton **Simone Signoret:**
Alice Aisgill **Laurence Harvey:** Joe Lampton **Heather
Sears:** Susan Brown **Donald Wolfit:** Mr. Brown

A Room with a View 1985
Genre: Drama/Romance **Duration:** 117 min **Color:**
Color (Technicolor) **Country:** UK **MPAA Rating:** Not
Rated **Studio:** Goldcrest Films International **Director:**
James Ivory **Maggie Smith:** Charlotte Bartlett **Helena
Bonham Carter:** Lucy Honeychurch **Denholm Elliot:**
Mr. Emerson **Julian Sands:** George Emerson

Rounders 1998
Genre: Drama **Duration:** 121 min **Color:** Color
Country: USA **MPAA Rating:** R **Studio:** Miramax Films
Director: John Dahl **Matt Damon:** Mike McDermott
Edward Norton: Lester "Worm" Murphy **John
Turturro:** Joey Knish **Gretchen Mol:** Jo

Rules of the Game 1939
Genre: Comedy/Drama **Duration:** 110 min **Color:**
Black and White **Country:** France **MPAA Rating:** Not
Rated **Studio:** Nouvelle edition française **Director:** Jean
Renoir **Nora Gregor:** Christine de la Cheyniest **Paulette
Dubost:** Lisette, sa camèriste **Mila Parèly:** Geneviève
de Marras **Odette Talazac:** Madame de la Plante

**The Russians Are Coming The Russians Are
Coming** 1966
Genre: Comedy/War **Duration:** 126 min
Color: Color **Country:** USA **MPAA Rating:** Not Rated
Studio: The United Artists **Director:** Norman Jewison
Carl Reiner: Walt Whittaker **Eva Marie Saint:** Elspeth
Whittaker **Alan Arkin:** Lt. Rozanov **Brian Keith:** Police

Sabrina 1954
Genre: Comedy/Romance **Duration:** 113 min **Color:**
Black and White **Country:** USA **MPAA Rating:** Not
Rated **Studio:** Paramount Pictures **Director:** Billy Wilder
Humphrey Bogart: Linus Larrabee **Audrey Hepburn:**
Sabrina Fairchild **William Holden:** David Larrabee
Walter Hampden: Oliver Larrabee

The Sand Pebbles 1966
Genre: Drama/War **Duration:** 179 min **Color:** Color
Country: USA **MPAA Rating:** PG-13 **Studio:** Twentieth
Century-Fox Film Corporation **Director:** Robert Wise
Steve McQueen: Holman **Richard Attenborough:**
Frenchy **Richard Crenna:** Collins **Candice Bergen:**
Shirley

Seabiscuit 2003
Genre: Drama/Sports **Duration:** 141 min
Color: Black and White, Color **Country:** USA **MPAA
Rating:** PG-13 **Studio:** Universal Pictures **Director:**
Gary Ross **Tobey Maguire:** Johnny "Red" Pollard **Jeff
Bridges:** Charles Howard **Chris Cooper:** Tom Smith
Elizabeth Banks: Marcela Howard

Serpico 1973
Genre: Drama/Crime **Duration:** 129 min
Color: Color (Technicolor) **Country:** Italy/USA **MPAA
Rating:** R **Studio:** Artists Ent. Complex/Produzioni De
Laurentiis Intl. Manufacturing Co. **Director:** Sidney Lumet
Al Pacino: Officer Frank Serpico **John Randolph:** Chief
Sidney Green **Jack Kehoe:** Tom Keough **Biff McGuire:**
Capt. Insp. McClain

The Seventh Seal 1957
Genre: Drama **Duration:** 96 min **Color:** Black and White
Country: Sweden **MPAA Rating:** Not Rated **Studio:**
Svensk Filmindustri (SF) **Director:** Ingmar Bergman
Gunnar Björnstrand: Jöns **Bengt Ekerot:** Death
Nils Poppe: Jof **Max von Sydow:** Antonius Block

Shadow of a Doubt 1943
Genre: Comedy/Drama **Duration:** 108 min
Color: Black and White **Country:** USA **MPAA Rating:**

PG **Studio:** Universal Pictures **Director:** Alfred Hitchcock
Teresa Wright: Charlotte "Charlie" Newton
Joseph Cotten: Uncle Charlie **Macdonald Carey:**
Jack Graham **Patricia Collinge:** Emma Newton

Shakespeare in Love 1998
Genre: Comedy/Romance **Duration:** 123 min **Color:**
Color **Country:** USA **MPAA Rating:** R **Studio:** Universal
Pictures **Director:** John Madden **Joseph Fiennes:**
Will Shakespeare **Gwyneth Paltrow:** Viola de Lesseps
Geoffrey Rush: Philip Henslowe **Colin Firth:**
Lord Wessex

Shampoo 1975
Genre: Drama/Romance **Duration:** 109 min **Color:**
Color **Country:** USA **MPAA Rating:** R **Studio:** Columbia
Pictures Corporation **Director:** Hal Ashby **Warren
Beatty:** George Roundy **Julie Christie:** Jackie Shawn
Goldie Hawn: Jill **Lee Grant:** Felicia Carp

Shine 1996
Genre: Drama/Biography **Duration:** 105 min **Color:**
Color **Country:** Australia **MPAA Rating:** PG-13
Studio: Australian Film Finance Corporation **Director:**
Scott Hicks **Geoffrey Rush:** David Helfgott as an
adult **Justin Braine:** Tony **Sonia Todd:** Sylvia **Chris
Haywood:** Sam

Silkwood 1983
Genre: Drama/Biography **Duration:** 131 min
Color: Color (Technicolor) **Country:** USA **MPAA Rating:**
R **Studio:** ABC Motion Pictures **Director:** Mike Nichols
Meryl Streep: Karen Silkwood **Kurt Russell:** Drew
Stephens **Cher:** Dolly Pelliker **Craig T. Nelson:** Winston

Silver Streak 1976
Genre: Comedy/Action **Duration:** 114 min **Color:** Color
Country: USA **MPAA Rating:** PG-13 **Studio:** Twentieth
Century-Fox Film Corporation **Director:** Arthur Hiller
Gene Wilder: George Caldwell **Jill Clayburgh:** Hilly
Burns **Richard Pryor:** Grover Muldoon
Patrick McGoohan: Roger Devereau

Smiles of a Summer Night 1955
Genre: Comedy/Romance **Duration:** 108 min **Color:**

Black and White **Country:** Sweden **MPAA Rating:** Not Rated **Studio:** Svensk Filmindustri (SF) **Director:** Ingmar Bergman **Ulla Jacobsson:** Anne Egerman **Eva Dahlbeck:** Desiree Armfeldt **Harriet Andersson:** Petra the maid **Margit Carlqvist:** Countess Charlotte Malcolm

Smoke 1995
Genre: Comedy/Drama **Duration:** 112 min **Color:** Color **Country:** USA **MPAA Rating:** R **Studio:** Miramax Films **Director:** Wayne Wang **Harvey Keitel:** Augustus "Auggie" Wren **William Hurt:** Paul Benjamin **Harold Perrineau Jr.:** Thomas "Rashid" Cole **Forrest Whittaker:** Cyrus Cole

Sons of the Desert 1933
Genre: Comedy **Duration:** 68 min **Color:** Black and White **Country:** USA **MPAA Rating:** Not Rated **Studio:** Hal Roach Studios Inc. **Director:** William A. Seiter **Stan Laurel:** Stanley Laurel **Oliver Hardy:** Oliver Hardy **Charley Chase:** Charley Chase **Mae Busch:** Mrs. Lottie Chase Hardy

South Park: Bigger, Longer, and Uncut 1999
Genre: Musical/Comedy **Duration:** 98 min

Color: Color **Country:** USA **MPAA Rating:** R **Studio:** Warner Bros. Pictures **Director:** Trey Parker **Trey Parker:** Stan Marsh/Eric Cartman/Satan/Mr. Herbert Garrison, etc. **Matt Stone:** Kyle Broflovski/Kenny McCormick **Mary Kay Bergman:** Liane Cartman/Sheila Broflovski **Isaac Hayes:** Chef

Speed 1994
Genre: Action/Adventure **Duration:** 116 min **Color:** Color **Country:** USA **MPAA Rating:** R **Studio:** Twentieth Century-Fox Film Corporation **Director:** Jan de Bont **Keanu Reeves:** Officer Jack Traven **Sandra Bullock:** Annie Porter **Dennis Hopper:** Howard Payne **Jeff Daniels:** Det. Harry Temple

Stage Door 1937
Genre: Drama **Duration:** 92 min **Color:** Black and White **Country:** USA **MPAA Rating:** Not Rated **Studio:** RKO Radio Pictures **Director:** Gregory La Cava **Katharine Hepburn:** Terry Randall **Ginger Rogers:** Jean Maitland **Adolphe Menjou:** Anthony Powell **Gail Patrick:** Linda Shaw

Star Wars: The Empire Strikes Back 1980
Genre: Sci-Fi/Adventure **Duration:** 124 min **Color:** Color Country: USA **MPAA Rating:** PG **Studio:** Twentieth Century Fox **Director:** Irvin Kershner **Mark Hamill:** Luke Skywalker **Harrison Ford:** Han Solo **Carrie Fisher:** Princess Leia **Billy Dee Williams:** Lando Calrissian

Stranger Than Paradise 1984
Genre: Comedy/Drama **Duration:** 89 min **Color:** Black and White **Country:** USA **MPAA Rating:** R **Studio:** Cinesthesia Productions **Director:** Jim Jarmusch **John Lurie:** Willie **Eszter Balint:** Eva **Richard Edson:** Eddie **Cecillia Stark:** Aunt Lotte

Strangers on a Train 1951
Genre: Drama/Thriller **Duration:** 101 min **Color:** Black and White **Country:** USA **MPAA Rating:** PG **Studio:** Samuel Goldwyn Company **Director:** Alfred Hitchcock **Farley Granger:** Guy Haines **Ruth Roman:** Anne Morton **Robert Walker:** Bruno Anthony **Leo G. Carroll:** Senator Morton

Swing Time 1936
Genre: Musical/Comedy **Duration:** 103 min **Color:** Black and White **Country:** USA **MPAA Rating:** Not Rated **Studio:** RKO Radio Pictures **Director:** George Stevens **Fred Astaire:** John "Lucky" Garnett **Ginger Rogers:** Penelope "Penny" Carroll **Victor Moore:** Everett "Pop" Cardetti **Helen Broderick:** Mabel Anderson

There's Something About Mary 1998
Genre: Comedy/Romance **Duration:** 119 min **Color:** Color **Country:** USA MPAA **Rating:** R **Studio:** Twentieth Century-Fox Film Corporation **Directors:** Bobby Farrelly and Peter Farrelly **Cameron Diaz:** Mary Jensen **Matt Dillon:** Pat Healy **Ben Stiller:** Ted Stroehmann **Lee Evans:** Tucker/Norman Phipps

The Thin Man 1934
Genre: Comedy/Crime **Duration:** 93 min **Color:** Black and White **Country:** USA **MPAA Rating:** Not Rated **Studio:** Metro-Goldwyn-Mayer (MGM) **Director:** W.S. Van Dyke **William Powell:** Nick **Myrna Loy:** Nora **Maureen O'Sullivan:** Dorothy **Nat Pendleton:** Guild

The 39 Steps 1935
Genre: Drama/Thriller **Duration:** 86 min **Color:** Black and White **Country:** UK **MPAA Rating:** PG **Studio:** Gaumont British Picture Corporation **Director:** Alfred Hitchcock **Robert Donat:** Richard Hannay **Madeleine Carroll:** Pamela **Lucie Mannheim:** Miss Annabella Smith **Godfrey Tearle:** Professor Jordan

A Thousand Clowns 1965
Genre: Comedy/Drama **Duration:** 118 min **Color:** Black and White **Country:** USA **MPAA Rating:** Not Rated **Studio:** United Artists **Director:** Fred Coe **Jason Robards:** Murray N. Burns **Barbara Harris:** Dr. Sandra "Sandy" Markowitz **Martin Balsam:** Arnold Burns **Gene Saks:** Leo Herman **Barry Gordon:** Nick

Tom Jones 1963
Genre: Comedy/Adventure **Duration:** 128 min **Color:** Color (Eastmancolor) **Country:** UK **MPAA Rating:** Not Rated **Studio:** Woodfall Film Productions **Director:** Tony Richardson **Albert Finney:** Tom Jones

Susannah York: Sophie Western **Hugh Griffith:** Squire Western **Edith Evans:** Miss Western

Touch of Evil 1958
Genre: Drama/Thriller **Duration:** 95 min **Color:** Black and White **Country:** USA **MPAA Rating:** PG-13 **Studio:** Universal International Pictures (UI) **Director:** Orson Welles **Charlton Heston:** Ramon Miguel "Mike" Vargas **Janet Leigh:** Susan "Susie" Vargas **Orson Welles:** Police Capt. Hank Quinlan **Marlene Dietrich:** Tanya

Unforgiven 1992
Genre: Drama/Western **Duration:** 131 min **Color:** Color (Technicolor) **Country:** USA **MPAA Rating:** R **Studio:** Warner Bros. Pictures **Director:** Clint Eastwood **Clint Eastwood:** William "Bill" Munny **Gene Hackman:** Little Bill Daggett **Morgan Freeman:** Ned Logan **Richard Harris:** English Bob

Viva Zapata! 1952
Genre: Drama/History **Duration:** 113 min **Color:** Black and White **Country:** English **MPAA Rating:** Not Rated **Studio:** Twentieth Century-Fox Film Corporation **Director:** Elia Kazan **Marlon Brando:** Emiliano Zapata **Jean Peters:** Josefa Zapata **Anthony Quinn:** Eufemio Zapata **Joseph Wiseman:** Fernando Aguirre

Waking Ned Devine 1998
Genre: Comedy **Duration:** 91 min **Color:** Color **Country:** UK **MPAA Rating:** PG **Studio:** Tomboy Films **Director:** Kirk Jones **Ian Bannen:** Jackie O'Shea **David Kelly:** Michael O'Sullivan **Fionnula Flanagan:** Annie O'Shea **Susan Lynch:** Maggie O'Toole

Wall Street 1987
Genre: Drama/Crime **Duration:** 125 min **Color:** Color **Country:** USA **MPAA Rating:** R **Studio:** Twentieth Century-Fox Film Corporation **Director:** Oliver Stone **Michael Douglas:** Gordon Gekko **Charlie Sheen:** Bud Fox **Daryl Hannah:** Darien Taylor **Martin Sheen:** Carl Fox

What's Up Doc? 1972
Genre: Comedy/Romance **Duration:** 94 min **Color:**

Color **Country:** France **MPAA Rating:** G **Studio:** Warner Bros. **Director:** Peter Bogdanovich **Barbra Streisand:** Judy Maxwell **Ryan O'Neal:** Dr. Howard Bannister **Madeline Kahn:** Eunice Burns **Kenneth Mars:** Hugh Simon

Whatever Happened to Baby Jane? 1962
Genre: Horror/Thriller **Duration:** 134 min **Color:** Black and White **Country:** USA **MPAA Rating:** Not Rated **Studio:** Warner Bros. Pictures **Director:** Robert Aldrich **Bette Davis:** Baby Jane Hudson **Joan Crawford:** Blanche Hudson **Victor Buono:** Edwin Flagg **Wesley Addy:** Marty McDonald

Wild at Heart 1990
Genre: Comedy/Adventure **Duration:** 124 min **Color:** Color **Country:** USA **MPAA Rating:** R **Studio:** PolyGram Filmed Entertainment **Director:** David Lynch **Nicolas Cage:** Sailor Ripley **Laura Dern:** Lula Fortune **Willem Dafoe:** Bobby Peru **J.E. Freeman:** Marcelles Santos

Witness 1985
Genre: Drama/Thriller **Duration:** 112 min **Color:** Color (Technicolor) **Country:** USA **MPAA Rating:** R **Studio:** Paramount Pictures **Director:** Peter Weir **Harrison Ford:** Det. Capt. John Book **Kelly McGillis:** Rachel Lapp **Josef Sommer:** Chief Paul Schaeffer **Lukas Haas:** Samuel Lapp

Witness for the Prosecution 1957
Genre: Drama/Crime **Duration:** 116 min **Color:** Black and White **Country:** USA **MPAA Rating:** Not Rated **Studio:** United Artists **Director:** Billy Wilder **Tyrone Power:** Leonard Steven Vole **Marlene Dietrich:** Christine Helm **Charles Laughton:** Sir Wilfrid Robarts **Elsa Lanchester:** Miss Plimsoll

Women on the Verge of a Nervous Breakdown 1988
Genre: Comedy/Drama **Duration:** 90 min

Color: **Color Country:** Spain **MPAA Rating:** R **Studio:** El Desceo S.A. **Director:** Pedro Almódovar **Carmen Maura:** Pepa **Antonio Banderas:** Carlos **Julieta Serrano:** Lucía **María Barranco:** Candela

You Can't Take It with You 1938
Genre: Comedy/Romance **Duration:** 126 min **Color:** Black and White **Country:** USA **MPAA Rating:** Not Rated **Studio:** Columbia Pictures Corporation **Director:** Frank Capra **Jean Arthur:** Alice Sycamore **Lionel Barrymore:** Grandpa Martin Vanderhof **James Stewart:** Tony Kirby **Edward Arnold:** Anthony P. Kirby

Z 1969
Genre: Drama/Thriller **Duration:** 127 min **Color:** Color **Country:** France **MPAA Rating:** PG **Studio:** Office National pour le commerce et l'industrie ciné./Reggane Films/Valoria Films **Director:** Costa-Gavras **Yves Montand:** Zei **Irene Papas:** Helena (Zei's wife) **Jean-Louis Trintignant:** The examining magistrate **Jacques Perrin:** The photojournalist

Index